# JOE'S BOOK OF MUSHROOM COOKERY

TO CINDY AND MARTY,

GOOD COOKING!

*[signature]*
3/22/97

# Joe's
## BOOK OF
## MUSHROOM COOKERY

*Jack Czarnecki*

WILD MUSHROOM PHOTOGRAPHY BY
*Joseph L. Czarnecki*

FOOD PHOTOGRAPHY BY
*Sally Shenk Ullman*

FOOD STYLING BY BARBARA FRITZ

Atheneum
NEW YORK
1988

The author acknowledges with thanks permission to use the following recipes: *Stir-Fried Chicken with Dried Russulas* (pages 266–267) and *Marge Stafford's Mushrooms-in-the-Field* (pages 265–266) used by permission of Marge Stafford; *Chanterelles with Ham—Cream Style* (page 129), *Pickled Mushrooms Monterey* (page 139), and *Quick-Fried Cepes* (page 121) used by permission of Roy Thomas; *Stuffed Mushroom Caps Winiarski* (pages 135–136) used by permission of Warren and Barbara Winiarski; *Chanterelles en Vol-au-Vent* (pages 128–129) and *Champignon aux Duxelles* (pages 134–135) used by permission of Ted Balistreri; *Helen Turley's Sautéed Enoki with Apples and Cellophane Noodles* (page 122) and *Cream of Blewit Soup* (page 260) used by permission of Helen Turley; *Blewits with Pernod* (page 258) and *Fresh Cepes—Heitz Style* (pages 260–261) used by permission of Joe and Alice Heitz; *Oriental Mushrooms* (page 262) used by permission of the Mycological Society of San Francisco; *Stuffed Russula Xerampelina* (pages 264–265) used by permission of David Bruce.

Atheneum Publishers
Macmillan Publishing Company
866 Third Avenue, New York, N.Y. 10022
Collier Macmillan Canada, Inc.

Library of Congress Cataloging-in-Publication Data
Czarnecki, Jack.
Joe's Book of mushroom cookery.
Bibliography: p.
Includes index.
1. Cookery (Mushrooms)  I. Title.  II. Title:
Book of mushroom cookery.
TX804.C9   1988        641.6'58        88-16633
ISBN 0-689-70742-8

Macmillan books are available at special discounts for bulk purchases for sales promotions, premiums, fund-raising, or educational use. For details, contact:

Special Sales Director
Macmillan Publishing Company
866 Third Avenue
New York, N.Y. 10022

10 9 8 7 6 5 4 3 2

First Paperback Edition

Printed in the United States of America

*This book is for the two most wonderful women in the world:*

**MY WIFE, HEIDI,**
**AND MY MOTHER, WANDA**

# *Acknowledgments*

This book would not be possible without the enormous influence of my mother and father, who were responsible for my interest in cooking, particularly with mushrooms.

The desserts for this book are the results of the combined talents of my wife, Heidi, and my mother. The work herein on the mysterious world of baking and sweets was done by Heidi, who spent many hours perfecting their execution for this book.

Special thanks to George Lang, who encouraged me and waded through my first stumbling efforts at a manuscript, making suggestions and corrections along the way. Again, a heartfelt thanks to George and his wife, Jenifer Harvey Lang.

A special note of appreciation to my California "family," those friends whom Heidi and I have come to cherish, and who contributed to this book: Heidi's mother and father in Monterey, Patti Ballard of Bargetto Winery, Warren and Barbara Winiarski of Stag's Leap Winery, Joe and Alice Heitz of Heitz Wine Cellars, Roy Thomas of Monterey Peninsula Winery, David Bruce of David Bruce Winery, Marge Stafford, and Ted Balistreri of the Sardine Factory Restaurant in Monterey. Also thanks to Helen Turley, who showed me new ways to prepare enoki and blewits (also known as woodblewits).

*ACKNOWLEDGMENTS*

Thanks to John and Marie Simmons for their encouragement and suggestions on recipes and methods of presentation.

To the staff of Joe's, my toughest critics, whose unabashed comments led to many revisions.

Thanks to Sally Shenk Ullman for her fine work on the food photography and to Barbara Fritz for the food styling.

And lastly, to my editor, Susan Leon, whose patience and guidance I could not have done without.

To all the aforementioned I raise a glass of thanks!

# A Special Word of Caution

Mushrooms run the gamut from edible and excellent to deadly poisonous. Only about a dozen or so types, out of some thirty thousand species, are considered *deadly*. These few types, however, can grow in great quantity, often among harmless species. They also include some of the most attractive mushrooms in the forest, being pure white or bright in color and elegant in stature. There are about another hundred or so species that are considered poisonous to a lesser degree. Still other species are edible but never considered for culinary purposes, being either too small or bitter or offensive for reasons like texture or smell. Then there are those varieties that make excellent eating and are the subject of this book.

In no way does this book attempt to describe mushrooms for the purpose of identification, which is a science best left to the experts; nor does it encourage beginners to pick their own. The last chapter, "Caveats and New Friends," provides a more detailed explanation of the dangers inherent in picking wild mushrooms. It also suggests a way to get you started in your own pursuit of edible wild mushrooms by listing the names and addresses of various mycological clubs around the nation.

Be very careful when receiving gifts of wild mushrooms from friends or neighbors. Make *absolutely* sure they know what they are doing and what they are picking. Reject any offers from strangers who seem to sell wild mushrooms casually, and don't assume mushrooms are safe because you "bought" them. Mushroom picking and buying cannot be casual; the known integrity of your local merchant and his supplier's knowledge are essential.

One last word to the wise: avoid eating *any* mushrooms that are raw or barely cooked as this can cause severe distress or allergic reactions in some individuals.

# Contents

# JOE'S BOOK OF MUSHROOM COOKERY

**CHAPTER ONE**

# *Introduction*

This book began in a moment. The moment occurred on a hot August afternoon about twenty years ago. I was with my father (then a second-generation proprietor of Joe's, our family restaurant in Reading, Pennsylvania) in the front seat of our jeep, and we bumped and jolted over a backwoods dirt road about ten miles outside town. June and July had ravaged the forests around Berks County with a merciless string of blisteringly hot days. It was the third year of a drought that had sent us very occasional periods of snow in the winters, reluctant showers in the spring, and unrelentingly dry summers. Drought is hard on wild mushrooms.

On this particular afternoon our hopes of finding any mushrooms for the restaurant were as bleak as the parched leaves strewn like litter on the forest floor. Still we looked and bumped and looked, running our eyes over every leaf, rock, fern, and bit of fallen debris of the midsummer woods. We searched, straining our eyes forward to the depth of the forest and right back to the wheels of the jeep as we slowly crawled ahead on that dusty road. It was another day of looking for mushrooms, another fruitless search, hoping to locate something we knew we wouldn't find.

I remember plenty of other days just like it and plenty of successful days, too, when my mother and father would go out and fill their baskets with various kinds of mushrooms. Whatever the outcome of the day's excursion, however, I was invariably unmoved. A few years before I had discovered

America's favorite pastime. I was now a teenager and a confirmed Phillies fan, who fidgeted at the prospect of spending my summer afternoons on those interminably long and totally boring wild mushroom hunts. Fresh air was no big deal, and nature was a given of life, as predictable as my father's insistence that I accompany the family to the woods every Sunday. The more he tried to tell me how wonderful the outdoors was, the more intransigent I became. I much preferred to stay in the car and listen to radio broadcasts of the Phillies games while my parents went deep into the woods to pursue this damn passion of theirs, which I hated, and which I knew would return us home too late to see "The Twentieth Century" or even "The Ed Sullivan Show." My only revenge against the injustice of it all was curling up inside the car, getting into the game, and not being "out there." I suppose at some point my father gave up on me, because I remember listening to a lot of Phillies games and running down the battery in the family car.

My father always said that the mushrooms don't come to you; you have to go out and get them, which was his way of giving me a sort of mini-lecture on life. (He was right, by the way—about the mushrooms, that is.) So here we were again, on another expedition, only this time my father would not stand for my protests. Our restaurant's supply was practically depleted, and we were growing desperate. We needed mushrooms. So we went bumping through the woods on this rock-marked dirt and grass road somewhere in the state game lands. We were about a mile into the woods when the road forked. We crawled forward to the right, and as I was peering out the window in another weary look-see, I spotted some tan-colored fleshy caps about twenty feet away from our jeep.

"Hold it!" I yelled to Pop, and the jerk on his brake jolted us both forward in our seats. I opened the door and jumped out and on my way spotted two more mushrooms to my immediate right, then three more larger caps underneath a fern by my feet, and then about ten in a cluster among some fallen leaves, all on the way to the original few I had seen. I could hear my father just reaching the edge of the woods about twenty feet away from where I was standing, but close enough to hear, "Oh my God, it's loaded." We were experiencing a rare phenomenon in mushroom hunting, a forest full of mushrooms in a season of unrelenting dryness—and at a time when we were in need of a miracle. Biblical scholars have proposed that the manna that fell from the heavens and fed the Israelites on their long journey to the Promised Land was a fungus that sprang up overnight. Indeed, the *Boletus subglabripes* we found that day would have filled their needs nicely, being of excellent flavor and robust quantities.

Since I was the one who had spotted these mushrooms, I felt as if I had practically saved the business from extinction, and, in fact, my father and mother treated me like a hero for the next few days. From then on my attitude changed. I sensed something positive and, weirdly enough, futuristic about this whole business of hunting mushrooms. I also felt that it was one of the closest moments I'd ever shared with my father.

There is a footnote to this episode. Since that summer, but for one or two loners, we have never again ever found that mushroom in that spot, or anywhere else; we've found lots of other kinds, but not that one. I recall that day as if time had never passed, picking alongside my father and filling our baskets up high and going back for more. But most of all I recall sensing my father's deep, inner joy as we picked in silence, and I knew that this was a day reserved for just the two of us, a day that became a memory while it was still happening.

After that day there was no question about what I would do for a good part of my life. I was going to be in the restaurant business. When my wife, Heidi, and I graduated from college in 1974, we returned to Reading, where I learned about cooking at my father's side. The two of us would stand over a large, butcher block table while he tried to teach me about cuts of meat and characteristics of different wild mushrooms, and I tried to sound smarter than I was. It was not easy for him. Eventually, though, he got enough across to me to retire from the business in 1978. Heidi worked with my mother and learned all the desserts and pastry techniques that she had developed over more than thirty years in the business.

My father taught me about the different types of wild mushrooms and their varied flavors. It was he who showed me that the magic and secret of dried mushrooms was in the rich liquor derived from reconstitution. He patiently explained all that he had learned from years of working with mushrooms. Gradually we integrated more and more different kinds of mushrooms into our dishes in the restaurant, and when we got a large quantity of fresh mushrooms, we would serve them alone, braised, in their own sauce.

We began coming up with new recipes for mushrooms. Yet the more we looked for new ideas in existing cookbooks, the more we realized that mushroom cookery had not advanced much beyond the classic concepts of the French masters as collected in *Larousse Gastronomique*. This involved little more than adding them to a dish, declaring what great and unique flavors they have, then dousing them with wine, cognac, vermouth, and ten different spices. Similarly, we were troubled because many of the recipes of the new cuisine we saw seemed to include mushrooms as window dressing, not as flavor enhancers themselves. ("Oh, look, a morel! How darling!")

Mushrooms *do* have unique flavors, and the intention of this book is to alter your culinary perceptions about mushrooms and to show you how to prepare them to maximize their delicate and subtle flavors. This does not mean the recipes are difficult; on the contrary, most are easy to follow once a few basic techniques have been mastered. In addition, most of the recipes in this book contain not more than six or seven ingredients, our theory being that the fewer the ingredients in the dish, the greater their emphasis on the flavor of the mushrooms themselves.

Moreover, you do not have to be an avid picker of mushrooms to enjoy wild mushroom flavors. Whether they are derived from fresh, dried, or canned forms, a treasury of flavor is concealed in commercially available mushrooms, an ever-growing variety of which may be found at your local supermarket or food specialty store. This book is therefore written as much for the beginner as for the chef experienced in mushroom cookery, and as much for the person who has no interest in picking his own mushrooms as for the hunter who has gathered them for years.

Good cooking depends on the right preparation, and to guide the reader in his exploration of an unfamiliar cooking territory, I have provided a section on selected species of edible mushrooms and their culinary characteristics. There are also sections on the theory and practice of cooking with mushrooms, discussions on what sorts of flavor complement mushrooms, things to watch for when purchasing them, and descriptions of the various forms in which mushrooms can be made for use in the kitchen: duxelles, extracts, purees and so forth. I hope you will read these sections carefully before you begin cooking; they will help you to understand what makes the particular dishes in the recipe sections distinctive and exactly what problems may be encountered in preparing them.

## A Note on the Recipes in This Book

The recipes are described as preparations for four people, except where indicated otherwise.

In most recipes, the salting technique—a combination of salt, sugar, and soy sauce—is specific. These recipes have been made according to my own taste. You should adjust the proportions to suit your own taste.

All eggs are U.S. Grade A large (2 ounces).

All measurements are standard level.

The body of the recipes is designed to use mushrooms that are readily obtainable in grocery or specialty food stores, like dried morels and cepes. Although many recipes specify the variety considered to be most suitable for that particular dish, substitutions may be made to allow for fluctuations in availability.

## A Special Note

Many of the receipes for sauces use dried mushrooms. This is because morels, cepes, and the like are seasonal and, even in season, are not as readily available as their dried versions. If you are fortunate enough to have fresh mushrooms available, you may still use these recipes by substituting eight parts fresh mushroom for one part dried. The liquid yield, however, must remain the same, so I advise that you *reduce* the water called for in the recipe by one-fourth. Then proceed as directed.

CHAPTER TWO

# Definitions and Culinary Characteristics of Selected Mushrooms

## Mushroom Words and Roots

The word *mushroom* has a roundabout origin. From the Greek word *mykēs,* we get our word *mycology,* the study of fungi. Hence, a mycologist is one who studies fungi, to which plant group mushrooms belong. A mycophagist is one who eats mushrooms, a mycophile is one who loves mushrooms, and a mycophobe is someone who fears mushrooms. The word *champignon* is the French for mushroom, related to the word for field, *champ,* and used to refer to the species *Agaricus campestris,* a common field mushroom. Later the term came to embrace all forms of fleshy fungi, large and small, molds, parasites, etc. A similar process accounts for the nomenclatural origin of the St. George's mushroom, which was known in France before 1200 as *mousseron* from *mousse,* a Teutonic word for moss. In England following the Norman conquest of 1066, the name became *muscheron* by 1440 and *mushroom* by 1563. The name stuck and thereafter was applied to most varieties of fleshy fungi.

A mushroom itself is the fruiting body of a fleshy fungus that is composed of small, threadlike fibers called hyphae. A larger grouping of these hyphae is called a mycelium and composes the network we can see when we remove earth to discover the fungi beneath its surface. Somewhere along this network of filaments a mushroom pushes up through the surface of the earth and becomes visible and recognizable as a mushroom.

Unlike most plants, mushrooms require no sunlight to grow and therefore produce no chlorophyll. Their nutrients come from the plants and matter upon which they feed. In actuality mushrooms are fleshy molds that grow in association with other living matter, either in a symbiotic relationship that is beneficial to both host and mold, or parasitically, aiding in the decay of the host. Mushrooms often grow in what is termed a "mycorrhizal" relationship with the roots of specific trees. This is why many species can be located—at the right time of year and with enough moisture—by simply locating the types of tree with which the mushrooms are associated.

The biological purpose of the mushroom is to carry and disperse its spores, which are the genetic information carriers for the fungus. These spores are different for every mushroom, and their microscopic characteristics often determine their identification. This is why the hobby or science of mushroom identification must remain the province of the specialist.

Nevertheless, much of the identification of wild mushrooms comes from macroscopic features such as size, shape, and color of the various components of the mushrooms in question. As related to their use in cooking, it is useful first to discuss the characteristics that make the mushrooms appropriate or inappropriate for a given culinary purpose.

## Selected Mushrooms and Their Culinary Characteristics

The first character to take into account is relative availability. Basically, mushrooms fall into one of two categories: those mushrooms that are commercially available in this country (whether fresh, canned, or dried) and those mushrooms that must usually be picked wild but may be seen occasionally on the commercial market.

Another characteristic is the flavor of the mushroom, and although this seems to be an obvious characteristic, it is the one—as I have suggested previously—that is generally ignored in cookbooks. This will be discussed in more detail in describing the individual mushrooms.

A third point is texture and the way a mushroom changes when cooked. Some mushrooms are quite delicate and quickly wilt on cooking. Others are brittle when raw, then hold together better after they have been blanched. Some require very long cooking to become tender. These traits will be pointed out where relevant.

9

Yet another consideration from a culinary standpoint is the condition of the cap and its suitability for cooking and ingestion. Some mushroom species, like the slippery jacks, have viscous caps that can cause indigestion and must therefore be peeled before cooking. The vast majority of mushrooms that you use do not need to be peeled, and this includes the domestic market mushroom. The ones that do require it will be pointed out. Also, mushrooms with viscous caps do not make suitable blanching extracts. The liquid that is left is slimy and unappetizing and, in some cases, difficult to digest.

A fifth factor is the best method for cooking the mushrooms you have. In the following chapter two methods of sautéing will be discussed, the low-heat method and the high-heat method (see pages 50–51). The recommended method for each mushroom described will be pointed out there. Some mushrooms are useful only for their aesthetic qualities of color and/or shape and may be suited best for simple salads. Others, like the Chicken-of-the-Woods, can be used as meat substitutes. Most of the mushrooms considered here will be suitable for almost all of the methods described in the chapter on basic preparations and for the recipes listed in the body of this book. What *you* should become sensitive to are the sometimes subtle, sometimes obvious differences among the varieties of mushrooms. Most mushroom hunters are aware of these, but a large majority of professional cooks fail to appreciate these differences.

The last factor to point out is the method of preservation. This is an area that need concern primarily the avid mushroom picker, but it is useful to know the means and pitfalls of keeping mushrooms. You may face a situation where you are the sudden recipient of some fresh mushrooms, or you may choose to buy a quantity of them from a store and wish to preserve them for the future.

# The Major Varieties of Edible Mushrooms

The following types of mushrooms are arranged in their rough order of market availability, the common commercial mushrooms discussed first, followed by their more exotic cousins. The exception to this is when a wild type closely related to a domestic type is discussed, i.e., when the mushrooms are species of the same genus, one being common and available, another being more exotic. This is done so that the culinary characteristics of mushrooms in the same genus can be discussed together.

You can expect to pay considerably more for truly wild types of mushrooms than for the common domestic type. But you should also be aware of the fact that some types are not as wild as they once were. Shiitake, oyster mushrooms, and enoki are all being cultivated commercially nowadays, are sold fresh, and are forming a new class of mushrooms I call the "cultivatable exotic mushrooms," a category that did not exist several years ago. Bear in mind that these mushrooms will continue to decrease in price as they are made more widely available in stores. These are the supermarket varieties of the future, and it is well worth your while to do some comparison shopping before you buy these at your favorite corner gourmet shop, because you may get a better price elsewhere. The other wild mushrooms discussed, however, will always demand a premium price because their presence is seasonal and dependent on weather conditions for their growth. It is not until they become "cultivatable" that they will be less in price.

### A Note on Mushroom Names

All mushrooms are designated by their genus and species names. For example, *Agaricus brunnescens* is in the genus *Agaricus* (note capital letter beginning) and is the species *brunnescens* (note lower-case letter beginning). A *variety* is a variant of a species. The botanical family to which various genera belong is simply indicated by an English term like *bolete* or *agaric* rather than long scientific names like Boletaceae or Agaricaceae. The word *type* is used as it relates to characteristics of a culinary nature as opposed to a scientific or taxonomic one.

### *Agaricus brunnescens (bisporus)* (Common Domestic Mushroom and Related Species)

Let's begin the discussion of the specific types of mushrooms with the one we know best—the common supermarket variety, *Agaricus brunnescens* (formerly known as Agaricus bisporus). It has been described as mealy, dirty, rich, earthy, mushroomy, and bland, depending on whether you are discussing it on its own merits or comparing it to other mushrooms. We shouldn't think too harshly of this easy-to-buy fungus, which has found itself snuggled amidst onions and gravy as a complement to meat, or awash in a quagmire of tomato sauce, mozzarella, and pepperoni atop pizza. After all, it is from the millions of caps of humble market mushrooms now in our memories and digestive systems that we have developed an interest in wild mushrooms.

The tendency in any discussion of wild mushrooms is to denigrate the

**11**

market variety. It suffers by comparison to the rich and often complex flavors of some of the more exotic varieties and is downgraded in any serious discussion of mushrooms in general. Yet when we think of mushrooms, and specifically their flavor, it is the taste of the common market variety that we bring to mind from the realm of our sensory memory. We know that familiar taste and texture, whether we like it or not, and it determines whether we "like mushrooms" or not. It is our standard of comparison by default, because it's been the only mushroom commonly available to us from our retail stores.

The *Agaricus brunnescens* (formerly called *A. bisporus*) was first cultivated by French horticulturists around 1700. It was fashionable at that time to grow one's own melons and pineapples in hotbeds of composted manure. Many gardeners found their hotbeds producing an unplanned-for "weed," now known as *Agaricus brunnescens*. This accidental appearance suggested a method for cultivating these "wild mushrooms"—and that's exactly what they were in those days—for mushrooms had never been domesticated before. The conditions for controlled fruiting were perfected, and the caves outside Paris became the earthy womb that was to produce centuries of delicious offspring.

These mushrooms came to be known as Champignons de Paris, and for the first time could be counted on to grace the French table any day of the year. The practice of mushroom cultivation spread slowly at first, because a rigid cult of secrecy surrounded this new industry. Most of the work on mushroom diseases and methods of propagation had to be literally rediscovered elsewhere. But once introduced, the idea of mushroom cultivation spread rapidly, reaching Sweden and England during the late eighteenth century. Serious work began in this country about 1900; today the United States is one of the world's leading growers of cultivated mushrooms. And all this was not for some bland-tasting fungus of no repute.

The flavor of *A. brunnescens* is what most of us know as "the mushroom flavor." Indeed, there are many who believe that all mushrooms taste alike. I am often asked the question in my restaurant, "Do wild mushrooms *really* taste different from cultivated ones?" Yes, of course they taste different. But the taste of *Agaricus brunnescens* is not a bad flavor by any means, earthy and creamy. Some people consider it a bit slippery, which has led to the unfortunate practice of adding lemon juice to mushroom dishes.

The texture is reassuringly firm when raw, softer when cooked but still firm by mushroom standards. The cultivated mushroom must be cooked for a relatively lengthy period of time for it to become as soft and limp as most wild types become in a few short minutes. And this outstanding feature of the domestic mushroom cannot be overlooked. Its firm texture has allowed it to survive and flourish in a world where we like our food and our beliefs rigid and round like heavenly spheres. It's the wild mushrooms that are the broken, earthy arcs, imperfect, but ever so fascinating. In other words, these cultivated mushrooms fit our ideas of what a mushroom *should* be.

Other related species of the genus *Agaricus* share the basic characteristics of the domestic species, except that a few of them are not as firm. Some people maintain that the wild species taste better or nuttier, but my conclusion is that those nuttier flavors originate in the euphoria of picking and eating one's own fresh meadow mushrooms.

One difference that does exist between the wild and cultivated species is that the cultivated tends to maintain its rigidity longer. The caps of the wild *A. campestris* open more quickly than the cultivated types, and its texture is more pliable and resilient. This rigidity in the cultivated mushroom has led to its description as "chalky," because when pulled apart it breaks somewhat like a piece of chalk, whereas the wild type tends to tear unevenly. The resilient softness of the wild type seems to give it a silkier texture in the mouth. One "breaks apart" the cultivated mushroom in the mouth while one "chews" the wild type.

The wild species can grow to be quite large. We know, for example, that both the mature *A. arvensis* (aptly called the horse mushroom) and *A. augustus* can weigh several pounds. Imagine one mushroom feeding a whole family! The *A. campestris* (meadow mushroom) is the most common species, however, and it rarely reaches those heroic proportions. It is also the most frequently picked wild mushroom in the world along with the morel, blewit, and cepe. Refer to the bibliography for books on mushroom identification for this and other edible wild mushrooms.

Lastly, in regard to the cultivated mushroom, it should be mentioned that several varieties of this species may be available in the market at different times. The browner or darker mushroom is not necessarily (as many think) a spoiled version of the pure white variety. It is merely a different variety commonly referred to as the "cream" mushroom. There are other varieties as well; some are pure white, some have a hirsute cap surface, others a scaly surface. These are varieties of the *Agaricus brunnescens* and appear on supermarket shelves either because of the time of year or because they are coming from a supplier from whose location that variety is grown. The flavors vary slightly but not significantly. The snow-white varieties appear to be the most popular, possibly because they seem "cleaner" to us.

Overall, the commercial market mushroom and its wild relatives rank above average in quality, flavor, and texture.

## Cooking with *Agaricus brunnescens*

When you are buying domestic mushrooms, never purchase those whose dark gills can be seen. These are older mushrooms. At their best, the cap should completely enclose the upper part of the stem. This is referred to as a closed cap. Do not purchase mushrooms that have browned from exposure. This sort of browning is different from mushrooms that have a natural brown pigmentation. This browning means the mushrooms are beginning to rot from too much exposure and is a sign of imminent decay.

Domestic mushrooms can be cooked by various methods. As with most mushrooms, they yield high amounts of water during cooking and shrink, so be sure that you have enough mushrooms to start with. Savory is an excellent herb to use when preparing these mushrooms, because it tends to intensify the natural flavor of the *Agaricus*. Use onions to round out the flavor and to cut the buttery-earthy character usually counteracted with lemon juice. Lemon juice may be used, but very sparingly, because a dish too acidified with it will be ruined.

These mushrooms are ideal for stuffing because the cuplike caps hold the filling during baking or steaming, and unlike some mushrooms, the stems are completely edible and digestible. Often they are discarded in favor of the caps, but are very useful for one of the most versatile forms of flavoring preparations—duxelles. Simply chop them and follow the directions for making duxelles (see pages 59–67). Also, an extract can be made from the stems by blanching them (see page 73–74).

### *Volvariella volvacea*
### (Straw Mushroom)

Known commonly as the straw mushroom or the padi-straw mushroom, this is the mushroom most often seen in a stir-fried dish in your favorite Chinese restaurant. It is a remarkably silky-textured mushroom, and the entire mushroom, stem and cap, are eaten together. The flavor is mild and of no great culinary significance except that it is one of the few mushrooms other than the domestic kind that is easily obtained—and it is a pretty mushroom, a feature welcome in any dish.

The straw mushroom always comes in cans. Since all the shrinkage that can take place has already occurred during the sterilization process, what you see is what you get after cooking. These mushrooms are obviously good for stir-frying, but in our restaurant we use them pickled in martinis, and they are also suitable in stews and casseroles.

Don't look for miracles of flavor from this mushroom. But when you need a visual pickup in a stir-fried dish or in a salad, this is your mushroom. Make sure to buy the "peeled" straw mushrooms, which will be indicated on the can.

## *Flammulina velutipes*
## (Enoki or Enokitake)

The *Flammulina velutipes* is generally imported from Japan, although some people are cultivating it in this country. The commercial variety of the mushroom is very small and works best in salads and dishes where appearance is more important than flavor. The flavor is very mild and slightly applelike, perfect for a sauté with Calvados as was suggested to me by Helen Turley, a winemaker in the Napa Valley (see recipe, page 122). The mushroom can be bought fresh, but caution must be used when buying, since these mushrooms are often oxidized or well into a browning stage, especially at the lower part of the stems, by the time they reach market. It is, in fact, this perishability factor that has kept the *Flammulina* from becoming popular. The wild species also lacks a "meaty" quality. But its flavor is pleasant, though mild, and like its commercial variety it should be considered for salads and stir-frying.

## *Lentinus edodes*
## (Shiitake, Black Forest Mushroom, Golden Oak)

Together with the *Pleurotus ostreatus* (oyster mushroom) the shiitake is becoming the most widely available cultivatable exotic mushroom in the food market. Although you may not see it in your local supermarket, this mushroom is catching on fast in specialty food stores. Until a few years ago it was available only in dried form from Japan, which is still the world's largest exporter of it. But in recent years shiitake farms have sprung up in the United States and Canada, and these mushrooms are being brought to restaurants and stores fresh. You must wait for chanterelles and morels to come into season, but shiitake are now available all year. Eat only the caps, because the stems are fibrous and tough, usable for extract and little else. These caps are a little spongy in texture, and this contrast to the chewy domestic mushroom accounts for some of their popularity. The flavor is pleasantly smoky and distinct, and the extract from shiitake is a great base for a soup (Chapter 3) or sauce (Chapter 4).

When buying shiitake, try to pick the youngest specimens (those that measure 4 inches or less across the top of the cap) because these will have more usable flesh than the older ones, about 15% of which will be nonusable stem. With the very smallest ones, you can even eat the stem, which will be crunchy rather than fibrous and chewy. Remember that you will be paying for this mushroom by the pound and that the stem is included in that cost; so make sure that you are buying enough *caps* for your purpose.

Because their smoky flavor and aroma add an element of Oriental intrigue to any dish, shiitake are excellent for any general mushroom use. Butter, garlic, and a variety of the stronger spices, particularly chili, coriander, and pepper, go well with shiitake. It is one of the few mushrooms that will stand up to these spicy flavors, and, in fact, they tend to enhance the shiitake flavor. The mushroom's versatility makes it a natural complement to almost all foods, including sausage. Because shiitake are available fresh, the dried version is not as highly thought of as it once was. Although reconstituted shiitake do not come back like the fresh form, the liquid from the reconstitution is a rich source of flavor and can be combined with fresh shiitake in a dish to reinforce its flavor.

### *Pleurotus ostreatus* and *Pleurotus Sajor-Caju* (Shimeji, Tree Oyster, Phoenix, Pleurotte, Oyster)

This mushroom has long been a favorite of wild mushroom seekers. Until a few years ago it could be found only wild, growing from trees from midsummer to midfall. Now, thanks to the efforts of American mycological researchers, it has begun appearing commercially on the shelves of specialty food stores and, in some localities, in local supermarkets. For texture the oyster mushroom is one of the choicest commercial varieties available. The entire body of the mushroom can be used, and it is a wondrous silky mushroom that is a joy for use in almost any mushroom dish. The smoky-gray cap is very attractive and can be sliced raw into salads. The oysterlike flavor that gives the mushroom its name is best brought out by the use of butter; one of my favorite ways of making this mushroom is deep-frying it and serving it as my own mock Fried Oysters (see pages 131–132). It is also excellent for stir-frying in oil and for duxelles, and although it makes a good extract, its virtues as a fresh mushroom are limitless. If you are a seasoned and experienced mushroom hunter and you find this mushroom wild, sauté it, and if you have enough left over to preserve, freeze it.

### *Auricularia polytricha* and *auricula* (Cloud-Ear, Wood-Ear, Jew's Ear)

The genus *Auricularia* comprises several species suitable for cooking. The two most common are the *A. polytricha* and *A. auricula*. *A. polytricha* is called *mou leh* in China, where it is cultivated. The *A. auricula* is commonly called the Jew's-ear or tree-ear. The terms "wood-ear" and "cloud-ear" have been assigned to them both. These distinctions are not critical, because they are similar in character, being partly gelatinous when wet, and hard and firm when dry.

The only way I have seen this fungus is in the dried form, as it is sold in Oriental grocery stores. To reconstitute them, place an ounce of the fungi in a quart of boiling water and let them simmer for several hours, replacing the water when necessary. You will be surprised to see how their size increases. These fungi are very crunchy and will not soften further beyond this texture with more boiling. When you are cooking with the *Auricularia,* slice them very thin and use them in stir-fry dishes or for stuffings that require some interesting textural contrast. In our restaurant I use them for stuffing fresh shad along with green onions and five-spice sauce (see pages 152–153). Alas, the liquid from the reconstituted fungi is dark but not particularly flavorful.

### *Cantharellus cibarius* and *Craterellus cantharellus* (Chanterelle)

The best known and loved chanterelle is the common *Cantharellus cibarius,* the beautiful, egg-yellow, almost flowerlike mushroom otherwise known in France as the *girolle*, in Germany as the *pfifferling*, and in Poland as the *kurka* or *liszka*. Chanterelles have also become enormously popular in the United States, where the industry of harvesting and selling them has expanded greatly.

The popularity of the chanterelle derives from a combination of factors. First, it has a distinctive, fruity, and peppery nutlike flavor that stands out in any dish and adds a rich complexity to it. Second, it tends to grow in large numbers when it fruits and can be preserved for the future by canning. Third, it is easy to spot in a forest, owing to its bright orange color, contrasting with the green-brown undergrowth of the forest floor. Moreover, chanterelles are not easily mistaken for other mushrooms (with the exception of the jack-o'-lantern, which is poisonous). Fourth, they are common and plentiful in most areas of Europe and North America. These factors make the chanterelle one of the most popular and widely picked wild mushrooms in the world.

Strictly speaking, the chanterelle is the species *Cantharellus cibarius.* But another mushroom, *Craterellus cantharellus,* is also considered a chanterelle because of its similarity in appearance and flavor to *C. cibarius.* Indeed, the two are not far apart genetically or taxonomically; *C. cibarius* has definite gill lines running down from the cap onto the stem, while the *Cr. cantharellus* gills are much smoother and less well defined, giving the underside an almost

**17**

gill-less appearance. I have used both, and the flavor characteristics are very similar. The texture of chanterelles is smooth and slightly chewy, with the younger, tinier caps being crunchy. The flavor of chanterelles bursts forth onto the palate, and it is this distinction that makes it so prized in cooking. The stem is slightly more fibrous and chewy than the cap, but not significantly so—the whole mushroom can and should be used. The smell and flavor strongly resembles apricots, with a slightly peppery finish.

When buying chanterelles from the market, pick the freshest-looking and youngest specimens. These will be firm to the touch and a light orange to red-orange in color. This mushroom often looks "dead" on the shelves, because the thin and slight edges brown and dry rapidly. They can be revived very quickly under water, but do this only when you are ready to use them. Otherwise, refrigerate them in a paper or plastic bag as soon as you get home. Do *not* let them sit out on your kitchen table. When ready to use, clean them by removing the obvious dirt.

The chanterelle is a mushroom that needs a minimum of help from other ingredients to get its point across, so be careful how you use it. It gives casseroles and soups a distinct chanterelle flavor, so use it sparingly. On the other hand, it goes very well indeed with fowl and game, especially when the preparation includes nuts. It does not go well with beef because its fruity flavor does not blend well with the flavor of beef; I would also advise caution when using it with fish. Simply think of the chanterelle somewhat as a fruit rather than a mushroom when you are deciding whether or not to use it.

The three ingredients I use when preparing chanterelles are butter, onions, and chopped, dried apricots. These are the components of Chanterelle Duxelles, which is described on page 66. Chanterelles lose their moisture during sautéing, but not quite as much as do other mushrooms. Therefore use the high-heat method of sautéing to maintain as much of the texture as possible. Chanterelles can also be baked, with bacon wrapped around them. If you find a large quantity of chanterelles, preserve them by canning or brining. Do not dry them, since the liquid from the reconstituted dried chanterelles is very difficult to use, unless the chanterelles are reconstituted in a veal or chicken stock. However, there are two situations in which dried chanterelles are very useful. Making an aperitif is one. Place an ounce of the dried chanterelles in a fifth of vodka and let it sit for a week. This is a typical method for making mushroom liquor. The second situation is when you want to enhance a stew or soup with an exotic flavor.

Related good and useful species are the *Cantharellus lateritius* and *Cantharellus clavatus,* the latter being a very large mushroom when mature. Other recommended species are *Cantharellus tubaeformis, Cantharellus minor, Cantharellus xanthopus, Gomphus clavatus,* and *Polyozellus multiplex.*

The *Cantharellus cinnabarinus* is another species of chanterelle, but it is much smaller, only an inch or two high and an inch or less across the cap. The color is bright red-orange, making it one of the prettiest mushrooms in the summer forest, growing in areas where there is a considerable amount of moisture or water flow, as on banks of very wet roadsides. This mushroom usually grows in some quantity but even several handfuls will not get you very far in satisfying a voracious appetite. They are best used in salads, and have a distinct, peppery flavor that really stands out. They are also striking in a jellied madrilene served in a clear wine goblet.

### Craterellus cornucopioides
### (False Truffle, Trumpet-of-Death, Horn-of-Plenty)

Despite its rather grim-sounding name this mushroom is excellent and commonly picked in Europe. As the name "false truffle" implies, the species is often used to mimic truffles because of its dark color. The *Craterellus* is related by genus to the chanterelle, but it is a much more delicate mushroom in texture if not in flavor. In the wild it looks like a fragile, gray-black flower, and can grow to a height of over three inches. The stem and cap are continuous, and there is no difference in their texture or flavor; therefore, the whole mushroom is usable.

It has an excellent flavor, which is revealed only once it is dried and then reconstituted. The outstanding quality of this extract is its rich, buttery character. It makes one of the few mushroom sauces that go exceptionally well with fish. The best method for preserving the mushroom is drying, and it can then be used for extract or can be crushed and powdered in a mortar and pestle and saved in that form as an addition to cream or clear sauces for fish or veal.

### Morchella esculenta and Related Species
### (Morel)

Like lone aristocrats, morels break earth long before most other edible mushrooms. They and their relative, truffles, stand apart from these other families of mushrooms in more ways than one. Most commonly known mushrooms are classed as basidiomycetes, which means that their spores (reproductive information carriers) protrude from a clublike structure called a basidium. In morels and truffles, however, these spores are contained in a closed structure called an ascus and are therefore classed as ascomycetes. It is as if from birth morels and truffles exist in their own sheltered environment and simply do not mingle with the masses. It might be successfully argued that morels are not mushrooms at all, being so different taxonomically, but that argument is considered esoteric, and most experts are happy to include them in all general discussions of wild mushrooms. Whether the morels are happy is another matter.

Morels (also called sponge mushrooms, spongies, and, in eastern Pennsylvania, corncob mushrooms) include several different species of the genus *Morchella*. French chefs I have spoken to in this country bemoan the fact that our domestic morels are not of the high quality they are used to in France, the implication being that American soil is simply inferior to that of French. Their complaints are not unfounded but probably not for the reason they so patriotically believe. Imported morels are usually smaller, darker, and of a smokier quality. This latter aspect is important, especially where dried mushrooms are concerned, because it suggests that the European method of drying morels involves some smoking as well as air drying. Also, American morels are mostly of the species *M. esculenta,* which is a larger, tan-colored mushroom. *Esculenta* is usually referred to as the light, yellow, or tan morel, as opposed to the black morel, which is one of the species *conica, angusticeps,* or *elata;* these latter comprise the bulk of imported morels. All of the above grow in both Europe and America, as well as in India and Pakistan, where many "European" morels originate. Both imported and domestic morels are picked commercially, the difference being in the preponderance of each species and the method of drying. All of them share common flavor characteristics and for that reason will be discussed as a group.

Morels have distinctive caps and stems, but they are different from most other wild mushrooms in that the stem and cap are both hollow. The stem is slightly tougher than the cap and should therefore be cut away before using the cap in a dish, although the stem itself should be saved and used for duxelles. The cap is regular in shape and is comprised of a series of round or oval involutions, from which the name "sponge mushroom" is derived. The regularity of the cap shape is important because it distinguishes it in appearance from the *Gyromitra esculenta,* which resembles a squashed version of the morel and is therefore called the false morel. The *Gyromitra* can also do a great deal more harm than visually mimic the real thing—it is poisonous. Also, the *Gyromitra esculenta* is marketed quite frequently, and I have seen it in cans labeled "morels." There is a common belief that it loses its toxicity on cooking or drying, but there is no reason for you to chance proving or disproving that thesis. Stay away from it!

Morels are most often purchased dry, and the only thing to watch for is worm holes. These holes indicate that the mushrooms will have large numbers of tiny bugs crawling out of them during reconstitution. If fresh morels are available at your market, check for rotting. When morels are shipped fresh and become exposed to heat, the innermost section of the carton of mushrooms builds up heat faster than the outer perimeter, which is exposed to some air. The enzymatic process of rotting begins and spreads from the center outward. Smell the fresh morels. They should be virtually odorless or slightly nutty and should have no signs of moisture on any part. You might notice some drying along the edges but don't worry about that. It's moisture that causes problems. Also remember when buying morels that the stems are tough, so select the ones with the shortest stems. Refrigerate them in a paper or plastic bag immediately on returning home. They will keep like this for several days. When preparing them for use, wash them to remove any sand or dirt. Morels, whether fresh or dried, often come from sandy areas and should be cleared of any residue before use.

Prepare the fresh morels as indicated in the recipes. Extract made from dried morels is rivaled only by that made from cepes. The extract can be stored and frozen, but do not salt it until ready to use. The reconstituted mushrooms can sometimes be used in the same dish as the one in which the extract was used for the flavor. The recipe for making morel extract is listed in the section on sauces; when sautéing morels, use the low-heat method (see page 119) to evaporate as much liquid as possible to maximize their flavor. There are two ingredients that support and bring out the flavor of morels because of their similarity to the morel flavor. The first is sweet green or red pepper. Use it sparingly so you don't overwhelm the morel flavor; it is remarkable how similar the two flavors are, and combining them is the best way of expressing the morel taste. The second ingredient is caraway seed, which harmonizes well with the earthy character of the morel. Experiment with them both and use them together with morels to make the morel taste more like itself than when used alone. Garlic also goes well with morels, especially in combination with cream sherry or Madeira, but the use of either ingredient creates a different flavor from that of pure morels—as distinguished from pepper and caraway, which support the morel flavor itself. Another character of the morel, its hollowness, makes it very suitable for stuffing with a mousse of pheasant and parsley.

If you discover a cache of fresh morels, dry them. Canning does nothing for them, but drying promises future dishes redolent of their singular flavor. This simple and uncomplicated process is explained in Chapter 16.

### *Clitocybe nuda*
### (Blewit)

Blewits are very popular among avid wild mushroom hunters. The English, who, as a group, pick very few mushrooms, have gathered blewits to their breasts and have embraced them with great affection. One reason for their popularity is that they are aesthetically attractive, light blue to violet color, both on the cap and in the gills underneath. The taste is subtle and typical of the genera *Clitocybe, Lepista,* and *Tricholoma.* Both cap and stem are usable. The methods for using the blewits are the same as for the genus *Agaricus* (see pages 13–14). They are excellent in soup or sautéed by the low-heat method and served over buckwheat groats (kasha).

The lesser-known but equally excellent *Clitocybe irena* is a mushroom well worth the effort of seeking out.

## The Boletes

This is the large family to which the *Boletus edulis,* or cepe, and *Suillus luteus* belong. It is called the family Boletaceae, which is distinguished from the family Agaricaceae by the presence of pores beneath the cap as opposed to gills. From a culinary standpoint these pores can be troublesome when the mushroom is fairly old, a condition characterized by its having a very soft, spongy underside, readily depressed when squeezed. In this case the pores should be cut away and discarded before the mushroom is used. On younger specimens the pores are tight enough to retain a pleasantly spongy, but somewhat firm texture.

Mycologists have subdivided this group of mushrooms several times in the past few decades but the list below represents the current names of old favorites. As for cooking boletes, refer to the section on *B. edulis* (the cepes, pages 23–24), and cook them the same way. Aside from the pores, the flesh is generally firmer than that of the agarics (gilled mushrooms), and these mushrooms have a more buttery and nutty flavor. The stem is fully usable but best for duxelles. The preferred method of preservation is drying, and all of the boletes make a distinctive extract that should be treated in the manner prescribed in the section on sauces (pages 73–74). Grilling is an excellent method for making the larger varieties of boletes, such as *B. Edulis* or *Tylopilus alboater.* The dried versions can be added to any soup, stew, or casserole for added flavor and interest. A consommé can be made from any type of bolete, using the salting method described on page 53.

The best edible boletes are the following: *B. affinis, B. badius, B. ballouii, B. cromapes, B. cyanescens, B. griseus, B. bicolor, B. edulis, B. separans, B. speciosus, B. variipes, B. subglabripes, Leccinum aurantiacum, Leccinum scabrum, Boletinellus merulioides, Strobilomyces floccopus* (old Man of the Woods), *Suillus americanus, S. brevipes, S. granulatus, S. grevillei, S. luteus, S. pictus, Tylopilus alboater.*

22

## *Boletus edulis*
## (Cepe, Steinpilz, Porcino, Borowik)

The *Boletus edulis* is the most universally loved and utilized mushroom in Europe. I will refer to it as the cepe, from the French word *cèpe* (and that, in turn, is from *cep,* which means "trunk" in Gascon, for the fat stem of the mushroom), because most people recognize it by that name. Indeed, the French and the Poles share an especially unbounded respect for its flavor and body, with the rest of Europe in almost equal reverence of its properties. No other mushroom combines flavor with meaty texture as does the cepe. As with morels, popular terminology is confused. Several distinct *Boletus* species enjoy the flavor and aromatic characteristics of the *Boletus edulis.*

It should be pointed out that genetically the *cèpe* (France), *Steinpilz* (German for "stone mushroom"), and *porcini* (Italian for "piglets") are all the same mushroom, although their relative sizes can differ markedly. The porcini, I have heard, can grow to as large as five pounds or more; indeed, the Italians slice off pieces from these mushrooms and grill them with cheese and spices. My friend Roy Thomas of Monterey Peninsula Winery told me he once found a California cepe that had to be rotated out of the ground and weighed over five pounds.

The average cepe, however, usually grows to a cap width of three to five inches and stands about two thirds of its cap width in height. The stem is tender and bulbous and is ideal for making duxelles. The flesh of the cap is the best meat, while the spongy mass of pores beneath the cap can be used if the specimens are young. If a mature cepe is picked when wet, then the pores will surely be water-soaked, and the mushroom will be hard to work with. But, as with most boletes, these pores are easily removed (as opposed to poly-pores, which we will get to later). The taste of a raw cepe has the characteristic butteriness of many wild mushrooms, and not until it is cooked does it reveal its wonders. The most amazing thing about it, though, is the remarkable extract it produces from the dried state.

When choosing fresh cepes in the market, search for worm holes, which, if present, will be most visible at the bottom of the stem. Commercial wild mushrooms are actually graded in Europe according to the percentage of worm holes they have relative to the overall surface of the stem. If you see more than 10 percent of the base of the stem ringed with holes, then don't buy it (this goes for any wild mushroom that you find on the market). The bugs work their way up the stem into the cap and spread out from there. Feel the stem. It should feel firm, not hollow or delicate. If the stem feels delicate, then you can be sure the mushroom is infested with bugs.

By far the most common form in which cepes are available is dried. Dried cepes, usually displayed in oversized apothecary jars, have become an almost obscenely expensive staple in specialty food stores. Oddly enough, the best buy is probably the most expensive—whole caps as opposed to slices—because they are pure *Boletus edulis,* usually with no stems. Sliced mushrooms (of whatever *Boletus* species) contain more stems by weight than caps, and the stems are always considered less desirable. Furthermore, sliced cepes are often adulterated with less fine species. So, although you can expect to pay a premium for whole caps, what you see is what you get.

The only way to check for authenticity is to smell the product. Pure cepes are known by their strong and distinctive odor, clean and earthy. If the mushrooms you are smelling have only a faint odor, then they're probably not cepes. The only exception to this rule are the porcini, which seem to have a fainter character than their northern cousins; but this is offset by the fact that porcini, even sliced, are usually unadulterated—the Italians are very scrupulous in what they market. Cepes can come from any country in Europe and America, too, and their aromas all differ; just be sure to follow your nose in deciding whether to buy or not. I would strongly recommend that you invest some money in a few ounces of pure, whole caps (usually Polish) of *Boletus edulis* to familiarize yourself with the smell. After a while it will become part of your sensory library, and you will be able to detect forgeries with a whiff.

If you are lucky enough to find fresh cepes, use them as indicated for the recipes that require fresh mushrooms. Most of you will only be able to obtain them dried, but this is far from second best. The derived extract of *Boletus edulis* is one of the finest cooking liquids in the world—meaty, fragrant, and lusty, far more complex than a beef or veal stock. Directions are given in the chapter on soups and sauces for making this extract, and I urge you to pay some attention to it. The dried cepe is excellent added to a casserole or stock pot; its rich body carries its flavors well and allows it to stand up to other flavors and improve them. Once the cepe is reconstituted, however, the mushroom itself becomes leathery and tough; but it can be used chopped, or sliced (very thinly because of its texture).

Meat stocks and onions go well with cepes. The mushroom and its extracts are especially well paired with beef, veal, pork, lamb, furred and feathered game, and with rice and pasta dishes. Its flavor is too strong to be used with most fish (swordfish, tuna, and shark being exceptions), and it should never be paired with fruit of any kind in a dish.

Drying is the best method of preserving cepes, as it is with any of the mushrooms in the *Boletus* category. Salting and canning are also good because they maintain the essential texture of the mushroom.

## *Suillus luteus*
### (Slippery Jack, Forest Mushroom)

The slippery jack plays the proverbial second fiddle to its famous cousin, the cepe. It is much less expensive than the cepe, but it has a strong and distinctive flavor all its own and is not much less tasty than the cepe. The character can be described as very musty as opposed to the cepe, which is very clean. Often sold in cheap plastic bags under the name "forest mushroom," the slippery jack is, in fact, a very good mushroom—the most commonly used diluter of commercially sold cepes.

When fresh and wet the cap is slimy and should be peeled before eating. The stem is firmer than the cap, and some do not think it is very good for eating. The pores beneath the cap are tight and compact and can be eaten with the flesh of the cap. Dried slippery jacks make an excellent extract, but one that is slimy if the caps are not peeled before drying. Use this mushroom as you would the cepe, in the methods described on page 24. One last thing worth noting is that this mushroom grows in great quantity throughout the world and may be the largest-selling commercial mushroom in circulation. It may only be a matter of time before it becomes popular as a commercial variety in this country.

## *Armillariella mellea*
### (Honey Mushroom)

The Poles call this mushroom *podpinki* and, along with various types of *Tricholoma*s picked in pine forests, it is among the most widely sought. In this country, it grows in deciduous forests, coming up in September in the East, in greatest quantities after heavy rains. One year I picked several bushels myself in a little over an hour and that was just caps, the stem of the *Armillariella* being fibrous and not usable. The flavor is meaty and robust, and the smallest caps are excellent for pickling. The larger caps tend to become bug-infested quite fast and should be checked carefully before being deposited in your basket.

Use these mushrooms for any of the general mushroom recipes. The caps are viscid, and although this does not adversely affect the eating character of the mushroom, it does affect the blanching extract, which is not good and should be discarded. As with the *Tricholoma*s, one of the best ways to prepare this type is to sauté them with onions using the longer low-heat method, and then to add *crème fraîche*. The acidity from the *crème fraîche* counteracts the sliminess of the cap. Canning is the best method of preserving *Armillariella mellea.*

### *Armillaria ponderosa* (Matsutake)

Also called *Tricholoma ponderosum,* the matsutake is probably the most popular of the Japanese wild mushrooms. It is sold fresh in Japan and exported dry, and is not common in this country except on the West Coast, where it is sold commercially. Use these mushrooms the same way you would the *Tricholoma*s (see pages 29–30).

### The *Russula* Group

This is a genus that contains many fine, edible species. These are summer and fall mushrooms, and because they come up in warm weather, various bugs in the soil tend to get to them very fast, which is why they are so often buggy when found. But when fresh, bug-free specimens are discovered (and these mushrooms can come up in enormous quantity in wet weather), there is no greater culinary treat than to cook them up immediately and eat them by themselves.

The best species in this group include *R. subdepalans, compacta, cyanoxantha, delica, nigricans, olivacea, virescens, aeruginea, alutacea, decolorans, flava, integra, lutea, vesca, xerampelina,* and *mariae.* When picking *Russula*s remember that the caps are often very brittle. Don't pile them on top of each other in your basket because the mushrooms at the bottom will turn to crumbs. On blanching this brittleness disappears, and the mushrooms become resilient.

The blanching extract from *Russula*s is fair and makes a good consommé. Sauté *Russula*s by the high-heat method to maintain their delicate texture. The smaller caps are excellent for pickling and stir-frying and are especially good when sautéed and added to scrambled eggs; slice the larger caps before proceeding. Because the flavor of the *Russula*s is distinct, they should not be mixed with other mushrooms when being prepared for recipes. Brining is the best method of preservation, although canning is almost as good.

## The *Lactarius* Group

Closely related to the *Russula* is the genus *Lactarius*. The species in this genus are generally firmer and larger than those of the genus *Russula*. What sets them apart taxonomically from the *Russula*s is the fact that when the flesh is broken, it exudes a milk (lactate), hence the name. One mushroom, the *L. piperatus*, yields a milk hotter than Tabasco sauce. Another, the *L. deliciosus*, is among the finest wild mushrooms in the forest and exudes an orange milk. This mushroom is often prepared by being wrapped in bacon and placed in a hot oven for five minutes. The crunchiness of the mushroom and the smokiness of the bacon combine for a burst of sensory joy.

Other excellent species include *L. camphoratus*, which smells like maple when dried, *L. subpurpureus*, which is a light and shiny reddish color, *L. vellereus, volemus, corrugis, chelidonium, fuliginosis, indigo* (particularly good pickled in salads), and *sanguifluus*. All of these varieties are excellent eating mushrooms. They do not become as buggy as the *Russula*s, and they are not as brittle. The flavor characteristics are similar to the *Russula*s, however, and they can be prepared in any of the ways for fresh wild mushrooms. The blanching extract is average in quality. Brining and canning are the best methods of preservation, except for the *L. camphoratus*, for which drying is best.

## The Genus *Amanita*

Despite the fact that this genus contains the most deadly poisonous mushrooms known, it also contains a few gems. Among the *Amanita*s most frequently eaten are the *A. caesarea* (Caesar's mushroom), *A. calyptroderma, A. crocea, A. vaginata,* and *A. rubescens*. Of these, the most widely picked and eaten is the *A. calyptroderma*. In Italy these mushrooms are eaten while the cap is still hidden within the delicate, sheathlike veil that encases the mushroom; as the *Amanita* matures, this veil ruptures, and the remnants form scales on the cap of the mushroom, and also form the volva, the enlargement or enclosure at the base of the stem. The mature mushroom is quite good as well, but this egglike youngster is the most highly prized form of this species.

On the other hand, the *A. crocea* is similar to the *calyptroderma* and to the *caesarea* but has no ring on the stem and has a "sugar-frosted" look on the yellow gills. These three comprise the best-eating *Amanita*s. Additional species to note are the *A. vaginata*, which is gray in color, also has no ring on the stem, and is commonly found on lawns (we eat it with scrambled eggs when it comes up in front of our house), and the *A. rubescens,* which is widely

**27**

picked in Europe and England, but not in this country perhaps because it is easy to mistake it for *A. brunnescens,* which is poisonous.

I cannot emphasize too strongly that this genus is dangerous and life-threatening and should be left completely alone except by professional mycologists or advanced amateurs, who are able to make positive identification. But if you belong to one of those categories, the experience of eating the *Amanita caesarea* should not be forsworn. *Amanita caesarea* sautéed with shallots in a bit of butter is the supreme mycophagous experience.

The edible *Amanita*s are good for general purposes. Use the low-heat method of sautéing to maximize flavor, since texture is not one of their strong points. Brining is the best method of preservation, and canning is also acceptable. Drying is not.

### The Genus *Coprinus*
### (Inky Cap)

The members of this group of mushrooms are commonly found on suburban lawns near tree stump remains and constitute some of the mushrooms which are called weed fungi because of their persistence. As these mushrooms begin to deteriorate, the caps liquefy from the gills, leaving an inky residue from which their name derives. Two types are important from a culinary viewpoint. The first, *C. atramentarius,* is an excellent eating mushroom with one serious drawback—it causes an unpleasant physical reaction when taken with alcohol, because the mushroom inactivates an enzyme that detoxifies alcohol in our systems. The condition, which causes tingling of the fingers and toes, nausea, and headaches, is not permanently harmful and abates within a couple of hours. Still, alcohol of any kind should be avoided for several days before ingesting this mushroom. The second, *C. comatus* is the famous shaggy mane, which is excellent served alone or as a vegetable side dish. This is the best mushroom for making mushroom catsup because of the dark, inky gills. *C. comatus* is best served alone, and steaming for a brief period is a good method of preparation. Sauté only the small caps, using the high-heat method to keep the pleasing crunchiness intact. Onions and sweet red peppers are good flavor companions. These mushrooms do not preserve well by any method because of their delicacy, so eat all that you pick or purchase.

### *Marasmius oreades*
### (Fairy Ring Mushroom)

This rather attractive lawn mushroom has enjoyed continuous popularity in Europe for many years. It is called *faux mousseron* ("false mushroom")

by the French. It has a pleasant if somewhat farinaceous odor and is more widely used to add color to stews and sauces than flavor. These mushrooms can be preserved by drying, and they yield a good extract and sauce when combined with shallots and butter. (The stems should be discarded.) *Marasmius alliaceus* is also an excellent mushroom for flavoring, as is *M. scorodonius*, which is distinguished by its garliclike smell and taste.

## The *Tricholoma* Group

This genus encompasses many species that are picked and loved, particularly by the Poles. These are the mushrooms of my childhood which I knew only by the names *gąski* and *siwki*. On many a Sunday afternoon in late fall I would lie collapsed in the middle of a pine forest somewhere in the Blue Mountains north of Reading, exhausted and arms aching from carrying my basketload of gray and yellow mushrooms from one patch to another. On a good afternoon the family would pick up to a dozen bushels.

When I got older and began working in the restaurant, we would take along several bottles of restorative liquid (also known as California Zinfandel) and use it to wash down Hunter's Potatoes (see page 251), which we would cook out in the forest, having generously sprinkled them with some of the morning's fresh-picked mushrooms. Nevertheless—considering the abundance of the *Tricholoma*s we picked in some years—I remember a year so dry that not a single one was found. Then our supply for the restaurant dwindled, and we simply prayed like farmers for a better harvest the next year. Yet when they were abundant, no mushroom could coat the forest floor the way they could.

In forests of white pine, no mushroom could actually be seen. They grew in the space between the forest floor and the thick ground layer of white-pine needles, so our only clues were telltale humps around the bases of the trees. Hump after hump would be investigated, and sometimes as many as fifty caps would be found in a continuous network stretching as far as twenty feet—and this from a single mound that revealed not a single visible cap.

Perhaps no other mushrooms take on the flavor and odor of their surroundings as do the various *Tricholoma*s. The ones that grow in pines have the resin-scented character of the pine trees below which they grow. An excellent extract can be made from blanching the fresh mushrooms and saving the slightly viscous liquid. This extract will be slightly green and needs only to be lightly salted to bring out the flavors of the pine forest. You may also add a slice or two of fresh green onion, but be careful that the onion flavor does not predominate. Do not concentrate the extract of these mushrooms because they lose their character if too intense and do not come back when rediluted. The mushrooms themselves are best preserved by brining, but canning is also acceptable. Do not dry them. The *Tricholoma*s are good in any dish calling for wild mushrooms, and they are especially so in game dishes because of their piney flavor. Savory is the complementary herb to use with them. Remember that the cap is naturally viscous in many species and that this does not mean that the mushroom is spoiled. The best way to prepare these mushrooms by themselves is with *crème fraîche* and onions. Save the tinest caps for pickling.

The best *Tricholoma*s for eating are the *T. columbetta, aggregatum, flavovirens, portentosum,* and *terreum.* Be warned that this genus does contain some poisonous species.

### *Lepiota procera* (Parasol Mushroom) and *Lepiota naucina*

The *Lepiota procera,* or parasol mushroom, is one of the better-known wild mushrooms and is popular because of its distinctive, musky taste. It is one of those mushrooms that should be eaten alone because of its singular character. Breading and frying seems to be the method most preferred, and this is indeed a wonderful way to prepare the parasol mushroom. The cap should be brushed before using to remove the hirsute layer of matter on the surface. The stem is fibrous and, like the shiitake stem, unusable.

The *Lepiota naucina* (now called *L. naucinoides*) is often mistaken for the common field mushroom, *Agaricus campestris.* Both are white and grow in grass. The difference is that the naucina is a slightly taller mushroom with a longish stem while the field mushroom has a thicker, squatter stem and grows closer to the ground. There are other generic differences, but this is the most obvious. The *Lepiota naucina* has an indistinct flavor and is therefore best used as the type of mushroom you would add to a dish more for appearance than flavor. Preserve by salting or canning.

Extracts prepared from both of these mushrooms are only fair and not recommended.

### *Lycoperdales*
### (Puffball)

Of all the fungi that cause surprised wonder in the forest, puffballs are the most-often cited. The sight of these orbs in a summer forest creates the impression that they have fallen from the sky rather than grown from the ground. Their round shape and white color are a stark contrast to some of the more suspicious-looking species of the woods and fields.

Puffballs are always friendly, of course, interesting, and worth a good glass of wine or two at lunch. Now comes the bad news: Puffballs are bland and tasteless.

I don't mean to put you off about this much-used fungus. I am simply stating a fact that holds true for veal and spun sugar as well. There's no taste there. But that doesn't mean that you shouldn't pick and eat them. It means that you will have to find some interesting way to use puffballs as the center-piece of a dish while some other flavor carries the delectableness. Like veal, puffballs are neutral, and thus their use is limited only by the creativity and embellishment of the chef. Treat them like eggplant (which is also bland). Sauté them in butter and onions, and savor the flavor of the butter and onions. Make a puffball parmesan or lasagne, and revel in the flavors of the tomato and cheese and the "idea" of the puffball. This species is best enjoyed with the imagination.

Be sure to use it only when the interior is pure white. The larger varieties are the best and last the longest. Dry them, and they will look like tofu—and, indeed, can be used in the same recipes for which you use tofu, specifically stir-frying. Don't bother canning or salting a puffball. Drying is best. Use the high-heat method of sautéing, with onions, butter, and green peppers.

The best species are *Calvatia caelata, craniiformis, cyathiformis,* and *gigantea.*

## *Laetiporus sulphureus* and Related Species
### (Chicken-of-the-Woods)

The common name of this is a fungus derives from the fact that, when cooked, this mushroom has the texture of fresh chicken breast. The fungus is one of a larger group of fungi known as polypores—similar to boletes in that the underside of the cap is composed of pores rather than gills. In most cases polypores are inedible because of their woody texture. Some, however, are quite good to eat, and the chicken-of-the-woods is among the best known. It is also known as the sulfur mushroom because the underside of the cap is a bright yellow color. The top side is a striking red-orange, which makes it very easy to identify.

These fungi can be seen growing out of fallen and rotting trees from summer to late fall. Older specimens take a long time to cook because of their woody texture. Younger specimens take just a short time to make them soft and chewable. The part of the fungus farthest from the base is the most tender. The thick core, or stem, can be used for extract but will usually be too tough to eat, except in a very young specimen.

True to its common name, prepare it by boiling it in strong chicken broth, to which onion and salt have been added. When it is tender, it is done, and the cooking time may vary from one-half hour to several hours. You can then sauté it or use it as you would any other mushroom. I like to slice it thin and then sauté it with green onions and butter. Or it can be added to some of the liquid in which it was cooked, after which you can thicken the whole thing and serve over toast or croissants.

The following types are polypores and are the most often used:

The *Boletopsis subsquamosa* is used by the Japanese and is known there as *kurotake*. The mushroom is slightly acrid in flavor and can be used cooked and sliced very thin with Belgian endive in a salad.

*Fistulina hepatica,* known as the beefsteak mushroom, is much loved by avid mushroom hunters. It is sometimes compared to beef liver because of its shape, but you must remember that it is a polypore and should be cooked the requisite time to tenderize it. Its hearty texture makes it ideal for mushroom "steaks" smothered in onions. When cooking this mushroom, add a little sugar to the water to counteract its high acidity.

*Grifola frondosa* is known as hen-of-the-woods, or sometimes ram's head, probably because the chicken-of-the-woods needed a companion. Like the chicken, this polypore can grow to weigh fifty or more pounds. The two mushrooms are generally considered to be the best-eating polypores. The hen is more tender and does not require the long cooking time that the chicken does. Use the hen more as you would nonpolypore mushrooms, because it is a most delicate mushroom by polypore standards. Onions, butter, and green pepper are the best flavor companions for the hen.

*Polyporus umbellatus,* the umbrella polypore, is similar to the *Grifola frondosa* and should be treated in the same manner.

*Polyporus berkeleyi* is edible but inferior in both texture and flavor. It is usually found in great quantity.

In preserving polypores, remember that the flesh is very firm. But these mushrooms can be sterilized by blanching without fully cooking them. This way you can keep them without softening them too much. But you *must* blanch them about three times as long as regular mushrooms to make sure they are sterilized. Then proceed to can or salt them. Drying is also possible, but the extract from dried polypores is not especially good.

## *Tuber melanosporum, Tuber magnatum, Tuber gibbosum* (Truffle)

If a pure white *Agaricus brunnescens* plucked from a supermarket shelf is representative of our Puritan legacy in this country, then truffles are the fungi that best represent the European taste for the earthy and exotic. One does not simply like truffles; rather, as with tobacco and espresso, one becomes addicted to them. Truffles are usually thought of, with fois gras and caviar, as the most patrician of edibles, but fois gras and caviar appeal to the palate immediately, whereas truffles challenge the neophyte gourmet to find them disagreeable. Indeed, many people fail to get past their first bite of this dark seductress. But those who do find in this gritty sphere an incomprehensible satisfaction. The flavor suggests rather than states, and seems to pervade all the peripheral areas of one's sense while coyly evading the center. Thus one is unable to consider and analyze why he enjoys the truffle. This elusive quality accounts for much of the truffle's popularity.

The black truffle of Périgord (*Tuber melanosporum*) is the most famous truffle in the world, and Périgord is the region from which most truffles are exported. It was from this area that the history and hunting of truffles was carried to the rest of the world. From here came tales of pigs and trained dogs, and the flies that hover over the precious fungus buried many inches inside the earth in symbiotic harmony with mighty oaks. And it was in Périgord that the industry of truffle cultivation was born. The white truffle of Piedmont (*Tuber magnatum*) has just as many and loyal devotees as her French cousin, and I am not going to make a value judgment here as to which is superior. Both are distinctive and expensive. Neither is a poor substitute for the other.

When buying truffles, choose the cleanest specimens and avoid those with pitted wet spots, which are the beginnings of rot. The truffle turns a bluish color and becomes soft during the onset of decay. Truffles are sold either as peelings, which are the actual outer and coarser shell of the truffle, or whole, fresh or canned. The peelings are usually canned and are suitable for color or decoration, as in a pâté. A real truffle fancier will want his black diamond (as it was dubbed by Brillat-Savarin) whole and fresh. The volatile nature of the truffle is essentially what makes the canned product inferior. The processing involved in canning robs the truffle of its hearty but flighty character. It is an expensive decoration.

Whole, fresh black truffles cost about $190 per pound wholesale, and white truffles are double that. The white truffles have a stronger odor and character than the black, which accounts for their high price. Fresh truffles

**33**

must be handled with care. Keep the truffle covered at all times either in a hermetically sealed jar or in the classic manner—buried in a heap of uncooked rice. One thing you should remember, though, is that by the time you buy your truffle, it will have been buried in someone else's rice or jar for a while. French cookbooks suggest you bury your own truffle in rice and then cook the rice to get the truffle flavor. Or they tell you to bring the truffle into contact with fresh eggs so that the eggs take on the truffle character. These methods are sound and proved—but only for very fresh truffles. By the time you get *your* truffle, days or weeks after it has been pulled from the ground, there is precious little truffle aroma to permeate any rice or eggs. Chances are that rice or eggs cooked after contact with older truffles will taste like, well, rice and eggs, period.

In preparing truffles keep it simple and allow the truffle to take center stage (obvious advice considering the enormous expense required to buy one). Perhaps the best method of enjoying white truffles is to grate them onto freshly cooked pasta, or black truffles *en croûte* as it was prepared for me once at Le Lavandou in New York by chef Jean-Jacques Rachou. I submit that the French and Italians are the hands-down champions in truffle preparation. Still, you may want to try a version of Truffle and Bourbon Sauce (page 86) as an interesting variation on Sauce Périgeaux. Truffles are also excellent just slivered and fried in butter with fresh ground black pepper. Just remember to buy your truffles fresh. Recipes abound for their preparation, and a good Italian or French cookbook will guide you in the classic and well-traveled ways for maximum appreciation of this most enigmatic fungus.

The Oregon white truffle (*Tuber gibbosum*) is picked by a small group of tightly knit truffle hunters and sold in fair quantity on the West Coast. Their quality is not considered to be on par with the European version, since they have a strong, unusual odor. Still, it is all we have available now of this family in the United States.

## Selected Mushrooms and Comments

The following wild mushrooms are also picked regularly by mushroom hunters, and we have used them at one time or another in our restaurant. As a group these mushrooms are best preserved by canning or brining. Drying does not work well for them because they tend to shrivel and do not yield strong extracts. The low-heat method of sautéing is best for these mushrooms. As usual, butter and onions are the best complements.

**OUDEMANSIELLA RADICATA.** Formerly called *Collybia radicata,* this is a good mushroom with generous flesh in the cap. Use for stir-frying.

**CORTINARIUS ALBOVIOLACEUS.** This mushroom is frequently confused with the blewit (*Clitocybe nuda*). Its color is rather more intense than the blewits, and it can be used the same way the blewit is. A related species, *Cortinarius Violaceus,* is also picked but is a rare species. The flavor of the mushrooms in this genus is only fair.

**CHROOGOMPHUS TOMENTOSUS.** Formerly called *Gomphidius tomentosus,* this mushroom is common in the West. It is of average quality. A related species, *Gomphidius glutinosus,* is common over the entire country and can be used in the same manner as any of the boletes. The extract from blanching this mushroom will be slimy and cannot be used.

**HYGROPHORUS CANTHARELLUS.** This is a colorful, tiny mushroom that resembles the *Cantharellus cinnabarinus* and can be used in the same way.

**HYGROPHORUS RUSSULA.** A superb species of this genus, the *Hygrophorus* should be used the way you would any of the better *Russulas.*

**PSATHYRELLA VELUTINA.** This mushroom yields a dark but not intensely flavored extract. Use the mushroom and the extract for sauces. This species is also good for making mushroom catsup.

**FAMILY CLAVARIACEAE.** The fungi in this family are known as the coral fungi, because the species resemble underwater coral, being brightly colored and shaped like the latter. They are found covering the forest floor in wet weather and make a lively addition to any salad. They are also excellent pickled and dropped into a martini.

**GENUS AGROCYBE.** These mushrooms come up from the middle of the spring to fall. The *Agrocybe praecox* usually fruits just after the morel in the late spring and tastes and smells similar to the morel. It makes a good extract and is a good eating mushroom for all purposes. Other species in this genus worth eating are the *Agrocybe aegerita* and *A. dura.*

**LACCARIA LACCATA.** This rather pretty mushroom along with its generic cousin, *Laccaria ochropurpurea,* is a very firm and plentiful type ideal for use in casserole dishes. The flavor of these mushrooms is not very distinct, but the hard, gummy texture offers a departure from the usual mushroom texture.

35

**STROPHARIA RUGOSO-ANNULATA.** The *Stropharia* seems to be next in line for massive commercial cultivation, because it is one of the few species to have been raised successfully under laboratory conditions. When young, it is meaty and firm. As it matures, the ratio of gills to flesh becomes quite high, resulting in a flabby, soft overall texture. But the flavor is very good, and the stock it produces from blanching is very much like chicken stock, but darker, which makes it very attractive for sauces.

**DENTINUM REPANDUM.** A mushroom that is sold commercially on the West Coast and is enjoyed by mushroom hunters all over the country, the *Dentinum* is firm, with a fairly wide range of colored caps. The flavor is somewhat shrimplike and good for sautéing and use in casseroles. Look for occasional bitterness.

**GENUS COLLYBIA.** This genus has an interesting characteristic: It holds its shape well during cooking, one of the few mushrooms that do. Thus it is excellent for any dish where a firm mushroom texture is desired. The species best for eating are the *Collybia abundans, butyracea,* and *familia.*

**CLITOPILUS PRUNULUS.** Known as the sweetbread mushroom, this grows in great quantity when it comes up. It must be handled carefully in picking because the flesh is very brittle and breaks apart rapidly. This property is alleviated when the mushroom is blanched. A cousin, *Clitopilus abortivus,* is also good.

# A Summary of Selected Mushrooms and Their Culinary Characteristics

| NAME (QUALITY) | SOME COMMON NAMES | BEST COOKING FORMS AND METHODS | BEST USED WITH: | PRESERVATION METHODS OR MOST COMMONLY BOUGHT | COMMENTS |
|---|---|---|---|---|---|
| *Agaricus brunnescens (bisporus and related species (p. 11) (excellent)* | button, cream, domestic, market (*A. bisbrunnescens* or *A. bisporus*); champignon de Paris, common field mushroom, meadow mushroom (*A. campestris*—wild); horse mushroom (*A. arvensis*); the prince (*A. augustus*) | all methods described; basic mushroom for duxelles; one of the best mushrooms for stuffing, soups | all-purpose use with savory to emphasize flavor | canning; pickling | still one of the best all-purpose mushrooms available; firm, sturdy, and common; has distinct flavor, though not as interesting as some of the better wild types |
| *Volvariella volvacea (p. 14) (Good)* | straw; padi-straw mushroom | stir-frying | stir-fry dishes; stews, casseroles, salads (pickled) | canning; pickling | a good filler mushroom with average flavor; available in Oriental grocery stores |
| *Flammulina velutipes (p. 15) (average)* | enoki; Christmas, Enokitake, golden, velvet stem, winter | sautéing, raw | salads; quick-sautéed dishes | none | very mild flavor; best as eyebrow-raiser in salad; the wild variety is much prettier and slightly meatier |

# A Summary of Selected Mushrooms and Their Culinary Characteristics—Continued

| NAME (QUALITY) | SOME COMMON NAMES | BEST COOKING FORMS AND METHODS | BEST USED WITH: | PRESERVATION METHODS OR MOST COMMONLY BOUGHT | COMMENTS |
|---|---|---|---|---|---|
| *Lentinus edodes* (p. 15) (*excellent*) | shiitake, black forest mushroom, golden oak mushroom, doubloon | sautéing, braising, duxelles, sauces, soups | all-purpose with caution; smoky flavor can be used with stronger spices without losing character | drying; freezing (after braising) | the best-flavored commercial mushroom available; however, stem tough and inedible except in smallest mushrooms |
| *Pleurotus ostreatus and related species* (p. 16) (*very good*) | oyster mushroom (*P. ostreatus*); Phoenix sovereign (*P. sojar cazu*) | sautéing; braising; deep frying | good all-purpose mushroom; needs butter and onion to bring out flavor | freezing (after braising); canning | mild-flavored mushrooms, requiring onions and butter to bring out "oyster" flavor, good texture in cap and stem |
| *Auricularia polytricha; A. auricula* (p. 16) (*average*) | cloud-ear; wood-ear; Jew's-ear | sautéing; soups; sauces | stir-fry and sauté dishes; Chinese 5-spice good complementary flavor | drying | very crunchy even after reconstituting; faint flavor; best used for textural contrast in stir-fried dish; reconstituting liquid faint flavor |

| | | | | | |
|---|---|---|---|---|---|
| *Cantharellus cibarius and craterellus cantherellus (p. 17) (superior)* | chanterelle | sautéing; duxelles | fowl; wild game birds; furred game; match with chopped apricots and other fruit with fowl; stews, casseroles | canning; brining; pickling | earthy apricotlike flavor makes this one of the most sought-after wild mushrooms; peppery when raw; this mushroom is often marketed in dried form, making it difficult to use; extract fair; use dried chanterelles simply for adding to stews, casseroles, where heat will reconstitute them |
| *Related species of chanterelles (see p. 18) C. tubaeformis C. minor C. xanthopus Gomphus clavatus Polyozellus multiplex* | | sautéing | casserole; sauté dishes; omelets | canning; brining | this genus provides very good mushrooms of high eating quality |
| *Craterellus cornucopioides (p. 19) (superior)* | false truffle, trompettes, trompettes-des-morts, horn-of-plenty; trumpet-of-death; black trumpet | sauces; soups; powder (from dried) | fish; veal casseroles; complementary flavor; butter | drying | often overlooked as fresh mushroom; it is much better when reconstituted from dried form; extract dark, rich, and buttery, making excellent sauce or soup |

# A Summary of Selected Mushrooms and Their Culinary Characteristics—*Continued*

| NAME (QUALITY) | SOME COMMON NAMES | BEST COOKING FORMS AND METHODS | BEST USED WITH: | PRESERVATION METHODS OR MOST COMMONLY BOUGHT | COMMENTS |
|---|---|---|---|---|---|
| *Morchella esculenta and related species (p. 19)* (*superior*) | morel, sponge mushroom, spongy | sautéing; braising; soups; sauces; duxelles butter, puree; stuffing | veal; fowl; casseroles; stews; complementary flavors; sweet peppers, caraway; butter; onions | drying; canning | perhaps best-known wild mushroom in America; very distinct, nutty flavor; stem edible but usually tough; excellent extract from dried form for sauce |
| *Clitocybe nuda and related species (p. 21)* (*very good*) | blewit, woodblewit | sautéing, braising, soups | all-purpose; use onions when cooking | canning; brining | widely picked and abundant wild mushroom; fairly fleshy, a good mushroom to use as a "vegetable" because of relative abundance |
| *Boletus edulis (p. 23)* (*superior*) | cepe, *Steinpilz, porcini, borowik* stone mushroom, king bolete | all methods described; one of few wild mushrooms good for grilling and stuffing | meat; fowl; rarely with fish. | drying; canning | the best and most distinctive of all mushrooms, most versatile, intensity of flavor different, depending on origin; most intense: Polish, German, French; less intense: Italian, American; makes superior extract for sauce and soups |

| Species | Common name | Cooking method | Use | Preservation | Comments |
| --- | --- | --- | --- | --- | --- |
| *Related species of boletes. (see p. 22)* (excellent) | | as above | as above | drying; canning | the many cousins of *Boletus edulis* are often excellent if not quite as good as the king Bolete; this group is generally considered the best for drying along with morels, because of the rich extracts they usually produce; the pores, except for young specimens, should be removed before eating or drying |
| *Suillus luteus* (p. 25) (excellent) | slippery jack; forest mushroom | as above, except grilling and broiling | as above | drying; canning | not necessary to remove pores, but this mushroom has a slimy cap which should be peeled before using; very abundant and common |
| *Armillariella mellea* (p. 25) (very good) | honey mushroom | sautéing; braising | all-purpose *except* for soup, sauce | canning | a nonpeelable, viscous cap excludes this mushroom from use in soups and sauces; after boiling, discard extract |
| *Armillaria ponderosa* (p. 26) (very good) | matsutake | sautéing; braising | stews; casseroles; meats | drying | an Oriental mushroom picked wild in some parts of the West Coast |
| *Russula group* (p. 26) (very good to excellent) | | sautéing; braising | all-purpose | canning; fresh; brining | a very large group; some species are very firm and versatile, but most species delicate and crumbly until blanched; extracts fair |

## A Summary of Selected Mushrooms and Their Culinary Characteristics—*Continued*

| NAME (QUALITY) | SOME COMMON NAMES | BEST COOKING FORMS AND METHODS | BEST USED WITH: | PRESERVATION METHODS OR MOST COMMONLY BOUGHT | COMMENTS |
|---|---|---|---|---|---|
| *Lactarius group* (p. 27) (*very good to excellent*) | | sautéing; braising | all-purpose | canning; brining; pickling | much like *Russulas* for cooking purposes, but firmer and slightly larger |
| *Amanita group* (edible) *A. caesarea, A. calyptroderma* (p. 27) (*excellent*) CAUTION! | | sautéing | all-purpose | canning; brining | the poisonous species are in this genus, so this is for experts only |
| *Coprinus group* (p. 28) (*excellent*) | inky cap | sautéing; steaming braising, catsup | best eaten alone; use small, closed caps only | | firm, delicious; avoid *C. atrementarius* |
| *Marasmius oreades* (p. 28) (*very good*) | fairy ring mushroom | adding fresh or dried to sauces and casseroles | stews; sauces; veal; fish | drying | reconstitutes to original form; yields good extract from dried. *M. scorodonius,* related, has garliclike smell and taste |
| *Tricholoma group* (p. 29) (*excellent*) | piny; steely | sautéing; braising | all-purpose; creamed-style mushrooms | canning; brining; pickling | the *Tricholoma* found in pine forests take on flavor of pines; mushroomy-piney flavor excellent for consommé-style soup; some viscous caps in this group |

42

| Species | Common name | Cooking methods | Best served | Preservation | Notes |
|---|---|---|---|---|---|
| *Lepiota procera* (p. 30) (*excellent*) | parasol mushroom | sautéing, braising, frying | best served alone | none | hirsute cap which must be brushed clean before using; stem inedible |
| *Lycoperdales* (p. 30) (*average*) | puffball | sautéing, braising, deep frying, broiling, grilling | all-purpose | drying | the "eggplant" of the mushroom world; faint flavor but very adaptable; largest specimens best |
| *Laetiporus sulphureus and related species* (p. 31) (*very good*) | chicken-of-the-woods (*L. sulphureus*); Kurotake (*Boletopsis subsquamosa*); beef-steak mushroom (*Fistulina hepatica*); hen-of-the-woods (*Grifola frondosa*); umbrella polypore (*Polyporus umbellatus*) | boiling in flavored broth; then sautéing; grilling, broiling | casseroles; meat | canning | these fungi can take long cooking depending on water content, age, and section of mushrooms; species may *never* tenderize; buying these commercially is a dice throw; always boil in a flavored (chicken, veal) stock, then braise and thicken |
| *Tuber melanosporum, T. magnatum, T. gibbosum* (p. 33) (*superior*) | truffle | sautéing; light baking; sauces, soups | soak in fine liquor or brandy; beef, veal, fowl, game, pasta | canning | used often for decorative purposes as well as direct consumption; can be eaten by itself, but can stand with strong liquors and brandy to enhance flavor; called black diamond; use fresh when possible |
| *Clitopilus prunulus* (p. 36) (*very good*) | sweetbread mushroom | braising | all-purpose | canning; brining | crumbly, like *Russulas*; must be blanched; good all-purpose mushroom |

CHAPTER THREE

# *Starting Points: Buying, Keeping, and Cooking Mushrooms*

## A Guide to Buying Mushrooms

### Fresh

Mushrooms are sold commercially in three forms: fresh, dried, and canned. The common market variety, *Agaricus brunnescens,* is sold fresh and canned, but never dried because of its relative abundance in fresh form.

When buying fresh market mushrooms (the common domestic variety) always select the firmest caps that are *closed* around the stem. Be careful of any that show the dark gills underneath. These mushrooms are older and will not last for more than a day or two. Their flavor is a little more intense than that of the younger caps, and for some people this makes them more desirable.

When you are purchasing fresh wild mushrooms, use your common sense. If the mushrooms are frayed or dried around the edges or otherwise not fresh looking, why should you pay a high price for them? In this condition, they are an inferior product, and you shouldn't give in to temptation simply because the mushroom has a fancy or unusual name. *Be choosy* and take home only the freshest and brightest-looking specimens.

Do not be too concerned if the mushrooms are a little dirty, because the dirt can be removed later. However, the base of the stem where the mushroom was embedded into the ground should have been removed. Touch and smell the mushrooms before you buy them. Any mushroom that is wet or has an unpleasant odor is well into the process of deterioration. Also, with wild mushrooms, look for little holes where bugs may have burrowed their way inside. A few of these holes are no great disaster, but if they cover more than 10 percent of the mushroom, don't buy it. These holes will be found on the underside of the mushroom stem because this is where the bugs get into the mushrooms. There may also be some holes underneath the cap, so check there, too.

Fresh mushrooms are wonderful to have, whether domestic or wild, but there is one thing you have to take into account: They won't stay that way very long. So don't buy domestic mushrooms and expect to keep them in their fresh state for more than three to five days at the most. After that they will begin to get brown (oxidize) and take on a musty smell and taste. It's better for you to buy them strictly as needed.

The same is true if you happen to buy a wild variety. But with wild mushrooms, your chance of getting that particular species again soon might be uncertain, so you will have to think about buying them to preserve. (See Chapter 13 on preserving mushrooms.)

In general, mushrooms should be refrigerated as soon as you get them home. *Do not wash them until you are ready to use them.* Mushrooms break down from a natural enzymatic action while still in the ground, and this process (better known as rotting) accelerates once they are plucked from their habitat. The addition of water will hasten this. When you put them away, it's also advisable to keep the mushrooms covered or in a plastic bag to avoid having them take on a "refrigerator smell." Dry and protected, the mushrooms will keep for three to four days. If you have several species of mushrooms, separate them into like with like, because some types (like morels) break down more quickly than others (like shiitake) and have flavors and smells that can transfer rapidly to other types nearby, which are not as strong and which may thus lose their own characteristics in the mixing process.

If you find an unusual group of mushrooms on the market, you might buy them and upon returning home blanch them immediately, to stop the enzymatic breakdown of the mushrooms. This process (which I will discuss in further detail a few pages hence) allows you to keep the mushrooms for about a week in a cold refrigerator. You can also freeze mushrooms that have been blanched, covering them with some of the water used in the blanching; mushrooms sautéed or prepared in their own liquid can also be frozen and used as needed. Just remember to cover them with some liquid to prevent freezer burn. Do not freeze mushrooms directly unless they are covered, and do not freeze them at all unless you intend to use them in a day or two at most. Whole fresh mushrooms that are frozen can be excellent if kept for this limited period of time in the freezer, but the cellular structure begins to break down after that.

If you elect to ignore the mushrooms that you have bought and leave them out on the table at room temperature, they will last about a day in fresh condition before they dry and rapidly rot. Some of the more delicate types will begin to deteriorate in several hours. Again, refrigerate fresh mushrooms if you do not plan to prepare or process them immediately, and do not wash them until you are ready to use them.

### Canned

Very few types of wild mushrooms come canned, and those that do are hard to find. Their overall quality is good; they should keep for up to a year, and they can be compared to mushrooms that have been blanched as described above. Use them as you would blanched mushrooms, in casseroles, stir-fry dishes, or for almost any application requiring the use of mushrooms in a sauce or for a stuffing. You can even make duxelles (see pages 59–67) from canned mushrooms but this is one use that should be reserved as a last resort, when you can't get anything else.

The only drawback—and it is a considerable one—to the use of canned mushrooms is that they are limp and generally formless. They are cooked mushrooms that have been sitting in their own juices in contact with metal for God knows how long. A good deal of flavor was given up in the cooking and sterilizing process, and the juices in which they sit (compared to freshly made blanching liquid) have become equally devoid of flavor. Also, the mushrooms and liquid take on a "canned" flavor from the activity of the metal ions with which they mingle. Don't bother using the bland canning liquid—except perhaps canned truffle juice. So, the limitation to canned mushrooms is simple lack of flavor.

But often, especially in the case of straw mushrooms, the texture is still quite good, and the mushroom is rich enough to retain some of its original character. The same can be said of cepes and chanterelles, which can also be found in cans. Besides, there is nothing to prevent you from making a dish in which you use canned mushrooms for texture and dried mushrooms for flavor.

When buying canned mushrooms, do the normal checking you would for any canned product—namely, see if there are any bulges or leaks. If so, don't buy it. Even if the can looks satisfactory, after opening it *always boil the mushrooms for a half hour before using them.* This will eliminate the possibility of food poisoning (botulism) because the bacteria responsible for botulism are destroyed by high heat. Then proceed to use them as you would blanched mushrooms. Another note: I would caution against buying canned morels as these are often actually *Gyromitra esculenta,* or the false morel, which is generally considered poisonous. Cepes are also mimicked by using other types of boletes, inferior in quality and worth a fraction of the price. Always buy from a company with which you or your grocer are familiar. You'll get a more reliable product that way.

### Dried

The most common form in which wild mushrooms are sold is dried. You may wonder why they are so expensive, but when you consider that a hundred pounds of fresh mushrooms yield a maximum of ten pounds dried, you begin to get the picture. Mushrooms are primarily composed of water, and drying evaporates the "stuffing" in the mushroom. For a long time now drying has been considered the cheapest and *poorest* method of preserving mushrooms. There is certainly truth in the first assumption, because it is much easier and less costly to dry than to can. The second assumption that it is the poorest method comes from the fact that when a dried mushroom is reconstituted, it looks more like a remnant of a wet dishrag than the beautiful, full fungus it was when fresh. Therefore, because they *look* more like fresh mushrooms, canned mushrooms have usually been the preferred choice of cooks if the fresh product is not available.

My own opinion, strenuously held, is that the dried product is superior by far to the canned one for culinary purposes. The reason lies in two words: *Heat kills.* As I have just described, when mushrooms are canned, the heating that takes place from the sterilization process ravages the mushroom flavors so much that little is left *but the form.* Drying, on the other hand, requires a minimum of heat, and in many countries the mushrooms are even sun-dried. Although the mushroom is grossly shrunk, the components that bestow flavor on the mushroom are *concentrated* in the mushroom rather than cooked out and, as we shall shortly see, easily revive when the mushrooms are reconstituted for use.

When you shop for dried mushrooms, make sure that the product is free from worm holes. Also, buy caps whenever possible, because this is the surest way of getting what the sign says. Often, especially with cepes, sliced

47

versions are adulterated with other types, and the richness you expect may not be there because of the mixing. You will pay a premium, but whole caps insure the purity of the mushroom type.

Different mushrooms from different sources labeled the same can be very different in intensity. Thus, two mushrooms labeled "cepes" can come from different locations and reconstitute at different intensities. American and Italian cepes, or porcini, will usually produce lighter extracts. By the way, you can keep dried mushrooms for a fairly long period of time—a few months—but not indefinitely. Small bugs lay their eggs inside the mushrooms, and these eggs often survive the drying process. After a period of time these eggs will hatch and feed on your mushrooms! So check the mushrooms periodically. If some of these eggs hatch, you will see the bugs crawling around inside. Often you will not see them until you are reconstituting the mushrooms. (You will find them floating around in the water; they are usually white with little black heads, about one-quarter to one-half inch long, with striations along the body.) Don't worry about them; just pick them out and proceed with your recipe. They won't harm you even if you eat one or two.

When you bring the mushrooms home, be sure to keep them in a plastic bag to prevent them from getting any unwanted moisture. If the dried mushrooms are exposed to humid air, they will undergo a partial (if involuntary) reconstitution and may become moldy in the process. The best way to keep dry mushrooms for a long period of time is to pack them in a sealed plastic container and freeze them. The freezing prevents the egg larvae from hatching.

A final note: Many of the recipes in this book are built upon the extracted and concentrated flavors of mushrooms as they are derived from dried mushrooms. They are a rich source of flavor and will open for you, as they did for me, the real world of mushroom cookery.

## How Many Mushrooms Should You Buy?

Having discussed the properties of the various kinds of mushrooms available, it is important to consider the quantity of mushrooms you should purchase, especially since wild mushrooms can be very expensive.

When buying fresh mushrooms, remember that most mushrooms are around 90 percent water. That means that the mushrooms you purchase may lose up to half of their liquid during cooking and may shrink down to 20 to 40 percent of their volume during the cooking process. That fact might suggest that buying fresh mushrooms is not cost-efficient, but bear in mind that the lost liquid is rich in flavor and will add that flavor to the dish as a whole even though the mushrooms themselves will shrink. Exceptions to this rule are the polypores like chicken-of-the-woods or hen-of-the-woods and truffles, all of which tend to lose less water when being cooked because they contain less water in the first place.

Canned mushrooms are easiest to compute amounts with, because what you see is what you get. These mushrooms have already lost all the moisture they are going to. The liquid in the can, however, usually takes on a metallic-tasting quality and should be discarded.

Reconstituted dried mushrooms, however, will not come back in any form or fashion resembling fresh mushrooms. They will be wilted and flabby, or leathery, even though they may weigh as much as the fresh mushrooms. A good formula to remember is that an ounce of dried mushrooms will be sufficient in a sauce or soup for 4 to 6 people. This may vary depending on the mushrooms or the desired intensity of the dish, but it is a good rule of thumb, nevertheless.

The bonus with dried mushrooms is in the extract they produce, which will be discussed on pages 73–74.

## Methods of Cooking Mushrooms

Three factors should be kept in mind when cooking with mushrooms.

First, mushrooms contain well over 90 percent water. This means that on cooking you can expect them to shrink drastically. That's the bad news. The good news is that the more water that is cooked *out* of the mushroom, the more concentrated the flavor left *in*. Additionally, the liquid they exude is often rich in flavor and should be utilized as much as possible; this is especially so with the liquid that is used during reconstituting dry mushrooms: So don't feel cheated when you cook mushrooms and then try to find them.

Make sure you buy enough for the kind of dish you are making—about 4 ounces per person is a good average amount. Imagine that the mushrooms you see fresh in the store will look like about half, or even less, of that amount when cooked. When you prepare your fresh mushrooms for cooking, don't slice them too thin, either. Stringy-looking mushrooms don't look very appetizing. Never slice mushrooms thinner than ¼ inch and consider the fact that, aesthetically, whole caps make for a more attractive presentation. Finally, the high water content of the mushrooms correctly implies that the mushrooms cook very fast, since water conducts heat rapidly. This is why mushrooms are so easy to cook. They are relatively hard to burn because of their water content.

Second, a mushroom has its own flavor, different from that of other mushrooms and different from other foods as well. In the literally thousands of mushroom recipes I have read, this simple and obvious fact is often mentioned, but I have the distinct impression that it is not really believed. Many recipes use other ingredients and flavors that mask rather than support the mushroom's specific character. With wild mushrooms their visual presence seems more important than their flavor, and recipes in which they are used tend to utilize even more bizarre and varied ingredients, which further mask the mushroom's flavor. Taste some raw wild mushrooms when you get the chance. When fresh, many mushrooms exhibit a buttery-nutty character that has led many to believe that lemon juice is needed to counteract the almost slippery (as opposed to acidic) property of this flavor. On cooking, however, the mushroom flavors change and become more distinct and round; lemon juice, by thinning out its singular character, tends to rob the mushroom of its rich and earthy cooked flavor. There are, however, ingredients that can make mushrooms taste more like themselves and enhance their character. This aspect is discussed in more detail in the section ahead.

Third, mushrooms vary greatly in their texture—from the tough polypores that need long cooking to the delicate black trumpet chanterelles. Different parts of the same mushroom can be different in texture. The shiitake, for instance, has a tender cap but a tough and indigestible stem. Boletes have firm caps but spongy undersides, which may or may not be desirable to the person preparing them. Some types, like *Lactarius,* go crunch in the mouth, while the pliable chanterelle feels like silk on the palate.

These aspects of water content, flavor, and texture should be taken into account when making mushroom dishes or determining how many and which kinds to use for a specific dish. These details were, of course, listed in the previous chapter. A more complete discussion of basic techniques and procedures follows below.

## Specific Cooking Methods

SAUTÉING. This is the best-known and most often used method for cooking mushrooms. Two important considerations in sautéing are the method of sautéing chosen and complementary flavors used in the sauté.

There are two schools of thought for sautéing mushrooms. The first and more traditional method is to cook the mushrooms over low to medium heat until they lose most of their liquid, then continue to cook until the liquid is evaporated. For 2 cups of uncooked sliced mushrooms, this method takes about 10 to 15 minutes to yield ¾ cup. The argument for this method is that the mushrooms, in releasing their liquid, have a more concentrated flavor. Additionally, cooking usually diminishes their original crunchy texture. The end result is mushrooms which have been greatly reduced in volume, concentrated in flavor, and—unless they are of the very firm variety—diminished in fresh texture. The mushrooms are soft but have a rich mushroom flavor.

The second and more modern method of sautéing is to cook the mushrooms over high heat for a much shorter period of time. In this method 2 cups of sliced mushrooms can be done in about 2 minutes or less, and yield over a cup. What happens is that the oil used for sautéing seals in the water and maintains the crunchy texture of the mushrooms. But the water inside the mushrooms is for the most part not released, so that the mushrooms are not as concentrated in flavor as in the first method. The end result is a firm mushroom with less flavor. Of course, you do not have to use method one to the exclusion of method two but can vary the methods to suit your needs. You should be aware, though, of the difference between these two approaches and of the importance of retaining or cooking out the water in the mushrooms. The less water, the more concentrated the mushroom flavor and vice versa. The new California cuisine favors the latter method and the old European cuisine uses the former. You must decide for yourself whether flavor or texture is more important to your dish.

The second consideration in sautéing is the choice of other ingredients in the process. For oil I prefer butter, because the flavor of butter is such a good natural complement to the flavor of mushrooms. However, if you use butter with the second method, high-heat sautéing will burn the butter in the process. One way to minimize this problem is to use clarified* instead of whole butter; clarified butter will cook at a higher heat than whole butter without burning, but not at as high a heat as oil. Vegetable oil is best for high-heat sautéing, but the flavor is not as good, particularly for mushrooms. This is the reason why many recipes suggest using part oil and part butter. The butter flavor comes through, and the mushrooms can be sautéed at a higher heat than if butter alone is used. Thus, for high-heat sautéing use butter and oil in equal parts; for low-heat sautéing, plain butter is better.

As far as other ingredients are concerned, I almost always use something in the onion family for sautéing with mushrooms, either onions, shallots, scallions, or leeks. All have varying degrees of intensity but are suitable for sautéing. Leeks are the hardest to work with because of their texture and for this reason are the least desirable. Other ingredients can also be used in sautéing.

*Note: To prepare clarified butter, melt butter slowly over hot, not boiling, water. Pour off the clarified butter, which is the clear yellow liquid, and discard the milky residue left in the bottom of the saucepan or cup.

**BRAISING.** The term "braising" describes a specific method of cooking meat: After browning, it is placed in a pan with a little stock, wine, or water, then covered and cooked until done. Because this method can also be used for cooking mushrooms, I like to use the term when discussing certain similar preparations. Braising is related to sautéing as a method except for one vital difference—in braising you retain water, and the mushrooms actually create their own "sauce" during the cooking process. A small amount of water is added during braising, or veal or poultry stock may be substituted to yield a richer dish (but remember not to add too much or the dish will taste like meat soup). When braising mushrooms, try to use butter or margarine for the sauté part of a recipe. If you cannot, use only a small amount of oil. This oil remains in the dish and is not good for the finished result.

Braising is a good way to handle a large quantity of mushrooms if you want to preserve them by freezing. Simply omit the salting and thickening steps described in the regular recipe. You may add these when the mushrooms are defrosted.

**OVEN COOKING.** Baked mushrooms can be very good, but baking does not do much for the appearance of the mushrooms. Mushrooms sweat profusely and lose their moisture during baking—concentrating their flavor, but also becoming misshapen. The only time to bake mushrooms is when they are part of a larger dish that calls for baking, or when you prepare stuffed mushrooms. The stuffing keeps the mushrooms in their original shape. Do not bake at too high a heat unless browning is called for. Keep the oven at about 300° and bake until ready, usually 10 to 20 minutes. One traditional method used by the Poles is to wrap bacon around the cap of a wild mushroom (particularly the *Lactarius deliciosus*) and oven-bake it for 10 to 20 minutes in a 350° oven. The bacon bastes the mushroom as it cooks as well as adding its smoky flavor.

**BROILING OR GRILLING.** These two methods are virtually the same except for the direction of heat. This is an exceptional way to make large fresh wild mushrooms. The trick to broiling or grilling is to keep the mushrooms as close as possible to the flame—about 4 inches—until the mushrooms are warm all the way through. Mushrooms will cook very fast this way without burning because of their high water content. That water will also prevent them from burning quickly. If the mushroom does begin to brown too soon, just pull it away from the flame a bit and continue to cook. Mushrooms done this way are usually seasoned with salt, pepper, and sometimes cheese (Bonchampi or Parmesan). Mushrooms might also be broiled or grilled in conjunction with skewered meats. They will not burn while the meat is cooking.

However, it's a good idea to cut a few gashes along the edge of the cap to prevent the mushroom from curling during grilling. Mushroom kabobs can also be made with other vegetables or meats.

**DEEP FRYING.** Although this entails a very specific way of doing mushrooms, it is similar to high-heat sautéing in that the oil keeps the moisture of the mushroom locked in. The mushroom has first been lightly dredged in flour, egg, and a final coat of bread crumbs, and it gets its heat by conduction from the superheated breading. This warms the mushroom without shrinking it drastically, and it cooks quickly.

**BOILING. METHOD I—BLANCHING.** Boiling mushrooms by blanching is usually done for preservation or as a starting point for a soup or sauce. First clean the mushrooms, then bring water to a boil, add the mushrooms, and after the water returns to a boil, simmer them for about 2 minutes. Then remove and cool them under running water. If you have a large quantity of fresh mushrooms and nowhere to store them, blanching is the best method of keeping them (unless you wish to dry them). Blanched mushrooms can be kept for up to a week in the refrigerator and used when desired.

Most liquids left from blanching will take on the color of the mushroom or the mushroom spores. Thus a white mushroom like the market variety will yield a brownish liquid even though the mushroom itself is white. Some of the mushrooms with viscous caps like the honey mushroom yield a slimy water that must be discarded.

To test whether a blanching liquid will make a good consommé, salt 1½ cups of it with ½ teaspoon salt, or a combination of ½ teaspoon each of salt and sugar, and 1 teaspoon of soy sauce. This should bring out the mushroom characteristic. If the result is bland or tastes of the soy or salt (and not all mushrooms are rich in flavor), either cook down the mother liquid some more and try again, or discard the liquid.

Don't salt the liquid in which you are blanching the mushrooms; you can always adjust for salt later. Also, use just enough water to cover the bottom of the blanching pot, about an inch or so. Remember, most of the liquid should come from the mushrooms themselves. Be careful of the temptation to cook down or concentrate the liquid too much. I cooked down a blanching liquid too much one time and lost all semblance of mushroom flavor. When I diluted the liquid again, the character and flavor were simply gone.

The time for testing the flavor characteristics of the liquid is when the liquid takes on a distinctive color. This liquid can be a rich source of flavor because it takes with it much of the flavor of the mushrooms that were blanched in it, and it would be a shame to let it all go down the drain.

**BOILING. METHOD II—RECONSTITUTING DRIED MUSHROOMS.** Another type of boiling is the process involved in reconstituting dried mushrooms. Common wisdom says that the best way to reconstitute dried mushrooms is to soak them in warm water or milk for several hours, in order to preserve the flavor of the mushroom *in* the mushroom. The implication is that this method only "slightly" causes the revived mushroom to give up its flavor characteristics to the liquid, and that the liquid, once used, may therefore be discarded. But the theory is wrong, as is the method of reconstitution behind it. Historically, it has been the single greatest barrier to discovering the rich flavor of wild mushrooms. To begin with, any mushroom that is dried *never* reconstitutes to its original shape and *never* tastes at all like a fresh mushroom. In many cases the mushroom extract tastes better than the fresh mushroom itself did. This is because a fresh mushroom contains so much water that the actual flavors are diluted, and in the reconstitution liquid they are more concentrated and, therefore, more evident.

The key to this procedure, however, is *heat*. It is the use of heat that yields flavor in the broth. Once this concept is grasped, the rest of the methods for cooking with dried mushrooms are easy.

For proper reconstitution of mushrooms in liquid, then, the correct procedure is to cover 1 ounce of dried mushrooms with 3 cups of water in a saucepan and bring them to a rapid boil. Turn down the flame to low, loosely cover the saucepan, and simmer another 20 to 30 minutes. By this time most of the possible heat extraction will have taken place, and further heating will not be necessary. If the liquid is cooked down to 1½ cups it will yield a very strong broth.

Note that not all mushrooms have interesting reconstituted flavors. In some cases, as with the chanterelle, the flavor extraction into the liquid is easily obtainable but difficult to use. Some dried mushrooms simply lack any interesting flavor, and the reconstituting liquid is pale and bland. Refer back to Chapter 2 for specific details.

As also explained previously, blanching also yields an extract rich in flavor, although it is not quite as strong as from reconstituting dried mushrooms. Yet the principle is the same—the use of heat extracts flavor from the mushroom and concentrates it in the liquid.

The reconstituted mushrooms themselves may be sliced and used in a dish for texture or appearance. Ideally, they should be scattered about a dish whose sauce was made from the extract. For example, you prepare rice in a mushroom extract, then chop the mushrooms and toss them into the rice.

Reconstituted mushrooms are also very important in making a wild mushroom puree, which in turn is very handy for preparing duxelles (which

 54

gets its true flavor from being cooked in an extract but retains the solid presence of the mushroom itself), butters, or soufflés. More about this in Chapter 4.

## Mushrooms and Their Complementary Flavors

It would be great to declare that mushrooms have their own vigorous flavors and need no complement to their raw and savage presence on the plate and palate, and many recipes suggest just that. So why do I, who am writing about the wonderful variety of flavors in mushrooms, include a section on other substances that should be included in mushroom recipes? Because the flavor of mushrooms is greatly enhanced by certain other foods. They allow us to appreciate mushroom flavors better.

The first flavor component to consider is that of the mushroom itself. When raw, many mushrooms taste remarkably alike. The character of the flavor is somewhat buttery and nutty. It would be considered basic (alkaline) as opposed to acidic. The feel on the palate is slippery and mouth-filling and, in some cases, even bitter. Some mushrooms exhibit a peppery characteristic, but the buttery-nutty flavor is the most pronounced. Bite into a raw commercial mushroom. It is a good example of what I mean and is not much different from the raw flavor and feel of most wild mushrooms. When cooked, all that changes. Each mushroom type then exhibits its own characteristics, and it is at this point that complementary flavors enter the picture.

The taste of the individual cooked mushrooms is covered in the general discussion of Chapter 2 describing the different types.

BUTTER. Perhaps more than any other single ingredient, butter brings out the natural flavors of mushrooms. The salt from the whey obviates the need for further salting, but even without the salt the flavors come forth. Sautéing oyster mushrooms is a good example. The round flavor of these mushrooms simply is not evident until butter is added; then everything changes. Also, as mushrooms are sautéed slowly in butter, the liquid evaporates, and the butter influence becomes stronger in conjunction with the stronger, undiluted flavor of the mushrooms. When you are making a mushroom sauce, it is always a good idea to add some butter, if it does not harm the character of the sauce. Vegetable oil is good for sautéing mushrooms, but does little for their flavor. Nevertheless, the neutral flavor of vegetable oil does allow for experimentation with other flavors and spices that might otherwise be overwhelmed by the stronger taste of butter. If you prefer not to use butter for preparing mushrooms, you can still use vegetable oil along with some of the other ingredients described below. Bacon fat, however, is too obtrusive a flavor, except for the shiitake.

ONIONS. Onions are a good accompaniment to mushrooms and are used to enhance the overall flavor. But use them with caution; overuse of onions can mask those delicate mushroom flavors. Shallots and green onions are milder and preferable in some cases because of this. Generally, the more robust the mushroom flavor, the more safe it is to use onions. Hence, cepes, morels, and even chanterelles respond well to blending with members of this family.

GARLIC. Garlic has its own distinctive flavor, and the comments on onions refer to garlic also. The earthy, rich flavors of mushrooms are wonderful complements to garlic if the garlic is not overused. Generally the two flavors tend to stand up to one another and make a very good combination. Yet the use of garlic does not enhance the specific mushroom flavors.

LEMON. The use of lemon juice with mushrooms is one of the oldest and most accepted techniques of cooking with mushrooms. The reason is twofold: First, the acid from the juice tends to maintain the color of the mushrooms by keeping it from oxidizing; second, the acidity of the juice cuts into the heavy, earthy, buttery character of the mushrooms. As far as color is concerned, once the mushrooms are cooked (we are discussing domestic mushrooms here) color ceases to be a factor, so that argument holds only when raw mushrooms are considered. There is some merit to the addition of lemon juice as an acidic component, but when you do this, you are robbing the mushroom of its properties of fullness and body, and too much lemon juice wrecks the flavor altogether. Precious few recipes I have seen even indicate how much lemon juice to use, and I suspect that far too much is added in most cases. I recommend that you do *not* use lemon juice with mushrooms but rather try some of the other complementary flavors listed in this section first. The use of lemon juice with most *wild* mushrooms is entirely uncalled for.

FRESH SWEET PEPPERS. The use of fresh sweet peppers (green or red) is very underrated with mushrooms. In the case of morels, it actually enhances their flavor directly, because the two flavors are similar as well as complementary. When you use sweet peppers, always use some onion in equal parts to maximize their effect.

NUTS. Walnuts and pine nuts are great natural flavor and textural companions to mushrooms. They directly enhance the flavor of the mushrooms because the flavors are similar. They are especially good when you are using the high-heat method of sautéing.

SPICES AND HERBS. Almost any spice or herb used in moderation can be a good accompaniment to mushrooms, but there are several that are better than others, and one that specifically enhances the mushroomlike flavor of a dish. That one spice is savory. It goes equally well with wild or domestic mushrooms and should be added in the last minute or two of cooking. Marjoram is also excellent as it has a soft, full, buttery flavor, which are the very words I hear most frequently used to describe mushrooms. The combination of savory and marjoram is also excellent. Another combination that works very well is thyme and sage; this is perhaps the ultimate herb combination for mushrooms and lamb. Caraway seed is excellent for bringing out the flavor of morels. Most of the other spices are interesting but not as complementary as the ones listed above.

WINE. Being acidic, wine has a tendency to counteract rather than support the flavor of mushrooms. Tangy and zesty are the terms usually applied to wine, and thus it lends more acid to a dish than flavor. This characteristic is necessary in many cases, but for mushrooms wine should be confined to use in sauce. Mushrooms tend to counteract wine. Warren Winiarski of Stag's Leap Wine Cellars in Napa Valley, California, uses fresh raw domestic mushrooms as a palate cleanser during wine tastings, because the mushrooms tend to absorb the acid on the palate rather quickly.

I do not mean to imply that mushrooms and wine do not go well together, merely that the flavor and acidity in wine do not support the flavor characteristics of mushrooms. The argument is much the same as that made for the use of lemon juice above.

Wine and mushrooms contrast rather interestingly, though, in a dish that seeks complexity and activity. Dry sherry and Madeira are often the best types of wine to use because of their nutty flavors and lower acidities. The combination of morels, garlic, and cream sherry in a dish is one of the sublime wonders of the culinary world.

INGREDIENTS FOR SALTING. The very last step involved in almost any dish is the act of salting. Salt itself is an important ingredient that brings out flavor, but it is not enough by itself. A consommé or sauce can become steely or awkward before its flavors can be expressed when salt alone is used. The type

57

of salt can be either iodized or noniodized, sea salt or kosher salt. Kosher salt is best when used for marinating mushrooms to maintain a clear liquid or in a recipe calling for a clear sauce. Sea salt has the most intense and complex flavor and less should be used than regular salt.

The second ingredient needed to bring out mushroom flavor is soy sauce. The regular commercial kind in a good Chinese or Japanese brand will do fine. Do not use a heavy soy or a flavored soy, with the exception of Chinese mushroom soy, which is a thin type. Since soy sauce contains salt, why not just use it and skip the salt altogether? The answer is that, if soy is used as the sole source of salt, then too much soy sauce will have to be used. So you must get salt from a neutral source as well and use just enough soy to do its duty.

A third ingredient is sugar. I'm not talking about amounts large enough to suggest sweetness but rather a touch to round the edges brought on by the salt and the soy. If the dish or sauce is even the slightest bit sweet, then too much sugar has been used. Brown sugar can be used as well as white, but honey should be used with caution, because it imparts too much of its own flavor.

The idea here is give roundness and fullness to the *mushroom flavor,* and it cannot be obtained with any of the above ingredients *alone.* The combination of these three in proportions explained in the specific recipes will yield the result you are looking for: expression of true mushroom flavor: that is, salt, for palate responsiveness; soy, for mushroom flavor expression; and sugar, for roundness and body.

CHAPTER FOUR

# Duxelles, Sauces, Stocks, Extracts, and Other Basic Preparations

## Basic Preparations

Cooking of any sort involves some techniques and unique approaches, and mushrooms are no exception. In fact, the rich variety of mushroom cuisine is based on a number of different preparations, which are used in a great many ways. These include solid preparations that go into the making of dishes such as duxelles, purees, catsup, and butter, and liquid preparations, including sauces and extracts.

The most important thing to remember when making these preparations is simplicity. Mushrooms have a delicate flavor that is easily overwhelmed by spices, stocks, acids, etc. The recipes in this book are (as I have said elsewhere) designed to express those flavors that are unique to mushrooms, and so I have purposely avoided many of the classic mushroom dishes, sauces, and preparations. The reader of this book will find this chapter an important preparation for the recipes in the chapters that follow.

## Solid Forms for Preparing Mushrooms

### Duxelles

*Larousse Gastronomique* tells us that the word *duxelles* derives from the name of the town of Uxel in France and that some believe the dish was so called because it was created by the seventeenth-century chef La Varenne and named for his patron, the Marquis d'Uxelles. It then goes on to describe a recipe for mushroom duxelles. *Larousse* begs off when it comes down to defining what a duxelles actually is, and I have yet to find a proper definition. But somehow everybody knows that it is a cooked mixture of mushrooms and onions, but is this a *duxelles* or a *mushroom duxelles*? Can there be an asparagus duxelles wallowing in disrepute somewhere?

What can be said is that it is what the French call an *appareil*, or a simple mixed preparation that is to be used later as part of another recipe, and that duxelles is one of the most wonderful and versatile methods for using mushrooms. It is also one of the most flavorful mushroom preparations you can make. For our purposes I shall define duxelles as a mixture consisting of mushrooms, onions, butter, and salt components (a little sugar is added, as I have just explained). This may raise some hackles, since many chefs believe that tomato paste is as essential to duxelles as it is to Sauce Espagnole, the classic brown sauce. But I prefer the simplicity of this basic approach and will consider the addition of tomatoes as but one of the numerous variations on duxelles presented below.

There are three reasons for converting mushrooms into duxelles: First, the flavor is altered and improved by the addition of onions and butter, two of the best natural complementary ingredients for mushrooms.

Second, the form of the mushrooms changes into a paste, which can then be used directly on toast or meat, or combined with sauces or filling to enhance their character. Third, duxelles can be stored and kept for a long time. Duxelles will keep in a normal refrigerator for a week and for several months in a freezer. It can be kept frozen even longer, for that matter, but there is a possibility that the mixture will dry out on the top if it is not properly covered. Avoid this by pouring a little melted butter on the top of the duxelles before storing it. The butter forms an oil layer and keeps the air from the duxelles.

Keep in mind that duxelles is good without embellishments, but it can also be a great starting point for some interesting variations, depending on its use in a particular dish. I think of duxelles as falling into two distinct types, basic domestic duxelles and wild mushroom duxelles. First, the basic domestic form.

## Basic Mushroom Duxelles

APPROXIMATE PREPARATION TIME: 1 HOUR
MAKES 1 CUP

This recipe lends itself to the more interesting variations that immediately follow. Duxelles can be made in a food processor, but this is risky because too much processing will result in a puree. Truly good duxelles should come from mushrooms and onions, hand-chopped fine. The recipe yields 1 cup of finished duxelles.

If there is one preparation in this book that I believe everyone should have on hand in quantity, it's this one. Yes, it can be time-consuming to make a large quantity of it; nonetheless, duxelles cannot be topped for versatility and usefulness in the kitchen.

Most of the following duxelles recipes utilize this basic one by simply adding some ingredient to the primary recipe. Therefore, you're better off timewise if you can just pull a small quantity from the freezer, defrost it, and add the necessary ingredients for the variation. This recipe is for 1 cup, because that is the most useful amount for the majority of the recipes in this book. Multiply this recipe by ten, then store the duxelles in ten 1-pint plastic containers. Fill each container only half full, because the duxelles will expand as it freezes, and then freeze until ready to use. You won't regret it.

> *3 tablespoons melted butter*
> *⅔ cup chopped onions*
> *2 cups chopped mushrooms*
> *¼ teaspoon salt*
> *¼ teaspoon sugar*
> *½ teaspoon soy sauce*

1. Sauté the onions in the butter until they are just transparent.
2. Add the mushrooms and the rest of the ingredients and cook until these are well mixed. The mushrooms will begin to yield their water, and for a while the mixture will look like a swamp.
3. Continue cooking about 5 to 10 minutes, or until all the liquid has evaporated and a pastelike mixture is formed. This is duxelles. Let cool for ½ hour, and store in a jar or plastic refrigerator container.

The following represent some ideas on the further use of duxelles. Each of the following recipes will yield about 1 cup of duxelles. The time required to make these recipes will depend on whether you have some stored basic duxelles or must make that preparation from scratch.

### Tomato Duxelles

Add to the basic recipe 2 teaspoons tomato paste and adjust for sugar if desired, since the tomato adds acid to the mixture and should be offset by about ⅛ teaspoon more of sugar. This can be used the same way as the basic duxelles but goes particularly well in a sauce for pasta.

### Garlic Duxelles

While sautéing the onions in the basic recipe, add 1 teaspoon chopped garlic and proceed as directed for the remainder of the recipe. Some people prefer this approach to basic duxelles and will use the garlic in all the duxelles recipes. Others prefer the tomato as a constant or like them both. That is fine if it is to your taste. But if you decide to make your basic duxelles with tomato or garlic, or both, it will complicate the other variations that follow, and you should proceed with caution.

### Sweet Duxelles I—Chinese Style

To the basic recipe add 1 tablespoon hoisin sauce. This duxelles can be used on toast as a canapé or for stir-frying. Since the mixture is already thick, you do not need to add cornstarch for thickening the stir-fried items. Simply stir-fry the ingredients (pork and Chinese vegetables are ideal) and add the duxelles at the end to bind the whole, the same way you would add the hoisin by itself.

## Sweet Duxelles II

Prepare the basic recipe and add 1 tablespoon honey. This is really good as a finishing touch to game, which is quickly pan-fried to medium rare and then lightly coated with the duxelles. It is also excellent just spread on a fresh, warm croissant.

## Oyster Duxelles

To the basic recipe add 2½ tablespoons chopped fresh oysters and 1 teaspoon Chinese oyster sauce in place of the salt, sugar, and soy sauce. This duxelles is wonderful spread on swordfish that has been wrapped in parchment and baked. It is also good on fresh tuna, shark, or any fish substantial enough for its rich flavors. It is not recommended for delicately fleshed fish like sole.

## Smoked Salmon Duxelles

Add to the basic recipe 2½ tablespoons smoked salmon, chopped fine. This duxelles can be combined with a béchamel, a basic butter-flour-and-milk sauce (pages 126–127), to make a sauce for an egg dish like Eggs Benedict, or over fish quenelles, made of forcemeat bound with eggs (see Quenelles Sonja, pages 141–142). Lox can also be used, but the salt must be reduced in the basic recipe, or this mixture will be too salty. It can be used on a bagel with cream cheese as a variation on that classic combination.

## Herb Duxelles

Prepare the basic recipe and add 2 teaspoons fresh chopped herbs or ½ teaspoon dried herbs. Savory is a personal favorite of mine, since it is one of the spices that truly enhance the flavor of mushrooms. Nutmeg is added in some basic duxelles recipes, but I prefer it in combination with other herbs like savory or thyme. Bouquet garni (a mixture of parsley, thyme, and bay leaf) is also excellent. This is one kind of duxelles recipe where experimentation can yield marvelous results. Herb Duxelles prepared with basil is an excellent preparation for fish (see page 162). For example, make a smoked salmon duxelles and add freshly ground dill, a great start to a complex and daring sauce.

63

## Cream Duxelles

To the basic recipe add 2 tablespoons heavy cream and 1 tablespoon *crème fraîche*. This addition will thin the mixture and make it more spreadable. It will have a little zip from the *crème fraîche* and is great in a casserole with chicken and fresh mushrooms.

## Cheese Duxelles

To the recipe for cream duxelles (above) add 1 tablespoon Roquefort or other blue cheese, crumbled fine. Blend over heat until melted. The Roquefort-blue types are used, because they match the earthy quality of the mushrooms and their own strong flavors are natural companions. This duxelles goes well as a light coating over a preparation of snails in garlic butter.

## Mixed Vegetable Duxelles

Sauté together ⅓ cup carrots, ⅓ cup celery, and ½ cup parsley, all chopped fine, in 2 tablespoons butter. Add the basic duxelles. This mixture is best used as a base for a mushroom stuffing for pork, veal, or game birds.

## Meat Stock Duxelles

In this recipe, add to the basic recipe ½ cup very rich veal, beef, or chicken stock (see pages 72–73). Continue to cook until all the liquid has been evaporated. You will be left with a duxelles that has been enriched by the stock and can then be used on the meat from which the stock was derived. For example, if you want to make a dish in which this duxelles is placed between two layers of meat (e.g., Venison Rymanów; see pages 225–226), you would first make this type of duxelles, using a rich venison or veal stock. This kind of duxelles is also ideal for use with variety meats like kidneys or sweetbreads.

## Hot Duxelles

To the basic recipe, add 1 teaspoon hot chili peppers, chopped fine. Also excellent variations would be 2 teaspoons Thai hot sauce, or ¼ teaspoon cayenne pepper. This mixture is great on tacos or as a stuffing with refried beans for burritos. It is also recommended for a mushroom chili or a hot pasta dish.

## Wild Mushroom Duxelles

APPROXIMATE
MAKES 1 CUP, UNLESS OTHERWISE NOTED.

There are several approaches to achieving a wild mushroom duxelles. Before these are discussed, I would like to point out that the goal in preparing a duxelles made from wild mushrooms is to create a unique flavor of its own. Therefore, I do not think that variations from this type of duxelles is a good idea. The particular mushroom flavor should stand alone.

## Wild Mushroom Duxelles—Simple Method

To 1 cup of water, add ½ ounce well-rinsed dried cepes or morels. Bring to a boil, and simmer until the liquid is reduced to 2 ounces. Then add this rich mushroom liquid to the finished basic domestic recipe, and cook over medium-high heat while stirring until the liquid is evaporated. You can also chop the reconstituted mushrooms fine and add these to the duxelles. This will increase the yield by about ¼ cup.

## Cepe Duxelles—Fresh Method

Follow the recipe in Basic Mushroom Duxelles (page 61), using 2 cups of fine-chopped small cepes instead of the domestic mushrooms. If you are using older specimens, remove the pores first. This is a good duxelles for use with beef or veal.

## Cepe Duxelles—Dried Method

In a pot containing 2 cups of water, add 1 ounce dried cepes. Bring to a boil, and let gently simmer uncovered for 20 minutes. Remove the mushrooms from the water, and rinse thoroughly to remove grit. Chop fine, and rinse again. In another pan, sauté 1 tablespoon chopped onions in 2 tablespoons butter until transparent. Add the fine-chopped mushrooms, the strained liquid from the reconstituted mushrooms, ½ teaspoon salt, ¼ teaspoon sugar, and ½ teaspoon soy sauce. Cook until almost all the moisture is evaporated. This is a very rich duxelles, and it can be stretched by adding some domestic duxelles without losing too much of its character. This method is similar to the simple method. Makes ¾ cup.

## Morel Duxelles

This recipe can be used for fresh or reconstituted dry morels. The fresh morels will draw more water while cooking, however, and will take longer to finish. Sauté 1 tablespoon chopped onions and 1 tablespoon chopped green pepper in 3 tablespoons butter for 2 minutes. Add 1 cup chopped morels, ¼ teaspoon salt, ¼ teaspoon sugar, ¼ teaspoon soy sauce, and continue cooking until all the liquid has been evaporated. This is a good stuffing for veal or one of the more delicate fish. It can also be used for chicken, but avoid using it in meats or fish that have too strong flavors themselves, or the flavor of the morels will be lost. It is best served over a warmed croissant (see page 113).

## Chanterelle Duxelles

Chanterelles have an almost fruity nutlike quality, which lends itself to some experimentation. I am including just one here to give you the idea. This recipe uses dried apricots, since they support the flavor of the butter and onions and match the flavor and texture of the chanterelles. When combining the apricots and chanterelles, use 1 part apricot to 4 parts chanterelles (you can use fresh or canned). Sauté 4 tablespoons chopped onions in 4 tablespoons melted butter until almost transparent. Add 1 cup chopped chanterelles, ¼ cup chopped dried apricots, and a pinch of salt, and cook together for 2 minutes. The mushrooms will not draw much water, so this duxelles will be ready to use very soon and will not reduce to a paste. This duxelles is perfect for wild duck breasts or any fowl or game bird dish.

## Shiitake Duxelles

In 3 tablespoons melted butter, sauté ½ cup chopped green onions for 1 minute. Add 1 tablespoon fine-chopped Chinese sausage (which can be purchased in any Oriental grocery store) and 1 clove crushed garlic, and continue to sauté for another minute. Add to this mixture 1 cup chopped shiitake and 2 teaspoons hoisin sauce. Blend, and cook for another minute. This is best used as a filling for bao or Chinese bread, or just for spreading on toast or on a croissant. It is also excellent spread on a roast pork chop. Makes ¾ cup.

## Shiitake-Bacon Duxelles

Prepare as in above recipe but replace the Chinese sausage with 1 tablespoon of fine-chopped bacon. This duxelles is also excellent with pork. Makes ¾ cup.

## Dry Duxelles

This duxelles is always made with wild mushrooms, preferably with reconstituted dried mushrooms because these do not give off much water during the cooking process. In a saucepan, melt 3 tablespoons butter, and cook until the butter is slightly browned. Add to this butter ⅓ cup bread crumbs, and sauté until the crumbs are well browned (about 10 to 15 minutes). Add to this mixture ¾ cup chopped reconstituted dried cepes or chanterelles, and cook for another 5 minutes. Salt to taste. This duxelles is excellent over fish cooked in parchment.

## Duxelles from Mushroom Powder

See pages 71–72.

### Mushroom Purees

A mushroom puree is chiefly useful in making butters and soufflés. Purees are similar to duxelles, and the ingredients are exactly the same. The difference is that with duxelles the mushrooms and onions should be chopped and cooked down to a paste, whereas with a puree the mushrooms are simply placed in a blender and mechanically cut down to a puree. The difference is small, but a fine duxelles should really have evidence of mushroom and onion pieces, whereas a puree is expected to be part liquid.

Purees are easier to make and quicker than duxelles, because anything that fits into a food processor becomes a potential puree within seconds. Also, you eliminate the sauté step. This is illustrated in the following recipe in which all the ingredients of the puree are combined, then cooked together. One thing to keep in mind when making a puree from dried mushrooms is to wash the dried mushrooms thoroughly before processing them. Otherwise, the puree will have a gritty feel from the dirt or sand and will lose much of its appeal.

## Domestic Mushroom Puree

**APPROXIMATE PREPARATION TIME: 1 HOUR**
**MAKES 2 CUPS**

This is the puree you will be making most often because of the availability of market mushrooms. It may also be frozen and stored. If you plan to make mushroom butter, the time to do it is when the puree is freshly cooked. One part puree to 1 part softened butter is the recommended proportion.

*½ cup melted butter*
*1 small onion sliced*
*1 pound fresh domestic mushrooms, sliced*
*1 teaspoon salt*
*1 teaspoon sugar*
*1 tablespoon soy sauce*
*3 to 4 tablespoons water*

1. Put the butter in a sauté pan, and add the onions. Sauté until the onions become transparent.
2. Add the mushrooms to the pan, and continue to sauté over a low to medium heat for 5 minutes.
3. Add salt, sugar, and soy sauce, and continue to sauté for another minute.

4. While the mixture is still hot, place it in a blender or food processor, and add the water so that the mix blends. Add more water if necessary. When the mixture is smooth, transfer, cool, and store in a refrigerator or add to butter.

## Puree of Cepes

APPROXIMATE PREPARATION TIME: 1 HOUR
MAKES APPROXIMATELY ¾ CUP

This is the necessary first step in making Wild Mushroom Soufflé (pages 116–117). The result will taste slightly bitter in the mouth but don't worry about that: This recipe is not meant to be lovable by itself but rather as a step in other preparations, and in combination with butter and soufflés the bitter character fades. Purees can also be extended to sauces or soups and are a powerful source of flavor. They can be kept refrigerated for up to two weeks, and much longer if frozen. As in all purees, it is important to wash the dried mushrooms thoroughly before making the mixture, or you will have a gritty, sandy product that will follow through in all your subsequent preparations.

> *1 ounce dried cepes*
> *1 tablespoon chopped onion*
> *3 cups water*
> *¼ teaspoon salt*
> *½ teaspoon sugar*
> *1 teaspoon soy sauce*

1. Wash and thoroughly rinse the dried mushrooms.
2. Combine the mushrooms, onions, water, salt, sugar, and soy in a saucepan, and bring to boil, then lower the heat, and let simmer gently uncovered for 20 minutes. The liquid should become quite dark and be reduced to 2 cups.
3. Remove the mushrooms and onions from the liquid. Blend in a food processor, adding as much mushroom liquid from the reconstitution as necessary to make a smooth and medium thick (not too thick) puree. Reserve the remaining liquid from reconstitution for another soup or sauce. The resulting puree can now be stored for later use or frozen.

## Morel Puree

Prepare in the same manner as in the above recipe but add 2 tablespoons chopped red or green sweet pepper.

## Mushroom Catsup

APPROXIMATE PREPARATION TIME: **30** MINUTES
MAKES **1** CUP

Mushroom catsup originated in English cookery, where layers of fresh mushrooms were salted and skimmed over a period of three days to a week. During this time the salt would extract the liquid from the mushrooms, which would then be strained and seasoned. The resulting liquid would be cooked down to a syrupy extract, sealed, and sold as a condiment for meats or for a simple addition to sauces. It is found only rarely today, since this salting method is expensive, not to mention the fact that the catsup is very salty.

The following recipe, which combines mushrooms with standard tomato catsup, makes a flavorful sauce that can be used on sandwiches. Catsups made from wild mushrooms are a waste of time and energy, because the acidity of the tomato catsup eliminates most of the wild mushroom flavor (the exceptions to this rule are some of the dark-spored wild mushrooms like the *Coprinus atramentarius* [inky caps] or the *Psathyrella velutina,* which, because of their dark color, give the catsup a rich, finished look and good flavor). Domestic mushrooms, on the other hand, soften this acidity and are in fact the only proper mushrooms for making this condiment. You may vary the relative amounts of tomato catsup and mushrooms, increasing the mushroom puree to increase the mushroom character of the catsup. If you use too much, however, the color becomes an unaesthetic gray and loses eye-appeal. If you don't use enough, the color will still be red, but you might as well not have added the mushrooms for all the flavor you will get. Settle for this light red product, which allows for the flavor of the mushrooms to come through while maintaining a good color.

> *¾ cup sliced domestic mushrooms*
> *⅓ cup chopped onions*
> *1 tablespoon butter*
> *¼ teaspoon salt*
> *½ teaspoon soy*
> *Water*
> *⅓ cup tomato catsup*

1. Sauté the mushrooms and the onions in the butter in a skillet for 2 minutes.

2. In a blender or food processor, combine the mushrooms, onion, salt, and soy. Start to blend into a puree, adding only as much water as you need to get a puree that is fairly smooth.

3. Combine the puree with the tomato catsup. Store in a jar.

### Mushroom Butters

Mushroom butters are made by simply blending mushroom purees with softened butter. Minced mushrooms as well as minced garlic or onion can also be blended into the butters for appearance and texture. These are simple preparations but extremely useful ones for last-second spreading on light meats such as veal or pork and heavier types of fish such as swordfish, tuna, and even salmon. Another use for these butters is for general sautéing purposes when you want to integrate a mushroom flavor into a dish in a subtle way. A good example of this use is with scrambled eggs made with cepe butter. Simply use the cepe butter in place of regular butter while making your eggs, and slice in some fresh mushrooms for an interesting variation.

Various breads and other baked items like croissants and brioches are marvelous when spread with mushroom butter. Pasta served and tossed with wild mushroom butter is a simple, low-fat, and highly flavorful dish. The relative amounts of butter and puree to be used should be about equal, but this can be varied to your preference.

To make the butter, soften regular salted or unsalted butter so that it can be easily blended by light whipping, taking care not to let the butter separate by giving it too much heat. Prepare the puree of your choice (pages 67–70), and while the puree is warm, blend the butter and the puree with a whisk or in a mixer. The butter will keep for several weeks in the refrigerator and for months in the freezer. Store it in small containers if you are going to use it for many recipes over a period of time.

### Mushroom Powder

Mushroom powder is made by grinding dried mushrooms of any sort in a coffee grinder or spice mill. Powders are useful in soups and pastas where the powder can be combined with the flour for the pasta product. It can be used as a spice in virtually any dish to which you want to add a mushroom flavor without any physical evidence of mushrooms, as in a soup or stew. The only drawback to powders is that dried mushrooms often have bits of sand and dirt in them, and you will have to live with these in the powdered product. Powders can also be used in making butters in place of purees. When you do this, be sure to let the butter sit for several hours to absorb the mushroom flavor. For ½ pound of softened butter add 3 tablespoons mushroom powder.

To prepare a duxelles from mushroom powder, make one recipe of the Basic Mushroom Duxelles (page 61) with the following variation: Do not evaporate the liquid as described. Blend in some of the mushroom powder to absorb this liquid. Add enough powder to form the paste. This preparation will give you good wild mushroom-flavored duxelles without having to use a large amount of wild mushrooms.

# Liquid Forms for Preparing Mushrooms

Sauces constitute the most familiar of the liquid forms taken by mushroom flavors, although stocks, blanching liquids, and dried mushroom extracts are important, too. Liquids are a most effective means of covering the palate with flavor. Whereas solid food is tasty because it touches the palate at regular points, only liquids have the ability to "coat" the palate and maximize sensory awareness. Thickened liquids have an even more profound effect, because they linger on the receptive taste buds of our tongues. This fact should be borne in mind: The flavor of mushrooms is better conveyed by mushroom liquids than by solids. Here are the basic methods of extracting flavor from mushrooms into liquid. The place to start is with stocks.

## Stocks

Stocks are the key liquid ingredient for making meat- and poultry-flavored sauces. Several of the sauce recipes that follow require the use of veal stock. The classic procedure for making this stock involves adding vegetables such as carrots, celery, and onions to the broth. For the purposes of mushroom cookery, I recommend avoiding these as they tend to mask the flavor of the mushrooms. Stocks for mushroom dishes and sauces should be very plain in flavor but rich in body.

To make a stock, buy about 10 pounds of veal bones, preferably cut up, place them in a pot, and cover with about 1 gallon of water or enough to cover the bones by 2 inches. Do *not* add anything else. Bring the whole to a boil, skim as necessary, then cover, and let simmer for 6 to 8 hours. The stock

72

is ready for use when 1 or 2 teaspoons is rich enough to harden like gelatin after being placed in the refrigerator for 1 hour. If the test teaspoonful does not harden, continue to cook down the stock until it is rich enough to pass this test. Discard the bones.

A quicker but less reliable way of telling when it is rich enough is by noting the color. A concentrated stock will be a definite light golden-brown color and opaque, as compared to the clear tan color it has when it is just beginning to cook. The darker the stock, the more rich it is (assuming that you have not added any other ingredient that would affect its color). Your yield from 10 pounds of bones will be about 4 cups of rich stock.

The reason for keeping the stock so simple is to minimize the interference of other flavors with the mushrooms. You can always add other components, such as salt, later on; but the stock should be a source of *body*, period, not flavor. Stock is like the canvas of a painting, providing background and support for the creative concept.

This same technique should be used for preparing beef and other meat stocks. Chicken stock is good, too, but it must be cooked down (or reduced) sufficiently to yield a strong enough body. For purposes of mushroom cooking, fish stocks are not recommended.

When the stock is finished, it may be frozen in small containers and kept for up to six months. Defrost as needed.

## Mushroom Extracts

For sauces, soups, and consommés, extracts are the best way to derive concentrated mushroom flavor. Extracts can be made from fresh mushrooms, but richer and more complex flavors come from the dried form. Generally speaking, of the limited number of mushrooms available dried in most specialty food stores, the best extracts by far come from cepes and morels. After these in quality come black trumpet mushrooms, forest mushrooms, and shiitake. Bringing up the rear, and not very good, although usable, are the dried chanterelles and wood-ears.

To make a mushroom extract like a Boletus edulis extract, it is important to maximize the amount of color and flavor transferred from the dried mushroom to the liquid. Bring 3 cups of water, to which 1 or 1½ ounces of dried mushrooms have been added, to a rapid boil. Then reduce the flame and gently simmer 20 to 30 minutes, uncovered. The relative amount of mushroom liquid will determine the strength of the extract. One ounce for 3 cups of water yields a rich stock, but you can increase or decrease this amount as you desire. In most of the recipes, the liquid will be reduced to 1½ to 2 cups. Part of the released liquid will have been evaporated during simmering, and the rest will have been absorbed by the mushrooms themselves.

This 1½ cup of liquid is your mushroom extract. It may, in some recipes, serve as the base for light sauces; in others it may serve as a flavoring ingredient. The extract may be kept in the refrigerator for a week and may also be frozen and kept for up to six months. The reconstituted mushrooms themselves may be sliced and added to other dishes for texture and appearance; they may be rinsed thoroughly and pureed for use in soufflés and mushroom butters. Another means of using them is to make a dry duxelles (see page 67). But in any case, be sure to put them to use. They are still a rich source of flavor and useful for many mushroom dishes.

Finally, remember that, once extracts are salted, they cannot be kept for long periods of time, so do not salt until just prior to use. The method of salting is the same as for duxelles, using salt, soy sauce, and sugar (see pages 57–58).

### Sauces

We know sauces so well that we tend to overlook their function in a dish. Originally sauces were invented to hide the inferiority of food; a well-placed sauce could mask even putrid meats and fish. Like vermouth, which was spiced to disguise bad wine, sauces disguised bad food. Eventually, refrigeration and other preservation methods obviated the need for cover-up sauces, but by then their enhancement value had become so respected that they continued in use. Even meats and fish that were perfectly all right by themselves were improved with embellishment.

Today sauces are used to complement dishes without overshadowing them. What distinguishes them from other areas of cooking is that they are the only culinary form in which the cook controls the total "feel" of the food. When a cook produces a sauce, he adds all the ingredients from start to finish, including thickening, that affect the outcome of it. He determines the flavor and texture balance, which in turn determines whether the sauce will succeed or fail. Balancing these flavors, then, is the key to making a good sauce.

This is especially important in regard to mushroom sauces, where the mushroom flavor is very delicate and too often becomes overwhelmed by other ingredients. The point to making the mushroom sauces in the following recipes is to emphasize the mushroom flavor by using the other ingredients to support it. As with any sauce, the success or failure depends on the balance of the following components: body, acidity, salt, and flavor. Mushrooms have the properties of flavor and body; other substances must contribute salt and/or acid.

The bedrock to any good mushroom sauce is its extract, of course. (Blanching liquid made from fresh mushrooms, purees, and mushroom powder is an alternative source but its mushroom flavor is not as good as that of an extract.) Beyond that, you can do a certain amount of experimentation with flavorings. However, resist the temptation to use too much wine or too much spice for a mushroom sauce, and except with truffles and shiitake, never use any of the hard alcohols. And if you add fresh mushrooms to a sauce, remember that 90 percent of them is water, so add enough mushrooms to make their point.

### A Word on Thickening Sauces

Most of the sauces in this book are made from mushroom extracts and cannot be thickened by reduction. Nor are there recipes in which a pan is deglazed for sauce preparation, because deglazing requires the use of some sort of alcohol or stock to dilute the pan juices, which usually have a browned or burned taste to them; these flavors can mask mushroom flavors and therefore must be avoided. Most mushroom sauces (with some exceptions) have to be made separately from the meat or fish they are to complement. They are first made and then thickened. That way you can better control the flavor.

Thickening sauces requires the use of arrowroot or cornstarch. Arrowroot is expensive but preferable, because it yields a sauce that is clean and elegant looking, whereas cornstarch gives a shiny but opaque finish. (Flour, incidentally, should be avoided altogether, except in soups.) To make a thickening for a sauce, put 2 tablespoons of cornstarch or 1 tablespoon of arrowroot in ⅓ cup of cold water. When ready to thicken, mix the thickener and water together until the thickener is suspended in the water (it does not dissolve in the water; notice how it settles after sitting). Let the sauce come to a light boil. Slowly add the thickening solution to the sauce while stirring. Add about 1 teaspoon at a time. Stir until the milky white of the thickener disappears. Repeat with a little more thickening until you achieve the desired consistency. Never overthicken a sauce. A sauce underthickened is always more desirable than one overthickened. Sauces thickened with cornstarch will keep for a few days in the refrigerator, but those thickened with arrowroot may contain bits that have solidified during refrigeration, which do not come out easily with reheating.

Another way to thicken a sauce is by using a roux, a cooked mixture of butter and flour. Here I have followed the classic methods as explained in

75

the recipes. A few of the cream sauces are also thickened with egg yolk. First, whisk together 1 egg yolk with 2 tablespoons of cream to make what is called a liaison. Then add this slowly, while stirring, to about 1 cup of hot cream sauce. Remove from the heat to avoid curdling.

### Making Sauces from Fresh Mushrooms

What do you do when you have some fresh wild mushrooms and you want to make a sauce from them? This can be a tricky proposition, and the method explained here does not work for all wild mushrooms, simply because not all wild mushrooms have a lot of flavor. Still, the method is worth knowing and can be very useful. The first thing to do is to clean your mushrooms (about 1 pound) well. Then barely cover them with water in a saucepan. Bring the mushrooms to a boil, and then reduce to a simmer. Let the mushrooms blanch like this for 20 minutes, then remove them from the heat. Follow the directions on pages 72–73 for determining whether the mushroom broth is rich in flavor. Onions sautéed in butter can also be added to enrich the flavors, but this is recommended only for weaker-flavored mushrooms such as oyster mushrooms. The addition of soy, salt, and sugar is the method that is best for boletes, shiitake, and domestic mushrooms. Proceed to thicken and add back the mushrooms from the blanching. These sauces can be made much more elaborate by adding ingredients that support the hearty flavors of the mushrooms, such as garlic, onion, oyster sauce, and sometimes—and always sparingly—red wine.

### Cepe Sauce

APPROXIMATE PREPARATION TIME: 1 HOUR
MAKES 2 CUPS

This is an excellent all-purpose wild mushroom sauce. In this recipe the sauce is thickened with arrowroot, which gives it body without too much weight. In the velouté recipe that follows, where a big sauce is required, you simply thicken this sauce with roux. Clarified butter is used to maintain the clearness of the sauce.

> *1 ounce dried cepes*
> *3 cups water*
> *2 tablespoons chopped onions*
> *2 tablespoons clarified butter (see page 51)*
> *1 teaspoon sugar*

*1 teaspoon salt*
*1 tablespoon soy sauce*
*1½ tablespoon arrowroot mixed with ¼ cup water*

1. In a saucepan, add the cepes to the water, and bring to a boil. Let simmer for 20 minutes.

2. While the mushrooms are simmering, sauté the onions in the butter until the onions are transparent.

3. To the onions, add the cepes and the liquid, and the sugar, salt, and soy sauce. Simmer until the volume of the liquid is 1½ to 2 cups.

4. Strain the liquid through a fine sieve. Heat and thicken with the arrowroot mixture. If desired, return the mushrooms to the sauce and use immediately.

### VARIATION
## Naked Cepe Sauce

In this treatment, eliminate the step where the onions are sautéed. Otherwise, the procedure is the same as for the first sauce. Although onions complement the flavor of the mushrooms, they detract ever so slightly from the mushroom flavor itself. The true lover of raw, earthy mushrooms will want to try this sauce without the onions and butter. This sauce can be used in the same way as the first sauce and in all variations of it.

## Cepe Velouté Sauce

**APPROXIMATE PREPARATION TIME: 1 HOUR**
**USEFUL ADVANCE PREPARATION: PREPARE CEPE SAUCE (SEE PAGES 76–77)**
**MAKES 2 CUPS**

This is another all-purpose sauce that can easily be used in place of a recipe ingredient that calls for a beef or veal sauce. It possesses its own body and a distinctive flavor unmatched by anything else.

*1½ tablespoons clarified butter (see page 51)*
*1½ tablespoons sifted flour*
*2 cups Cepe Sauce unthickened*

1. Make a roux by combining the butter and the flour and mixing for about 5 minutes over medium heat in a sauté pan till the mixture becomes golden.

77

2. Add the unthickened Cepe Sauce to the roux, and stir until thickened. Strain and serve.

## Mushroom Juice for Beef

APPROXIMATE PREPARATION TIME: **30** MINUTES
MAKES 1½ CUPS

Two of the strongest-bodied ingredients for any sauce are combined here to give a flavor that is both powerful and elegant in its presentation. The two elements are *Boletus edulis* and veal or beef stock. The stronger the meat stock, the stronger the sauce. What sets this sauce apart from all others is the fact that it is not thickened, because of its natural body. It is superb with simple primary cuts of beef like prime rib or whole tenderloin of milk-fed veal. It also goes extremely well with rack of lamb.

> *1½ cups strong veal or beef stock (unsalted) (see pages 72–73)*
> *½ ounce dried* Boletus edulis *(cepes)*
> *1 teaspoon salt*
> *1 teaspoon sugar*
> *1 teaspoon soy sauce*

1. Combine and stir all the ingredients in a saucepan, and bring to a boil. Let simmer for a half an hour. Add water as needed to retain 1½ cups of sauce.
2. Remove mushrooms, and serve immediately. This sauce will chill quickly, because it is not thick enough to retain heat.

## Mushroom Cream Sauce I

APPROXIMATE PREPARATION TIME: **1** HOUR
USEFUL ADVANCE PREPARATION: PREPARE MUSHROOM EXTRACT (PAGES **73–**
      **74**) FROM *BOLETUS EDULIS* (SAVES **30** MINUTES).
MAKES 1½ CUPS

Here is an excellent sauce for veal, either poured over a chop or combined with the veal in a casserole. It also works well with pork. Any kind of fresh mushroom can be used for this sauce.

 78

*⅔ cup heavy cream*
*⅔ cup veal stock (see pages 72–73)*
*4 ounces* Boletus edulis *extract*
*¼ teaspoon salt*
*½ teaspoon brown sugar*
*1 teaspoon cream sherry*
*1 tablespoon sliced shallots or scallions*
*1 tablespoon mushrooms, chopped fine*
*2 tablespoons melted butter*
*2 tablespoons cornstarch mixed with ⅓ cup milk*
*Salt*

1. Combine the cream, stock, extract, salt, sugar, and sherry in a small bowl.
2. Sauté the shallots and mushrooms in the butter in a saucepan until the shallots are soft.
3. Add the ingredients from the bowl to the saucepan, and bring to a light boil, stirring constantly.
4. Thicken the above with cornstarch-and-milk mixture. Salt to taste.

**VARIATIONS**
## Mushroom Cream Sauce II

Follow the directions for Mushroom Cream Sauce I with the following difference: When sautéing the mushrooms and shallots, add 1 clove garlic, chopped fine. When the sauce is finished but not thickened, add ¼ teaspoon bouquet garni. Then thicken as described.

This sauce has more body than the first but should be used with dishes that already have strong flavors, like Venison Rymanów (see pages 225–226).

## Mushroom Cream Sauce III

This sauce is the same as Mushroom Cream Sauce I except that the veal stock is excluded. This allows the sauce to be used for vegetarian purposes; it also intensifies the character of the mushroom flavor.

Replace the veal stock in Mushroom Cream Sauce with more *Boletus edulis* extract in the same amount (i.e., use 1 cup total extract) and proceed as directed.

## Sauce Bonchampi

APPROXIMATE PREPARATION TIME: **45** MINUTES
MAKES 2¼ CUPS

Béchamel is the base for this rich sauce. It is made from that wonderful French cheese Bonchampi, still the best mushroom cheese on the market. The sauce is excellent for potatoes or pasta dishes.

*1 cup heavy cream*
*1 cup milk*
*3 tablespoons butter*
*3 tablespoons flour*
*6 ounces Bonchampi, rind removed*
*Milk*
*Salt*

1. Begin by combining the cream and milk in a double boiler. Start to heat.
2. Combine the butter and flour in a saucepan, and stir together until they form a paste; then cook for about 2 minutes. Do not let this roux brown. Remove from heat.
3. Cut the cheese into small chunks. Add to the milk and cream mixture. Continue to heat until a light skin begins forming on the milk. Stir in the roux while whisking vigorously, making sure that all the cheese has melted. Turn off the heat, and let stand for 5 minutes before serving. Add enough milk to thin the sauce if necessary. Salt to taste.

## Wild Mushroom Game Sauce

APPROXIMATE PREPARATION TIME: **1** HOUR
MAKES 1½ CUPS

This sauce is excellent for furred game, especially if the meat has not been marinated. It is very much in the traditional European Hunter's Style, which uses juniper berries and pickles. It was developed through the sixteenth and seventeenth centuries by cooks working on the great landed-gentry estates of France, Poland, and Germany.

*1 ounce dried* Boletus edulis
*2 cups water*
*2 ounces chopped, fresh onions*
*3 tablespoons melted butter*
*3 tablespoons flour*
*1 cup rich meat stock (see pages 72–73), preferably from the game*
*    being used; commercial variety also acceptable.*
*½ cup dry red wine*
*Salt and pepper to taste*
*6 juniper berries, crushed fine*
*2 allspice berries, crushed fine*
*1 teaspoon Dijon mustard*
*¼ teaspoon paprika*
*2 ounces diced dill pickles*

1. Clean mushrooms thoroughly under brisk running water.

2. Combine the mushrooms and about 2 cups of water in a saucepan, and bring to a boil. Then reduce the heat, and let simmer for 30 minutes. Remove reconstituted mushrooms from broth, and set aside for later addition to sauce.

3. Prepare a roux: Sauté the onions in the butter until they are almost transparent; add the flour, and stir for 1 minute.

4. Add the simmered mushroom extract, strained meat stock, and red wine to the roux mixture, and stir till blended and slightly thickened. Season with salt and pepper.

5. Add juniper berries, allspice, mustard, paprika, reconstituted mushrooms, and dill pickles. Simmer for 5 minutes. Add salt and pepper. The sauce is now ready to use.

## Mock Veal Velouté

APPROXIMATE PREPARATION TIME: 1 HOUR
MAKES 1½ CUPS

Here is a sauce that tastes like a veal or beef velouté. The trick is to assemble enough body ingredients to mimic the body from a meat stock. The use of garlic and sugar also aids in building the body of the sauce. It might make being a vegetarian a little easier.

> *¼ ounce dried* Boletus edulis *or dried morels, or dried forest*
>    *mushrooms*
> *2 cups water*
> *¼ cup soy sauce*
> *½ teaspoon garlic powder, or fresh, crushed garlic*
> *½ teaspoon salt*
> *1 teaspoon sugar*
> *3 tablespoons cream sherry or Madeira*
> *1 tablespoon chopped onion*
> *¼ teaspoon bouquet garni*
> *3 tablespoons melted butter*
> *3 tablespoons sifted flour*

1.  Combine all the ingredients except the butter and flour in a saucepan, and bring to a boil. Simmer for about 15 minutes. Cook mixture down to 1½ cups liquid.

2.  Strain this liquid, and set aside.

3.  Prepare a roux by blending the butter and flour, and cooking it to a light golden brown.

4.  Slowly add the liquid to the roux while stirring, and continue stirring till thick. Strain the sauce if necessary.


## Morel Sauce Rosenthal

APPROXIMATE PREPARATION TIME: **45** MINUTES
MAKES **2** CUPS

This sauce is named after Jack Rosenthal, a founder of the Culinary Institute of America. The sauce is elegant and full-flavored and goes ideally with veal or pork. The key to this sauce is the use of green peppers, whose flavor perfectly complements the flavor of morels.

> *1 ounce dried morels*
> *3 cups water*
> *3 tablespoons chopped onion*
> *3 tablespoons chopped green peppers*
> *2 tablespoons clarified butter*
> *1 teaspoon sugar*
> *1 teaspoon salt*
> *1 tablespoon soy sauce*
> *1½ tablespoons arrowroot mixed with ¼ cup water*

1. Add the morels to the water, and bring to a boil. Let simmer for 10 minutes.

2. Sauté the onions and green pepper in the butter until the onions are transparent.

3. Add the morels and liquid mixture and the sugar, salt, and soy to the onions and green peppers. Simmer until the volume of liquid comes to 2 cups.

4. Separate the liquid from the mushrooms, and thicken with the arrowroot-and-water mixture to desired consistency. Add the morels back to the sauce, sliced, if desired.

**VARIATION**
## Morel Velouté Sauce

Make this sauce the same way as the Morel Sauce Rosenthal, but thicken it with a roux made by combining 3 tablespoons flour and 3 tablespoons melted butter. This sauce will be quite light in color, so you may want to darken it with some food color. Use this sauce for beef dishes such as roulades.

## Morel and Veal Juice

**APPROXIMATE PREPARATION TIME: 45 MINUTES**
**MAKES 2 CUPS**

This recipe resembles the one for Cepe Sauce (pages 76–77). Here morels take center stage along with a rich veal stock. This sauce is best served with loin or leg of veal.

*1½ cups strong veal stock (see pages 72–73)*
*½ ounce dried morels*
*1 teaspoon salt*
*1 teaspoon sugar*
*1 teaspoon soy sauce*
*1 tablespoon chopped green pepper*
*Water*

1. Combine all the ingredients in a saucepan and bring to a boil. Let simmer for 30 minutes. Add back water as needed to retain 2 cup yield. Strain the sauce and serve immediately.

## Morel Cream Sauce

**APPROXIMATE PREPARATION TIME: 45 MINUTES**
**MAKES 1½ CUPS**

This sauce is ideal for casseroles or scalloped veal dishes. The combination of the garlic, sherry, and morels makes this one of my favorite sauces.

*1 ounce dried morels*
*1 cup strong veal stock or beef stock from bouillon cube*
*1 tablespoon chopped green pepper*
*1 tablespoon chopped onion*
*1 teaspoon salt*
*1 teaspoon sugar*
*1 teaspoon soy sauce*
*½ cup heavy cream*
*1 tablespoon sour cream or* crème fraîche
*1 tablespoon Madeira*
*½ teaspoon fresh, crushed garlic*
*2 tablespoons cornstarch mixed with ⅓ cup water*

1. Combine all ingredients from the morels to the soy sauce in a saucepan and bring to a boil. Let simmer for 20 minutes. Maintain 1½ cup quantity.

2. Add the cream and sour cream or *crème fraîche,* Madeira, and garlic to the liquid, and stir while simmering for another five minutes.

3. While stirring, thicken this sauce with the cornstarch-and-water mixture, a little at a time (you may not need it all), and keep warm.

## Morel and Caraway Sauce

**APPROXIMATE PREPARATION TIME: 45 MINUTES**
**MAKES 1½ CUPS**

Caraway seed is one of the ingredients whose flavor best complements that of the morel. They share an earthiness that in combination makes the morel taste more like itself. But be careful that you do not use too much caraway seed, or you will have a sauce that tastes like rye bread. This is a light sauce that goes well with medallions of veal or a heavier fish like swordfish or tuna.

*1½ cups water*
*½ ounce dried morels*
*4 to 6 caraway seeds*
*1 teaspoon salt*
*1½ teaspoons soy sauce*
*½ teaspoon chopped onion*
*½ teaspoon chopped green pepper*
*Water*
*1 tablespoon arrowroot, mixed with ¼ cup water*

1. Combine all the ingredients up to and including the green pepper, and bring to a boil in a saucepan. Let simmer for ½ hour, maintaining liquid level with added water.

2. Strain the liquid and add back the morels. The sauce may be thickened with some arrowroot to maintain clarity and add some body, but this sauce is meant to be delicate and subtle, so be careful with the thickening.

## Truffle Cream Sauce

APPROXIMATE PREPARATION TIME: **45** MINUTES
USEFUL ADVANCE PREPARATION: SOAK TRUFFLE IN MILK-CREAM PREPARATION
    (SEE BELOW) TO SAVE **30** MINUTES.
MAKES **1** CUP

This sauce is appropriate for any veal or game dish. Remember that, after the sauce is thickened, it must be removed from the heat immediately, or it will curdle. It is also excellent for pasta.

*½ truffle white or black, peeled or whole; fresh preferred but*
    *canned truffles acceptable (If canned truffles are used, add*
    *some of the juice from the truffles to the sauce.)*
*½ cup milk and ½ cup heavy cream combined*
*1 tablespoon chopped onion*
*1 tablespoon butter*
*1 teaspoon cream sherry*
*1 egg yolk*
*Salt and pepper and soy sauce*

85

1. Clean the truffle and chop. Let the truffle sit in the milk-cream mixture for an hour. Remove the truffle, and reserve the milk.

2. Sauté the onion in the butter for 1 minute. Add the sherry and the truffle, and continue to sauté for another minute.

3. Add ¾ cup of the reserved milk-cream to the sauté pan, and continue to heat gently for another minute.

4. In a small dish, add the other ¼ cup of reserved cream-milk mixture to the egg yolk, and whisk together well.

5. When the truffle-cream mixture begins to simmer around the edges, add the milk-cream-yolk mixture while stirring, and continue stirring until the sauce is thickened. Salt and pepper to taste, using some soy sauce to taste as well. Remove from the heat, and serve immediately.


## Truffle and Bourbon Sauce

APPROXIMATE PREPARATION TIME: **30** MINUTES
USEFUL ADVANCE PREPARATION: COMBINE TRUFFLES WITH BOURBON SEVERAL
      DAYS IN ADVANCE.
MAKES 1½ CUPS

This is my favorite recipe for truffle sauce. The body comes from the use of Chinese oyster sauce, which is readily available in Chinese grocery stores. Bourbon (I like Wild Turkey) for marinating the truffles is used to add body to the truffles. This sauce is a wonderful accompaniment for beef or veal dishes.

*½ truffle, fresh or canned, sliced; or 2 teaspoons peelings*
*Bourbon, just enough to cover truffles*
*1½ cups rich veal stock (see pages 72–73)*
*1 tablespoon Chinese oyster sauce*
*1 tablespoon soy sauce*
*1 tablespoon arrowroot mixed with ¼ cup water*

1. Cover the truffles with bourbon. Let sit at room temperature for several days in a sealed jar.*

2. Combine the stock, oyster sauce, and soy sauce, and bring to a simmer in a saucepan. Add the truffles and about 1 tablespoon of the bourbon. Thicken with the arrowroot and serve.

*Note: If this is not possible, then gently heat the bourbon in a small saucepan, add the truffles and let them simmer in the bourbon for ½ hour, and proceed as indicated.

## Shiitake Sauce

APPROXIMATE PREPARATION TIME: **45** MINUTES
MAKES **2** CUPS

Sauce made from dried shiitake is distinctly smoky. This character makes it one of the heartier mushrooms in terms of flavor, appropriate for many meat dishes. It is also excellent for smoked fish.

*1 ounce dried shiitake*
*3 cups water*
*1⅓ teaspoons sugar*
*1⅓ teaspoons salt*
*1⅓ teaspoons soy sauce (this is less than for other dried*
*    mushrooms)*
*1½ tablespoons arrowroot mixed with ¼ cup water*

Combine all the ingredients except the arrowroot in a saucepan, and bring to a boil. Lower the heat, and let simmer for ½ hour. The liquid should be cooked down to 2 cups. Thicken with the arrowroot-and-water mixture and serve immediately.

## Whiskey and Juniper Berry Sauce with Shiitake

APPROXIMATE PREPARATION TIME: **1** HOUR
MAKES **1½** CUPS

This is a light, elegant, sweet sauce that is best on game dishes like wild boar. It is derived from a basic Chinese sweet and sour sauce that supports the flavor of the juniper while masking its slight bitterness. The whiskey adds complexity and body to the sauce, and the shiitake lends it a smoky quality. I have used this sauce when preparing lion and antelope also.

*2 tablespoons peanut oil*
*1 clove garlic, chopped fine*
*1 teaspoon ginger, minced fine*
*1 shallot, sliced thin*
*12 caps shiitake mushrooms, sliced thin*
*1 cup meat stock (see pages 72–73)*
*1 ounce gin*

87

*1 ounce whiskey*
*1 ounce soy sauce*
*2 ounces lemon juice*
*4 tablespoons brown sugar*
*½ teaspoon crushed dried juniper berries*
*1 tablespoon arrowroot mixed in ¼ cup water*

1. In a sauté pan, heat the peanut oil till it smokes, and add the garlic, ginger, and shallots. Stir for 1 minute. Add the mushrooms, and sauté for 2 more minutes.

2. Add to the sauté pan the rest of the ingredients except the arrowroot mixture. Bring to a boil.*

3. When the sauce is simmering, add the arrowroot-and-water mixture until the sauce thickens to the desired consistency. Serve immediately.

*Note: If the sauce is not going to be used immediately, keep hot as an unthickened liquid.

## Domestic Mushroom Sauce

APPROXIMATE PREPARATION TIME: 1 HOUR
MAKES 2 CUPS

This is an approach like the one used to make a sauce from a batch of fresh mushrooms (see page 76), in that the extract is prepared from the blanching liquid rather than from dried mushrooms and is salted accordingly. This sauce is excellent on veal or chicken. Notice the use of savory in this recipe. It greatly enhances the mushroom flavor.

*2 pounds sliced domestic mushrooms*
*Water, enough to cover sliced mushrooms*
*1 teaspoon salt*
*1 teaspoon sugar*
*1 teaspoon soy sauce*
*½ teaspoon dried savory*
*1 tablespoon melted butter*
*1 tablespoon chopped onions*
*1½ tablespoons arrowroot mixed with ¼ cup water*

1. Place the mushrooms in a pot, and just cover with water. Bring to a boil, then let simmer for ½ hour.

 88

2. Add the rest of the ingredients, except the arrowroot, to the mushrooms. The yield should be about 2 cups liquid plus the mushrooms. Thicken with arrowroot-and-water mixture, and use immediately.

**VARIATION**
## Domestic Mushroom Cream Sauce

Make the mushroom sauce as in the above recipe but replace half of the water-base liquid with a ½ cup each of milk and heavy cream *before* adding the rest of the ingredients. Thicken and use.

## Chanterelle Sauce

APPROXIMATE PREPARATION TIME: 1 HOUR
MAKES 2 CUPS

Dried chanterelles are very difficult to use for sauces made in the same fashion as some of the previous recipes. Frankly, the best way to use chanterelles is to drop them into a casserole or sauce and let their flavor permeate the whole dish. The treatment below takes the route of a sweet and sour sauce, using apricot liqueur. This is a sauce for poultry or game birds.

*½ ounce dried chanterelles*
*2 cups water, or meat stock (preferably veal stock; see pages 72–73)*
*3 tablespoons chopped onion*
*2 teaspoons melted butter*
*2 ounces white vinegar*
*4 tablespoons apricot liqueur*
*4 tablespoons soy sauce*
*1 teaspoon salt*
*3 tablespoons sugar*
*1½ tablespoons arrowroot mixed with ¼ cup water*

1. Add the chanterelles to the water or stock, and bring to a boil. Let simmer for 20 minutes. Replace the liquid as necessary to retain 2 cups.
2. Sauté the onions in the butter until the onions are just transparent.

89

3. Add the chanterelle extract to the onions and butter, and bring to a boil. Add the chanterelles and the rest of the ingredients, except the arrowroot. Thicken with the arrowroot-and-water mixture.

## Wood-Ear Sauce with Five-Spice

APPROXIMATE PREPARATION TIME: 1 HOUR
USEFUL ADVANCE PREPARATION: SOAK DRIED CLOUD-EARS A DAY IN ADVANCE
      IN WATER.
MAKES 2 CUPS

Wood-ears or cloud-ears are found dried in Oriental grocery stores. On reconstitution, they are still quite chewy and firm, so slice them very thin for stir-fry or sauce purposes. The extract from the dried mushrooms is not very flavorful, but is of an attractive dark color, which should not go to waste. Here is a sauce that uses that extract as a base, then builds from it, using Chinese five-spice seasoning. Five-spice is very good on the oilier types of fish such as shad or mackerel and can be found in any Oriental grocery store. When reconstituting the fungus, use a good veal stock.

*1 ounce cloud-ears, dried*
*3 cups veal or beef stock (see pages 72–73)*
*1 cup water*
*2 teaspoons Chinese oyster sauce*
*2 teaspoons hoisin sauce*
*1/4 teaspoon five-spice seasoning*
*1/4 teaspoon fresh crushed garlic*
*1 1/2 tablespoons arrowroot mixed with 1/4 cup water*

1. Add the cloud-ears to the veal stock and water, and bring to a boil. Reduce to a simmer, and cover. Allow to continue simmering until the cloud-ears become chewable (this may take 1 hour or more). Remove the cloud-ears from the stock, and cut them into small slices. Return these slices to the liquid.

2. Add the rest of the ingredients, except the arrowroot, to the mushrooms and liquid. The amount of liquid should equal about 1 cup. Bring to a simmer, and thicken with the arrowroot-and-water mixture.

## Blood of the Beast

APPROXIMATE PREPARATION TIME: **20** MINUTES
MAKES **2** CUPS

Lamb with its burly flavors and heady aromas begs for a sauce of contrast and strong statement. This sauce satisfies that need. It also goes well with beef and is the sauce used for Jack's Spicy Beef Casserole, described on page 188.

*1 cup strong beef or veal stock (see pages 72–73)*
*1 cup red wine*
*6 tablespoons Chinese oyster sauce*
*1 tablespoon Tabasco or Thai chili sauce*
*2 scallions, sliced*
*12 caps wild or domestic mushrooms*
*1 tablespoon arrowroot mixed with ¼ cup water*

1. In a saucepan, combine all the ingredients except the arrowroot. Bring to a boil, stir and simmer for 5 minutes.
2. Thicken with the arrowroot-and-water mixture, and serve immediately.

## Miscellaneous Liquid Preparations—Beverages

## Mushroom Liqueurs

This preparation is very useful as another means of storing mushroom flavor. It can be used later for recipes that call for a high-alcohol ingredient plus a mushroom flavor. The recipe for Truffle and Bourbon Sauce is such an example. But the best way to enjoy Mushroom Liqueur is by itself with some friends who think you're a little crazy anyway.

The procedure is to add to a fifth of vodka 1 ounce of dried mushrooms. Cepes, morels, and chanterelles all work. You will taste their distinct characters while you sip. This can be served over ice or neat.

Truffle liqueur is made by adding fresh truffles to a good bourbon or whiskey, not vodka.

## Mushroom Coffee

This is a great waker-upper for someone who has had a few too many the night before. Add 1 part mushroom powder (see pages 71–72) and 2 parts fresh ground coffee. Mix well, and make the coffee the way you would regular coffee. The acidity of the coffee makes it difficult to taste the mushrooms, but the aroma is very distinctive.

**CHAPTER FIVE**

# Mushrooms in Soup

Mushroom soups should emphasize mushroom flavors and not become too complicated. Some of the best soups are simple flavored extracts. Others, like Joe's Wild Mushroom Soup, are heartier but still maintain rich mushroom character.

## Cepe Liquor

APPROXIMATE PREPARATION TIME: 1 HOUR
MAKES 4 SERVINGS

The method for making clear soup from dried mushrooms is the same for virtually all kinds of dried mushrooms. Simply salt the reconstitution liquid and serve with some thin-sliced scallions and sliced mushrooms, either fresh or reconstituted.

> *2 ounces dried cepes or forest mushrooms*
> *5 cups water*
> *2 teaspoons salt*
> *Pinch sugar*

*2 tablespoons soy sauce*
*1 scallion, sliced thin*
*1 tablespoon clarified butter (see page 51)*

1. Add the mushrooms to the water, and bring to a boil. Reduce to a simmer, and heat uncovered for another ½ hour.
2. Add to the liquid the salt, sugar, and soy sauce. Stir, add the scallion, and stir in the butter. Cook down to 4 cups, and serve.


## Christopher Soup

**APPROXIMATE PREPARATION TIME: 1 HOUR**
**MAKES 4 SERVINGS**

The idea of covering a cup of soup with puff pastry was introduced by the renowned Paul Bocuse when he made his truffle soup. The following is my own variation, using a morel liquid instead of truffles. Be sure to use ovenproof bowls for this soup. It is named after my son Christopher.

*2 ounces dried morels*
*5 cups water*
*1 tablespoon green pepper, chopped*
*1 tablespoon onion, chopped*
*2 tablespoons melted butter*
*2 teaspoons salt*
*2 teaspoons sugar*
*2 tablespoons soy sauce*
*4 pieces ready-to-use puff pastry\* cut into 3-inch squares*
*1 lightly beaten egg*

*Preheat oven to 450°.*

1. Add the morels to the water, and bring to a boil. Let simmer uncovered for ½ hour.
2. While the morels are simmering, combine the green peppers, onions, and butter in a sauté pan, and sauté over a medium heat until the onions and peppers are soft.

*\*Note: Recipe follows.*

 **94**

3. When the mushrooms are done reconstituting, add the liquid and the mushrooms to the onions and peppers along with the salt, sugar, and soy. Bring back to a simmer. Remove, and let cool before placing it in the bouillon cups.

4. While the mushroom, onion, and pepper mixture is simmering, roll out the pieces of puff pastry thin. Paint the outside edges of the cups with some beaten egg. Pour the soup into the cups, and cover with the puff pastry, making certain to overlap the cups with 2 inches of puff pastry, and press the pastry onto the outside of the cup where it is painted with the egg. Trim off excess puff pastry. Repeat for all the cups, and refrigerate.

5. After the soup has been refrigerated for 1 hour, place it in the oven, and bake until the puff pastry has risen and is golden brown. Serve

## Puff Pastry

APPROXIMATE PREPARATION TIME: **10** HOURS
MAKES **16** 8-INCH PUFF PASTRY SQUARES

> *2 cups all-purpose sifted flour*
> *2 cups sifted cake flour*
> *¼ teaspoon salt*
> *1 pound butter*
> *2 large egg yolks*
> *1 cup ice water*
> *1 tablespoon lemon juice*

1. Measure the flour, and sift with the salt into a large bowl.
2. Put butter into the flour, and cut into small pieces with 2 knives.
3. Beat the egg yolks, water, and lemon juice together in a small bowl. Add to the flour mixture. Mix lightly with a knife until all liquid is absorbed and the dough holds together. Place on floured board, and coat with flour.
4. Press with rolling pin, first one way and then the other. Roll into a sheet about 10 by 15 inches. Sprinkle flour under dough frequently to prevent sticking. Brush all surplus flour off top of dough.
5. Turn bottom ⅓ of dough over middle ⅓, removing excess flour.
6. Turn top ⅓ of dough over the other 2 layers, making 3 layers in all.
7. Turn the pastry with the open end toward you. Roll out again, and fold to make 3 layers.
8. Press firmly with rolling pin, and wrap in waxed paper. Store in refrigerator for 2 hours, then repeat the rolling and folding twice. Place in the

refrigerator for another 2 hours, and repeat again. (This will make six turns in all.)

9.  Store in refrigerator for 2 hours before using. When you are ready for final preparations, cut dough into 8 equal parts. Roll each piece on a well-floured board to a size of 9 by 18 inches. Trim the edges evenly, and cut in half. Squares should be 8 by 8 inches. Put between 2 layers of wax paper, and store flat in the refrigerator. Roll remaining dough the same way. There will be 16 pieces. I recommend that you make the puff pastry in this large quantity so that you do not have to do it too often. It may be stored in a refrigerator for 2 weeks, and in a freezer for up to 3 months.

## Puff Pastry Shells

These shells are very useful for holding mushroom preparations such as braised mushrooms or mushrooms in cream sauce. Lay out a sheet of puff pastry on a floured table and cut out, with a cookie cutter, any desired size or shape of shell you wish to have. You can even cut simple square or rectangular shapes with a knife if so desired. Place these cutouts on a baking pan covered with oven-proof parchment paper or wax paper. Coat each shape with some beaten egg applied with a pastry brush. Bake in a 425° oven until browned, about 10 to 15 minutes.

These will keep warm until ready to use, or can be refrigerated and reheated just before using. If the shells are going to be used to hold a preparation, then hollow out with a knife or spoon the interior of the shell and fill with the desired preparation. Or you can remove the top part of the shell in one piece by running a knife parallel to the table and keeping this top piece intact. Then hollow out the interior of the remaining shell. Fill with the preparation and cover with the top part previously removed.

## Joe's Wild Mushroom Soup

APPROXIMATE PREPARATION TIME: 2 HOURS
MAKES 4 SERVINGS

This is a hearty soup that captures the flavor of the cepe. It goes best with a full-bodied Zinfandel for a midday lunch.

*2 ounces dried cepes*
*1½ quarts water*

*3 medium-sized chopped onions*
*1 pound beef or veal bones*
*2 tablespoons sifted flour*
*2 tablespoons butter*
*Salt and pepper to taste*
*2 tablespoons crème fraîche*

1. In a large pot, bring the mushrooms to a boil in the water, then let simmer for ½ hour.

2. Strain the liquid through cheesecloth to remove any dirt, and wash mushrooms.

3. Puree the onions in a food processor, and add to cooking pan.

4. Add to the pot the mushroom liquid, the mushrooms, sliced, and the meat bones, and bring to a boil. Lower the heat, and simmer for 1 hour, covered.

5. Prepare a roux by combining the flour with the butter and heating until it forms a golden-brown paste.

6. Strain the liquid from the pot, and add to the pan with the roux, stirring, until thickened. (The liquid remaining in the stock pot should be about 2 to 3 cups. Reserve this for another use, such as sauce, etc.) Adjust seasoning with salt and pepper, and top each portion with ½ tablespoon of *crème fraîche*.

**VARIATION**
## Wild Mushroom Soup II—Quick Version

APPROXIMATE PREPARATION TIME: **45** MINUTES
MAKES **4** SERVINGS

This recipe utilizes a food processor for making wild mushroom soup. It is quick and tasty.

*1 ounce dried cepes, washed*
*3 cups water*
*½ cup chopped onions*
*2 tablespoons butter melted*
*½ cup rich beef stock or equivalent from bouillon cube*
*1 teaspoon salt*
*1 teaspoon sugar*
*1 tablespoon soy sauce*
*½ cup flour mixed with ½ cup water*

1. Boil the mushrooms in the water, then simmer for 20 minutes.

2. Remove the mushrooms but reserve the reconstituted liquid. Slice the mushrooms, then rinse them thoroughly. Place them in a food processor with the liquid from the reconstitution. Add the rest of the ingredients, except the flour, and blend down to a puree. This may have to be done in several stages if your blender does not have the capacity to contain all the ingredients.

3. If the puree has too many lumps, then strain it. (This soup should not have vegetable pieces floating around in it.) Place puree in cooking pot, and bring to a boil. Thicken by slowly pouring the flour-and-water mixture into the liquid through a sieve held over the soup pot. Stir while adding flour until desired thickness is reached.

## Slippery Jack Soup

APPROXIMATE PREPARATION TIME: **2** HOURS
MAKES **4** SERVINGS

Slippery jacks *(Suillus luteus)* are among the most abundant wild mushrooms on earth. Picked in great quantities in Europe, they suffer only in comparison to the *Boletus edulis,* of which they are considered to be poor cousins. Slippery jacks, however, have their own unique flavor, which many consider to be equal to cepes, and they are certainly less expensive. One of the scandals in the mushroom trade in recent years has been the substitution of these mushrooms for cepes in commercial dealings, in canned, dried, and powdered form, since the slippery jacks cost about one tenth as much as cepes. They take their name from their fresh form, in which they exhibit a shiny, gelatinous cap that is actually slippery to the touch. This cap is often peeled before using, since some people consider it to be slightly bitter. The dried form, when sold by itself, is often referred to as forest mushrooms and has a pungent, earthy odor that is wonderful in soups and sauces. I suspect we will see more and more of this mushroom fresh in our specialty stores since it is so abundant. Hence, the following recipe is for fresh slippery jacks. Note that some *crème fraîche* has been purposely added at the end to give the soup a tangy finish.

> 1 pound beef bones
> ½ pound soup vegetables (onions, carrots, celery, parsley), chopped
> coarse

*1 tablespoon salt*
*1 pound young, firm slippery jacks*
*1 onion, sliced thin*
*4 tablespoons melted butter*
*4 tablespoons flour*
*¾ cup heavy cream*
*Salt and pepper to taste*
*4 teaspoons crème fraîche or sour cream*
*1 teaspoon chopped dill*

1. Add beef bones and vegetables to a small (4-to-6-quart) stock pot; cover with water, and bring to boil.

2. Simmer this mixture for about 1 hour, skimming froth as necessary. Add about 1 tablespoon salt.

3. Clean slippery jacks by removing the slippery skin of the cap and any soil.* Slice the mushrooms.

4. In a skillet, lightly brown the onion in the butter, and add the mushrooms. Stir mixture over medium fire for 3 minutes.

5. Sprinkle the flour over this mixture, and stir till the flour mixture is smooth.

6. Strain the soup stock, and add 1 cup of stock to the mushroom mixture, stirring while adding.

7. Combine remainder of stock with soup mixture, and simmer for 10 minutes.

8. Add cream slowly while stirring. Add salt and pepper to taste.

9. Serve hot in heated bowls, adding the *crème fraîche* to each bowl, and top with the chopped dill.

* Note: To clean slippery jacks, rinse the mushrooms to remove any dirt. Then, using a paring knife, begin peeling the skin from the edge of the cap, until it is completely removed. Repeat for all the mushrooms.


## Sirloin and Mushroom Soup

APPROXIMATE PREPARATION TIME: 1 HOUR
MAKES 4 SERVINGS

This is a hearty winter's night soup that goes well with a mighty Zinfandel or a glass of port. Either fresh meat or leftover cooked meat can be used for this recipe. This soup is a one-dish meal in itself.

*12 cups rich beef or veal stock (see pages 72–73)*
*2 pounds fresh mushrooms*
*½ ounce dried mushrooms, preferably cepes*
*2 tablespoons soy sauce*
*1 tablespoon salt*
*2 teaspoons sugar*
*¼ pound butter melted*
*1 pound fresh sirloin, or ¾ pound leftover cooked meat, cubed*
*¼ pound smoked sausage, cubed small*
*¼ teaspoon dried savory*
*1 bay leaf*
*2 cloves minced garlic*
*1 medium onion, cubed small*
*Flour*
*Water*

1. Combine all the ingredients except the flour and water in a pot, and bring to a boil. Let boil for 1 hour. Remove bay leaf.

2. Combine about 1 cup of flour with about 3 cups of water and slowly add, straining the flour mixture through a sieve and stirring as it pours. Stop adding the flour mixture every time the soup becomes cloudy; then resume pouring when the soup clears. Continue in this manner until the soup is thickened. Adjust for salt, and serve.

## Vegetarian Soup with Cream of Wheat

APPROXIMATE PREPARATION TIME: **3** HOURS
MAKES **4** SERVINGS

This soup uses pure mushroom and vegetable flavors for its base; you may also add onions and herbs to it if you wish.

*3 ounces fresh mushrooms*
*3 quarts water*
*2 whole medium kohlrabi*
*1 medium carrot, cleaned, chopped coarse*
*2 ribs celery*
*1 handful chopped parsley*
*½ head savoy cabbage, chopped*
*1 cup cauliflower and asparagus pieces*

*1 cup uncooked Cream of Wheat*
*4 tablespoons butter*
*4 tablespoons flour*
*1 cup cold water*
*Salt and pepper*
*Chopped parsley and dill for garnish*

1. Wash mushroom caps thoroughly in warm water.
2. Put mushroom caps into a 5-to-6-quart pot, and cover with 3 quarts of water.
3. Add sliced kohlrabi, chopped carrots, celery, and chopped parsley, and bring to a simmer. Cook for 1 hour.
4. Strain out the mushrooms and vegetables, and puree them until smooth in a blender or food processor. Return to pot, and continue simmering.
5. Cook cabbage, cauliflower, and asparagus pieces separately until tender. Hold.
6. To the simmering broth, slowly add 1 cup Cream of Wheat, stirring broth as you pour.
7. In a skillet, prepare a roux of 4 tablespoons butter and 4 tablespoons flour. To it, add 1 cup of cold water, and stir. Add the roux to the simmering broth, and stir until smooth.
8. While pot is simmering, puree cabbage, cauliflower, and asparagus, and add to pot. Stir.
9. Correct seasoning, and add parsley and dill when serving.

## Fresh Wild Mushroom Soup

**APPROXIMATE PREPARATION TIME: 1 HOUR**
**MAKES 4 SERVINGS**

This is a very easy and satisfying soup to make. Prepare this recipe when you have some fresh wild mushrooms and wish to enjoy them as soon as possible. Simply clean the mushrooms, and then barely cover them with water in a pot. Turn the heat on, and cover the pot with a tight-fitting lid. When the water comes to a boil, turn it down to a simmer for 10 minutes. The mushrooms will have given off their liquid and literally made their own soup. For every 2 cups of liquid, add 1 teaspoon each of salt and sugar and 1 tablespoon soy sauce. Add 4 to 5 scallions, sliced thin, and 1/3 cup shoestring-cut potatoes. The soup is finished when the potatoes are cooked.

## Domestic Cream of Mushroom Soup

**APPROXIMATE PREPARATION TIME:** 1½ HOURS
**MAKES 4 SERVINGS**

The important thing to remember about making a good cream of mushroom soup is to let the mushrooms contribute their own liquid and flavor to the soup.

*6 tablespoons sifted flour*
*8 tablespoons melted butter*
*2 tablespoons chopped onions*
*2 pounds fresh domestic mushrooms, chopped*
*2 tablespoons water*
*1 cup heavy cream*
*½ teaspoon dried savory*
*2 teaspoons salt*
*2 teaspoons sugar*
*2 teaspoons soy sauce*

1. In a sauté pan combine the flour and 6 tablespoons of the melted butter. Heat over a low heat for 5 minutes. Set aside.

2. In another sauté pan, cook the onions in the rest of the butter until the onions are just transparent. Add the mushrooms and the water. Cover with a lid, and turn the flame down to low. You want the mushrooms to draw as much liquid as possible, and you do not want this liquid to evaporate.

3. After ½ hour, remove the lid from the onion and mushroom mixture, and add the cream (enough to make a total volume of about 5 cups), savory, salt, sugar, and soy sauce. Stir well, and bring to a simmer.

4. Thicken the mushrooms in cream with the flour-butter mixture. Serve immediately.

## Wild Mushroom Vichyssoise

**APPROXIMATE PREPARATION TIME:** 4 HOURS
**MAKES 4 SERVINGS**

This is a variation on the classic potato soup. The essence of the dried mushrooms gives the flavor another dimension, which is supported by the body and character of the potatoes.

*2 medium peeled potatoes, diced*
*2 cups water, or enough to cover potatoes*
*$\frac{1}{2}$ ounce dried mushrooms*
*2 tablespoons chopped onions*
*1 teaspoon salt*
*1 teaspoon sugar*
*1 tablespoon soy sauce*
*1 cup heavy cream*
*Milk (optional)*
*1 leek, chopped fine*

1. Begin boiling the potatoes in water.

2. In a saucepan combine the water, mushrooms, onions, salt, sugar, and soy sauce. Bring to a boil, then simmer down to 1 cup liquid. Remove the onions and mushrooms from the liquid, and puree in a food processor. Cool the liquid in the refrigerator for 1 hour.

3. Remove the cooked potatoes from the water. Begin mashing them in a blender, mixer, or food processor. Add the cream. Add the mushroom extract and puree, and blend well. Add some milk, if necessary, to thin down the soup.

4. Refrigerate the soup until well chilled. Serve topped with the leek.

CHAPTER SIX

# Mushroom Dishes for Light Lunch or Brunch

The following recipes are ideal for brunches, lunches, or light afternoon meals. The recipes for mushrooms and eggs can be used for breakfast, as can the recipes for mushrooms with croissants.

## Quiches with Mushrooms

### Quiche Chanterelle

APPROXIMATE PREPARATION TIME: 2 HOURS
USEFUL ADVANCE PREPARATION: MAKE OR PURCHASE ONE 9-INCH PIECRUST
      AND PREBAKE AS DIRECTED.
MAKES 4 TO 6 SERVINGS

This quiche is adequate for six people as a starter or for four as a luncheon main course. More exotic wild mushrooms can be substituted, provided they have the flavor to stand up to the other ingredients.

*1 9-inch piecrust*
*1 small onion, diced*
*2 tablespoons melted butter*

*2 ounces Canadian bacon, chopped coarse*
*¼ teaspoon bouquet garni*
*¼ teaspoon dried savory*
*3 ounces fresh or 1 ounce canned chanterelles, drained of juices*
*Salt and pepper to taste*
*½ cup milk*
*½ cup heavy cream*
*2 eggs*
*Dash cayenne pepper*
*3 ounces Gruyère cheese, grated*
*2 ounces Swiss cheese, grated*

*Preheat oven to 450°.*

1. Prebake pie shell for ten minutes in 450° oven. Check regularly to make sure the crust does not puff up and bake stiffened in that position. If it puffs, pierce crust with a fork several times. Do this as often as necessary to maintain a flat crust. Another method of prebaking shells is to line them with aluminum foil, then fill the foil with uncooked rice or beans to weight down the dough. The prebaking time will be slightly longer using this method.

2. Sauté onions in butter until transparent.

3. Add bacon, bouquet garni, savory, and chanterelles, and sauté for 2 minutes.

4. Add salt and pepper to taste, then set mixture aside.

5. Prepare the custard by combining the milk, cream, eggs, and cayenne thoroughly.

6. Place Canadian bacon mixture in pie shell, and cover with custard and Gruyère and Swiss cheese.

7. Bake pie at 450° for 10 minutes, then at 350° for 20 minutes. Check for doneness by piercing with a fork. If liquid custard is still on the fork, continue to bake for another 5 minutes, then check again. Repeat if necessary.

8. Remove pie from oven, and let cool 30 minutes before serving. Slice and serve.

## Morel Quiche

APPROXIMATE PREPARATION TIME: **2** HOURS
USEFUL ADVANCE PREPARATION: MAKE OR PURCHASE ONE **9**-INCH PIECRUST,
    AND PREBAKE AS DIRECTED.
MAKES **4** TO **6** SERVINGS

This recipe is a delicious illustration of one of the principles of cooking with morels: Always use a little green pepper when preparing them.

*1 9-inch piecrust*
*1 small onion, chopped*
*¹⁄₂ small green pepper, chopped*
*2 tablespoons melted butter*
*¹⁄₂ pound fresh morels or 3 ounces canned morels, drained, or 2*
    *ounces dried morels, reconstituted*
*¹⁄₄ teaspoon savory, dried*
*¹⁄₂ cup heavy cream*
*¹⁄₄ cup milk*
*¹⁄₄ cup morel extract (optional)*
*2 eggs*
*1 teaspoon salt*
*1 teaspoon sugar*
*1 tablespoon soy sauce*

*Preheat oven to 450°.*

1. Prebake pie shell for 10 minutes in 450° oven according to method described in Quiche Chanterelle recipe (see pages 104–105).
2. In a saucepan, sauté the onions and green peppers in the butter for 2 minutes.
3. Add the mushrooms (fresh, canned, or reconstituted), and continue to sauté for another 2 minutes. Fresh morels will give off liquid at this point. Pour it off while you are sautéing the mushrooms, and save to use for the extract. Do the same for extract from reconstituted morels.
4. Combine the savory, cream, milk, morel extract, eggs, salt, sugar, and soy, and mix well, making sure the eggs are thoroughly blended together with the rest of the ingredients.
5. Fill the pie shell with the onions, peppers, and mushrooms, and cover with the custard.
6. Bake pie at 450° for 10 minutes, and then lower the heat to 350° and continue baking for another 20 minutes. Check for doneness by piercing with

a fork. If liquid custard is still on the fork, continue to bake for another 5 minutes, then check again. Repeat if necessary.

7. Remove pie from oven, and let cool for ½ hour before serving.

VARIATIONS
## Quiche Bonchampi

APPROXIMATE PREPARATION TIME: **2** HOURS
USEFUL ADVANCE PREPARATION: AS INDICATED FOR QUICHE CHANTERELLE
      (SEE PAGES 104–105).
MAKES **4** TO **6** SERVINGS

Prepare this quiche exactly the way you prepare the Quiche Chanterelle, except use domestic mushrooms and the mushroom cheese, Bonchampi, instead of the other types. Actually, any kind of mushroom can be used for this quiche, because the flavor of the Bonchampi will predominate and give it a strong mushroom flavor.

## Domestic Mushroom Quiche

APPROXIMATE PREPARATION TIME: **2** HOURS
USEFUL ADVANCE PREPARATION: AS INDICATED FOR MOREL QUICHE (SEE
      PAGES 106–107).
MAKES **4** TO **6** SERVINGS

Prepare this quiche the same way you make the Morel Quiche except that in this recipe you are going to use domestic mushrooms, sliced. Place 1 pound of mushrooms in a saucepan and add ½ cup of water to them. Turn on the heat to medium, and cover the pan tightly. As the mushrooms cook, they will give off liquid. After 5 minutes, remove the mushrooms, and cook down the remaining liquid to ¼ cup. Use this as the extract liquid in the recipe above, and proceed as in that recipe.

# Mushrooms with Eggs

The combinations possible when these two versatile foods combine are numerous. The recipes included here are intended to give you just some ideas for joining the earthy complexity of the mushroom with the elegant, ladylike, and Rubensesque quality of the egg.

## Scrambled Eggs with Mushrooms and Onions

**APPROXIMATE PREPARATION TIME: 30 MINUTES**
**MAKES 4 SERVINGS**

Any kind of mushroom can be used here, but the complexity and interest of the dish will increase with the wilder types. The onion, that constant and faithful sidekick of mushrooms, is again an indispensable part of this preparation. Simply serve with toast points or croissants.

> ⅓ *cup chopped onions*
> 1½ *tablespoons melted butter*
> 1 *cup chopped mushrooms*
> ⅛ *teaspoon salt*
> ⅛ *teaspoon sugar*
> ¼ *teaspoon soy sauce*
> 8 *eggs*

1. Sauté the onions in the butter until they are just transparent.
2. Add the mushrooms and the rest of the ingredients except the eggs, and continue to cook until most of the moisture has evaporated, about 10 minutes.
3. Beat the eggs lightly and add to the sautéed mixture. Continue stirring until the eggs are not quite completely cooked, and take off the heat. The heat from the bottom of the pan will finish cooking the eggs while you continue to stir them. Serve with toast.

## Scrambled Eggs with Morels

**APPROXIMATE PREPARATION TIME: 30 MINUTES**
**MAKES 4 SERVINGS**

This delightful and distinctive dish is best with fresh morels. Dried morels can be used, however, since the flavor of the green pepper will support the flavor of the morels very effectively. Bagels or croissants go nicely with this dish.

*½ tablespoon minced onions*
*½ tablespoon minced green peppers*
*1½ tablespoons melted butter*
*½ cup fresh morels, sliced, or ⅓ cup dried and reconstituted*
*⅛ teaspoon salt*
*⅛ teaspoon sugar*
*½ teaspoon soy sauce*
*8 eggs*

1. Sauté the onions and green pepper in the butter until the onions are transparent.

2. Add the morels, and sauté for 1 minute.

3. Add the salt, sugar, and soy sauce, and continue to cook until the mixture has given up most of its liquid.

4. Lightly beat the eggs, add to the mixture, and cook until the eggs are done. Serve with bagels or croissants.

## Sunny Chanterelles

APPROXIMATE PREPARATION TIME: **30** MINUTES
MAKES **4** SERVINGS

This is a simple egg preparation made by just adding eggs to the sautéed mushrooms. The magic is in the combination of flavors. Serve with toasted whole wheat bread. It is important to prepare this dish in a nonstick-surface pan like Teflon, so that the finished eggs can be easily lifted out of the skillet.

*1 tablespoon chopped onions*
*1 tablespoon melted butter*
*½ cup chopped fresh or ¼ cup canned chanterelles, drained*
*8 eggs*
*Salt and pepper to taste*

1. Sauté the onions in the butter until transparent, and add chanterelles. Cook for 2 minutes, spreading the mushrooms evenly over the pan. (This recipe for 4 will probably have to be done at least twice unless you use a very large sauté pan. The eggs should not be packed too close together.)

2. Crack the eggs and pour over the mushrooms. Cook until done, sunny-side-up. Remove the eggs carefully with a wooden spatula. It is a good idea to cut the eggs into their serving portions while still in the pan, which will make it easier to remove them. Salt and pepper to taste, and serve.

# Mushroom Omelet I

APPROXIMATE PREPARATION TIME: 1 HOUR
ADVANCE PREPARATION: PREPARE MUSHROOM CREAM SAUCE I (PAGES 78–79).
MAKES 1 SERVING

There are basically three ways to incorporate mushrooms into omelets. The first method is simply to stuff them, as is done in this recipe. Again, the complexity of flavor here is directly related to the type of mushrooms used. The recipes for these omelets are for single servings.

*1 medium-sized onion, sliced thin*
*3 tablespoons melted butter*
*⅔ cup sliced mushrooms (⅓ cup if the mushrooms are*
    *reconstituted)*
*⅛ teaspoon salt*
*⅛ teaspoon sugar*
*¼ teaspoon soy sauce*
*3 eggs*
*1 teaspoon* crème fraîche *or sour cream (optional)*
*½ recipe Mushroom Cream Sauce I*

1. Sauté the onions in 1 tablespoon of the melted butter until transparent.

2. Add the mushrooms and continue to sauté, adding the salt, sugar, and soy as the mixture cooks. Set aside.

3. Beat the eggs and whip in the *crème fraîche* or sour cream if desired.

4. Make the omelet by putting the 2 remaining tablespoons of the butter in a saucepan (preferably Teflon). Spread the butter around the pan, and heat until the butter browns slightly. Add the eggs, and cook over a medium-high flame. The eggs will begin to set on the bottom of the pan.

5. Add the mushroom mixture to the center of the omelet, and flip one side on top of it. Then flip the other side over it. Invert the whole omelet with a spatula, and finish cooking for another 30 seconds. Serve alone or with the heated sauce, if desired.

VARIATIONS
# Omelet II

APPROXIMATE PREPARATION TIME: **20** MINUTES
USEFUL ADVANCE PREPARATION: PREPARE **1** SERVING BASIC MUSHROOM
        DUXELLES (SEE PAGE 61).
MAKES **1** SERVING

In this method the mushrooms are incorporated directly into the egg mixture. This can be done as is, or in conjunction with the first method, using the "mushroomed eggs" folded over a mushroom filling. The recipe here calls for using Basic Mushroom Duxelles, but any of the variations can be substituted. I particularly like the Garlic or Herb Duxelles (see pages 62 and 63) for this approach.

*3 eggs*
*2 tablespoons Basic Mushrooms Duxelles*
*1 teaspoon Mushroom Extract (optional)*
*2 tablespoons butter*

1.  Lightly beat the eggs and add the duxelles to them. One teaspoon of rich Mushroom Extract (see pages 73–74) can be added here to enrich the mushroom flavor. (Be careful not to add too much, or it will interfere with the cooking of the eggs.)
2.  Heat the butter in a Teflon pan, and add the egg-mushroom mixture, keeping the flame high.
3.  Finish the omelet by folding over, and serve alone or with a sauce.

# Omelet III

This recipe is for any omelet that is finished with a mushroom sauce. The sauce can be added to the first and/or second versions to give more mushroom flavor or to an herb or vegetable omelet to give it some complexity. I like cream sauces with omelets, and the easiest way to make one is by adding 1 tablespoon of any of the mushroom duxelles (see pages 61–67) to ½ cup béchamel sauce (see pages 126–127). Just heat and serve.

# Muffined Eggs with Mushrooms

APPROXIMATE PREPARATION TIME: 1 HOUR
MAKES 4 SERVINGS

Teflon muffin pans are best for this baked-egg recipe, to facilitate removing the finished eggs. They can be enjoyed as is, but I prefer to use them as the starting point for Eggs Benedict, adding ham or bacon and English muffins.

*⅓ cup chopped onions*
*1½ tablespoons melted butter*
*1 cup chopped mushrooms*
*⅛ teaspoon salt*
*⅛ teaspoon sugar*
*¼ teaspoon soy sauce*
*1 tablespoon heavy cream*
*1 tablespoon crème fraîche or sour cream*
*1 tablespoon Roquefort or other blue cheese, grated fine.*
*8 eggs*

*Preheat oven to 350°.*

1. Sauté the onions in the butter until they are just transparent.
2. Add the mushrooms, salt, sugar, and soy sauce, and cook until the moisture is evaporated.
3. Add the cream, *crème fraîche* or sour cream, and cheese and continue to cook until all the cheese is melted and blended, about 2 minutes. Remove from heat.
4. Butter well the bottom of a Teflon muffin pan. Crack 1 egg each into 8 of the muffin slots.
5. Place about 2 teaspoons of the cheese-mushroom mixture on each of the eggs. (You can reverse this order if you prefer: mixture first, eggs on top. This will look better when the eggs come out but will increase the possibility of the eggs sticking because of the cheese.)
6. Place the eggs in the oven until done, about 5 minutes. Remove the eggs from the pan and serve on toast or with a croissant.

 112

# Croissants and Mushrooms

This buttery baking miracle lends itself beautifully to the earthy flavors of mushrooms. Below are some ideas on this marriage.

## Croissants with Duxelles

In this recipe you can simply warm the duxelles of your choice, domestic or wild (see pages 59–67), and spread it on the croissant, as you would butter or jam. Or you can scoop out the center of the croissant while it is cold and spoon in some duxelles, then warm the whole thing in a toaster-oven.

## Mushroom Cheese Croissants

While making fresh croissants, fill them with Bonchampi cheese and, if you like, a little Virginia ham. Serve warm. This method can also be used in preparing croissants with the above duxelles.

## Morel Croissant

Split a croissant in half lengthwise. Cover bottom half generously with heated Morel Duxelles (see page 66). Place top half back on. Toast and serve croissant surrounded by Morel Velouté Sauce (optional) (see page 83).

## Croissants with Mushroom Butter

Prepare a mushroom butter (see page 71). Split 4 croissants in half lengthwise. Open out the croissants, and spread about 1 tablespoon of the mushroom butter inside each half. Place the croissants in a warm (350°) oven for 3 to 5 minutes. Remove when the croissants are warm and the mushroom butter is melted.

# Mushroom Snacks

### Hot Mushroom Sandwich

Sauté ½ cup sliced, fresh mushrooms and 2 tablespoons onion in 3 table-spoons butter. Split a croissant in half lengthwise and lay this mixture inside. Cover with the other half of the croissant. Place 2 thin slices of Bonchampi over the croissant, and put in toaster oven until the cheese melts.

### Mushroom Hamburgers

To make mushroom hamburgers, sauté some onions in butter until they are almost transparent. Add some fresh wild or domestic mushrooms, and sauté for another 2 minutes. Place on top of the hamburger, and serve.

Almost all the duxelles recipes may be used for hamburger toppings. The few exceptions would be the sweet duxelles. You can also work some duxelles into the meat while you are forming the hamburgers.

For a mushroom cheeseburger, substitute some Bonchampi or one of the other mushroom cheeses, such as a mushroom Gorgonzola, for your regular brand. Then top with some sautéed onions and mushrooms as described above. This can be served as an open-faced sandwich surrounded with Sauce Bonchampi (see page 80).

### Mushroom Tacos

Warm some prepared taco shells. Fill with sautéed beef, onions, cheese, to-mato, lettuce, and some Hot Duxelles (see pages 64–65).

### Mushroom Fritters

APPROXIMATE PREPARATION TIME: 1 HOUR
MAKES 4 SERVINGS

Here's a great mushroom snack! It's easy and fast. You can use fresh mushrooms, domestic or wild, and add some extract from wild mushrooms (see pages 73–74) to give the fritters some extra character. The important thing to remember is to use *sliced* mushrooms and *sliced* onions, not chopped. The result is misshapen-looking, but the texture is much better than if you mashed everything up. Canned or otherwise processed mushrooms are not recommended for this dish. The domestic variety works just fine.

> *1 egg*
> *1 tablespoon milk*
> *1 tablespoon heavy cream*
> *2 tablespoons mushroom extract (optional) but add 2 tablespoons*
>     *water if you don't use the extract to get the right consistency*
>     *for the batter.*
> *½ teaspoon salt*
> *½ teaspoon sugar*
> *½ teaspoon soy sauce*
> *Dash black pepper*
> *Dash cayenne pepper*
> *½ cup sifted flour*
> *¾ cup sliced mushrooms, domestic or wild*
> *½ cup sliced onions*
> *4 cups corn oil*
> *Mushroom Catsup (optional; see pages 70–71).*

1.  Beat the egg lightly in a mixing bowl. Stir in the rest of the ingredients except the oil, adding the mushrooms and onions last. Blend thoroughly.

2.  Begin heating the oil (use about 4 cups) until it reaches 375° or sizzles when a drop of water is added.

3.  Let the batter stand for 10 minutes, then add the mixture by the half-tablespoonful to the hot oil. Fry for about 2 minutes, doing 2 or 3 at a time if you use a wide skillet, 1 or 2 if you use a narrow saucepan or small skillet.

4.  Drain the fritters on a paper towel when done and serve, preferably with Sweet or Hot Duxelles or Mushroom Catsup (see pages 62–63, 64–65, 70–71).

**VARIATIONS**
## Morel Fritters

Follow the procedure for Mushroom Fritters but use ¼ cup sliced green or red sweet peppers in place of half the onions. If the morels are large, make sure the slices are no bigger than 3 inches long. Use a morel extract for this batter if handy (see pages 73–74).

## Truffle Fritters

To the basic recipe add 1 tablespoon truffles peelings and 1 teaspoon cognac.

# Wild Mushroom Soufflés

Mushroom soufflés derive their flavor from purees made from dried mushrooms (see Puree of Cepes, page 69). The rest is standard procedure for soufflé making. The soufflé can be served with or without a sauce. I like to accompany the larger soufflés with a cream sauce. This soufflé recipe can be used as well for forest mushrooms, which are much cheaper and make an excellent puree.

## Cepe Soufflé

APPROXIMATE PREPARATION TIME: 1 TO 2 HOURS
USEFUL ADVANCE PREPARATION: MAKE PUREE OF CEPES (SEE PAGE 69) AND
        DESIRED SAUCE.
MAKES 4 SERVINGS

This is an excellent dish for a light lunch. It is a good example of what to do with dried mushrooms whose extract has been used for another dish. For example you can make a Cepe Sauce (see pages 76–77) and puree the reconstituted mushrooms. Then pour the sauce into the soufflé. Morel Cream Sauce (see page 84) is also a good accompaniment for this soufflé. Serve this with a salad of Belgian endive and watercress.

*3 tablespoons melted butter*
*3 tablespoons sifted flour*
*¼ teaspoon salt*
*½ cup milk*
*½ cup heavy cream*
*½ cup Puree of Cepes*
*3 egg yolks*
*5 egg whites*

*¼ teaspoon cream of tartar*
*Butter for soufflé dish or dishes*

*Preheat oven to 375°.*

1. Make a roux by blending and cooking the melted butter, flour, and salt over a medium flame until a light gold paste forms.
2. Add the milk and cream, and cook until it reaches a medium consistency. Add in the puree, and blend until well mixed.
3. In a separate mixing bowl, beat the egg yolks until thick, add a little of the creme-puree sauce to it (2 tablespoons), and blend. Then add the egg yolks to the rest of the sauce, and blend well.
4. Beat the egg whites until foamy, and then add the cream of tartar. Continue to beat until the whites stand in stiff, smooth peaks.
5. Fold the beaten whites into the hot sauce until well blended. Fold these whites gently into the sauce because a soufflé rises or falls on the consistency of the whites.
6. Place the mixture either in a large 1½ quart soufflé dish or in individual soufflé dishes. In either case, the dish or dishes should be generously buttered on the bottom but not the sides and placed in a water bath for baking. If the large dish is used, 1¼ hours will be needed for the cooking time. If 2-to-3-ounce ramekins or dishes are used, the time required will be 10 to 15 minutes. Test doneness by carefully inserting a toothpick into the middle of the soufflé. If it comes out wet, then return it to the oven for another 5 minutes. Repeat until the toothpick comes out dry. Serve immediately. If a sauce is used for the soufflé, spoon it into the middle of the soufflé before serving.

## Morel Soufflé

APPROXIMATE PREPARATION TIME: 1 TO 2 HOURS
USEFUL ADVANCE PREPARATION: MAKE MOREL PUREE (PAGE 70) AND ANY
      SAUCE, LIKE MOREL SAUCE ROSENTHAL (SEE PAGES 82–83).
MAKES 4 SERVINGS

Use the same method as for Cepe Soufflé, substituting Morel Puree for Puree of Cepes. If you have additional morels, a nice touch is to fold in sliced morels during the last step before baking.

CHAPTER SEVEN

# *First Courses*

These recipes are grouped under First Courses because this is the way you will probably use them. However, like the light lunch and brunch dishes of the previous chapter, they can be served as main courses; simply increase the proportions of the ingredients. Some of the preparations can be made as side dishes, but these would only be those using domestic mushrooms.

Familiarity with the detailed discussion of the cooking methods described in pages 49–55 would be useful before you attempt these recipes, although it is not absolutely necessary.

### A Note on Cutting and Slicing

Mushrooms lose most of their volume during cooking, so take this into account as you prepare them. A raw, sliced mushroom will be reduced by sautéing or blanching to half its original size or less. Be sure that you do not slice mushrooms too thin—no thinner than ¼ to ½ inch thick. Any mushroom 2 inches or *less* across the cap will make a better presentation left whole.

# Mushroom Sautés

## Sautéed Mushrooms I
## Low-Heat Method

**APPROXIMATE PREPARATION TIME: 30 MINUTES**
**MAKES 4 SERVINGS**

Use this method of sautéing to extract maximum flavor from mushrooms. The long sautéing sweats out and evaporates the water, leaving a more concentrated flavor in the mushrooms. Use butter for your cooking oil, because you needn't be concerned with burning it as in the high-heat method. The recommended amounts of salt, sugar, and soy listed below are *approximate*. Some mushrooms will release more water than others and yield a smaller volume. Add salting ingredients a little bit at a time.

> *3 tablespoons butter*
> *½ cup sliced or chopped onions*
> *8 ounces whole or sliced mushrooms*
> *½ teaspoon salt*
> *½ teaspoon sugar*
> *1 teaspoon soy sauce.*

1. Melt the butter in a skillet, and add the onions. Sauté over a medium heat for about 1 minute.
2. Add the mushrooms, and continue to sauté over a medium heat for another minute. Then turn down the heat, and let cook, uncovered, until the mushrooms begin to draw water. Some types of mushrooms may become submerged in their own water but keep them on the heat, and slowly increase it until it comes to a light boil, and the water begins to evaporate.
3. Continue to cook until almost all the water has evaporated, and add the salt, sugar, and soy sauce. Serve alone or over a pastry shell, a puff pastry shell, toast points, or pasta (see Chapter 12).

## Sautéed Mushrooms II
## High-Heat Method

This method differs from the first in several respects. The point of Method I is to maximize the mushroom flavor. The point of Method II is to maintain the crunchy texture of the mushrooms. The ingredients are the same, except that in the second method you use half butter and half cooking oil. The oil has a higher heat tolerance than butter and can cook the mushrooms without burning. Oyster mushrooms are recommended for this style of sautéing.

*1½ tablespoons butter*
*½ cup sliced or chopped onions*
*1½ tablespoons cooking oil*
*8 ounces whole or sliced mushrooms*
*½ teaspoon salt*
*½ teaspoon sugar*
*1 teaspoon soy sauce*

1. Melt the butter in a skillet, and add the onions. Sauté over a medium heat until almost transparent. Add the oil, and bring the skillet to a high flame.

2. Add the mushrooms, and sauté over the high heat for ½ minute to 1 minute. Some water will be drawn out of the mushrooms, but this will evaporate almost immediately.

3. Add the salt, sugar, and soy sauce, and sauté for another 30 seconds. Serve alone or over a pastry shell, a puff pastry shell, toast, or pasta (see Chapter 12).

VARIATIONS
## Sautéed Morels

Prepare 8 ounces morels, whole or sliced, with the low-heat method, using a total of 3 tablespoons butter or cooking oil, or a combination of the two. Instead of using onions, use half green or red pappers (¼ cup), and half onions or scallions (¼ cup). Season with ½ teaspoon salt, ½ teaspoon sugar, and 1 teaspoon soy sauce.

## Stir-Fried Mushrooms

Stir-frying is really a method of sautéing. This is *not* generally recommended for wild mushrooms.

Begin heating a wok over a medium flame. Add 2 tablepoons peanut oil, then stir-fry ½ cup sliced scallions with ½ teaspoon minced fresh ginger for 30 seconds. Add 8 ounces small whole or sliced mushrooms, and continue to stir-fry them for a minute. Season with ½ teaspoon each salt and sugar and 1 tablespoon soy sauce. Serve with white rice.

## Quick-Fried Cepes

This dish is best with a hearty Zinfandel. It's from Roy Thomas of Monterey Peninsula Winery.

Thick-slice 2 cups of fresh cepes and set aside. Crush ¼ teaspoon caraway seeds and about 1 teaspoon of dried basil in a mortar and pestle. Heat 2 tablespoons oil in a skillet until it starts smoking, and add the caraway and basil. Quickly add the sliced cepes, and cook for about 30 seconds on each side. Salt to taste.

## Shiitake and Sausage Sauté

APPROXIMATE PREPARATION TIME: **30** MINUTES
MAKES **4** SERVINGS

Shiitake and sausage complement each other. This is also a very quick and satisfying dish for lunch or light supper. Serve over toast or warmed croissants.

*½ cup sliced onions mixed with ½ teaspoon crushed garlic*
*3 tablespoons butter*
*½ pound Polish sausage, sliced*
*1 pound shiitake mushroom caps*
*Salt*

1. In a skillet, sauté the onions and garlic in the butter for 1 minute.
2. Add the sausage, and lower the heat so that some of the fat is drawn out of the sausage.
3. Add the mushrooms, turn up the heat again, and sauté until the caps are tender, about 5 minutes. Salt to taste.

## Helen Turley's Sautéed Enoki with Apples and Cellophane Noodles

**APPROXIMATE PREPARATION TIME: 30 MINUTES**
**MAKES 4 SERVINGS**

This recipe was given to me by Helen Turley. It uses what the Japanese call enoki, a slender and delicate-looking mushroom usually reserved for salads. Helen's approach is much more interesting and exciting, however, than anything I have seen done with enoki thus far. Serve this with cellophane noodles.

> *1 quart water and 1 tablespoon salt*
> *6 ounces cellophane noodles*
> *2 cups enoki*
> *¼ cup fresh shallots, chopped*
> *2 tablespoons butter*
> *½ cup shoestring-sliced fresh apples*
> *1 tablespoon Calvados*
> *Salt and pepper to taste*

1. Bring salted water to a boil. Turn off heat, and add the cellophane noodles. Let them sit in the hot water until ready to use.
2. In a shallow sauté pan, sauté the enoki with the shallots, butter, and apples for 1 minute. Make sure the heat is fairly high for this preparation.
3. Add the Calvados, salt, and pepper, and continue to sauté for another minute. This should evaporate the alcohol in the Calvados. Remove, and drain the cellophane noodles. Place on a serving platter, and cover with the mushrooms.

## Morels Rosenthal

**APPROXIMATE PREPARATION TIME: 45 MINUTES**
**MAKES 4 SERVINGS**

This mushroom sauté is made a little more interesting by the addition of green peppers in butter to the usual shallots or scallions. The dish is even better if you use a morel extract in place of the water, to reenforce the morel flavor. Serve in puff pastry shells.

 122

*2 ounces onions, chopped*
*2 ounces green peppers, chopped*
*4 tablespoons clarified butter (see page 51)*
*1 pound fresh morels, sliced*
*1 cup water or morel extract*
*1 teaspoon salt*
*1 teaspoon sugar*
*1 tablespoon soy sauce*
*1 tablespoon arrowroot mixed with ¼ cup water*
*4 squares ready-to-use and warmed puff pastry shells (see page 96)*

1. Sauté the onions and peppers in the butter until the onions are transparent.

2. Add morels, and sauté on low fire for 10 minutes to draw water from morels.

3. Add water or morel extract to make about 1½ cups liquid. Add salt, sugar, and soy sauce, and simmer for 2 minutes.

4. Thicken with the arrowroot-and-water mixture. Serve in puff pastry shells.

## Shiitake in Burgundy Butter Sauce

APPROXIMATE PREPARATION TIME: **30 MINUTES**
MAKES **4** SERVINGS

The Burgundy Butter Sauce described here is quite strong, but shiitake is one of the few mushrooms that can stand up to it. The strength of the sauce actually improves the flavor of the shiitake.

*½ cup chopped onions*
*3 tablespoons melted butter*
*1 cup water*
*½ teaspoon ground coriander*
*½ teaspoon ground chili powder*
*1 teaspoon fresh, crushed garlic*
*1 teaspoon lemon juice*
*¼ teaspoon ground black pepper*

> *¼ cup red wine*
> *1 teaspoon salt*
> *1 teaspoon sugar*
> *1 tablespoon soy sauce*
> *1 pound shiitake mushroom caps*
> *1½ tablespoons cornstarch mixed with ⅓ cup water*

1. In a skillet, sauté the onions in the butter until they are just transparent. Stop the cooking by adding the water to the skillet.

2. Add the other ingredients, except the mushrooms and cornstarch, and stir for 1 minute.

3. Add the mushrooms, and turn the heat to low. Cover the skillet with a tight-fitting lid, and let simmer for 30 minutes.

4. Thicken the mixture with the cornstarch-and-water mixture, and serve alone or over rice.

## Mushrooms Braised

### Braised Mushrooms

APPROXIMATE PREPARATION TIME: 1 HOUR
MAKES 4 SERVINGS

Use this recipe for any mushrooms, domestic or wild. It is an excellent way of preparing domestic mushrooms and is also very good as a side dish for a main meal. But it can also be the entrée of a dinner, especially when the mushrooms used are extra special. Serve it in shells of puff pastry or regular pastry shells.

> *4 tablespoons melted butter*
> *½ cup chopped or sliced onions or scallions*
> *½ cup water or veal or poultry stock (see pages 72–73)*
> *8 ounces fresh mushrooms, sliced or whole*
> *1 teaspoon salt*
> *1 teaspoon sugar*
> *1 tablespoon soy sauce*
> *½ teaspoon dried savory, or 1 tablespoon fresh chopped savory*
> *2 tablespoons cornstarch mixed with ⅓ cup water*

1. Add the butter to a saucepan, and melt over a low heat. Add the onions or scallions, and sauté over a medium heat until they are almost transparent. Douse them with the water or stock, and bring to a simmer.

2. Add the mushrooms, and cover the pan with a tight lid. Turn the flame to low and let simmer for ½ hour, at the end of which they should be greatly reduced in size.

3. Add the salt, sugar, and soy sauce, and stir gently. Continue to simmer for 5 minutes, then add the savory.*

4. Thicken with the cornstarch-and-water mixture a little bit at a time, and serve over heated pastry shells (see page 96).

*Note: If you intend to freeze the mixture, proceed no further. Thicken it after it has been defrosted and is receiving its final preparation.

## Braised Mushrooms with Cepe Juice

APPROXIMATE PREPARATION TIME: 1½ HOURS
MAKES 4 SERVINGS

You may use any mushroom for this dish, but one good way is to combine wild and domestic types. The meat of the dish comes from humble domestic mushrooms while the character and flavor come from the liquor of the *Boletus edulis,* or cepe. This also makes a nice beef accompaniment: Just pour the finished mushroom preparation over roasted or broiled beef.

*½ ounce dried cepes*
*2 cups water*
*4 tablespoons melted butter*
*½ cup sliced onions or scallions*
*1 pound fresh domestic mushrooms, or any wild variety*
*1 teaspoon salt*
*1 teaspoon sugar*
*1 tablespoon soy sauce*
*2 tablespoons cornstarch mixed with ¼ cup water*

1. Reconstitute the dried mushrooms by adding them to the water in a saucepan. Bring the water to a boil, then simmer for 30 minutes. Allow the liquid in the saucepan to cook down to 1 cup.

2. Put the butter in a skillet, and add the onions or scallions. Sauté them for 1 minute, then add the finished cepe liquid.

125

3. Add the rest of the ingredients, except the cornstarch, cover with a tight lid, and let cook for ½ hour. Add the reconstituted dried cepes if desired, or save them for a duxelles.

4. Thicken with cornstarch-and-water mixture and serve alone (in a pastry shell; see page 96) or over steak.

# Mushrooms in Cream Sauces

Another popular way of making mushrooms for a first course is to combine them with cream. The standard method is to pour a white-type sauce such as Sauce Bonchampi (see page 80) over sautéed mushrooms, but there are other alternatives. Cream and mushroom extract thickened with egg yolk is one. Another is the use of sour cream or *crème fraîche* to make a piquant dish. Mushroom dishes done in cream sauce do not hold well so they must be made and served at once.

## Mushrooms in Béchamel Sauce I

APPROXIMATE PREPARATION TIME: 1 HOUR
MAKES 4 SERVINGS

Follow any of the previous recipes for sautéed mushrooms and set aside. In a small double boiler combine ½ cup each of whole milk and heavy whipping cream. Heat slowly. While the milk and cream are beginning to heat, combine ¼ cup sifted flour with ¼ cup melted butter, and blend until smooth in a skillet over a medium heat. Do not let this roux brown. When the milk-cream mixture begins to form a skin, add the roux slowly, while stirring. Whip the roux in if necessary with a wire whisk. As the mixture become hotter, the cream will thicken. Add the mushrooms, and adjust for salt, after the mushrooms have had time to blend with the sauce. Remove from heat. Pour over toast or croissant, and serve immediately.

VARIATION
## Mushrooms in Béchamel Sauce II

Prepare this dish the same way as Mushrooms in Béchamel I, but use ¾ cup of heavy cream and ¼ cup of extract made from dried mushrooms in place of the milk and cream used in the first recipe. Use a cepe extract for almost any mushroom except morels; use a morel extract for any morel dish. Correct for salt.

## Mushrooms Kraców Style

**APPROXIMATE PREPARATION TIME: 1 HOUR**
**MAKES 4 SERVINGS**

This is perhaps the best way to enjoy cepes, although the same preparation could be used for morels. The keys in this dish are the use of a rich extract and the thickening of the whole by means of egg yolks. This is one dish in which you can use canned drained wild mushrooms, as well as blanched ones. Serve this in a puff pastry shell as a main course with a big woody Chardonnay from Chalone or David Bruce.

*1 pound blanched or canned mushrooms, preferably wild, drained*
*⅓ ounce dried cepes*
*½ cup chopped onions*
*2 cups water*
*1 teaspoon salt*
*1 teaspoon sugar*
*1 tablespoon soy sauce*
*½ teaspoon sweet sherry or Madeira*
*1½ cups heavy whipping cream*
*4 egg yolks*
*4 puff pastry shells (see page 96)*

1. Rinse the blanched or canned mushrooms, and set aside.
2. Combine the cepes and onions in a saucepan with the water. Bring it to a boil, and let the mushrooms simmer uncovered for ½ hour. Remove mushrooms and onions from liquid. Cook down the liquid to ½ cup.
3. Grind the mushrooms and onions together in a blender or food pro-

127

cessor to a puree. Use this puree for another purpose, such as a Wild Mushroom Soufflé (see pages 116–117). You will use only the extract from step 2 in this recipe.

4. Add the salt, sugar, soy sauce, sherry or Madeira, and all but ⅓ cup of the whipping cream to the cepe and onion liquid. Put into a skillet. Begin heating this on a low to medium flame.

5. While the cepe-onion-cream mixture is heating, beat together the egg yolks with the remaining ⅓ cup cream, until well blended.

6. When the liquid is hot, add the mushrooms and continue to heat for another 3 minutes. When it starts to bubble around the sides, begin to add the egg-cream mixture slowly while stirring. Add all of the mixture, and heat until the sides begin to bubble or the mixture begins to thicken. Take off the heat immediately, and let sit for 5 minutes before serving. If the dish curdles, add some heavy cream and stir vigorously until smooth. Correct for salt. Serve over a shell of puff pastry.

## Chanterelles en Vol-au-Vent

**APPROXIMATE PREPARATION TIME:** 1 HOUR
**MAKES 6 SERVINGS**

This recipe was given to me by Ted Balistreri of the Sardine Factory in Monterey, California. It is a rich and elegant dish using cream and truffles for complexity. Serve with a California Pinot Blanc.

*1 pound butter in 4 quarters*
*3 pounds fresh chanterelles, sliced*
*1 shallot, minced*
*6 ounces flour*
*1 quart heavy cream*
*2 ounces truffles, cut into very thin slices*
*8 ounces dry vermouth*
*½ ounce lemon juice*
*Salt and pepper to taste*
*6 puff pastry shells (see page 96)*
*Watercress and saffron sprigs for garnish*

1. In a heavy-bottom pan, melt ¼ pound of the butter, and add sliced chanterelles. Sauté until limp. Drain the liquid, and reserve.

2. Add ¼ pound more butter, and melt with the chanterelles. Add shallot, and cook 3 minutes. Add flour, and cook 5 minutes.

3. Add heavy cream to chanterelles mixture, and cook 10 minutes, until thickened.

4. In a separate pan, heat the sliced truffles in the vermouth over a low flame, and add the cream mixture. Add the lemon juice, adjust seasoning, and simmer for 10 minutes.

5. Take remaining ½ pound butter, and cube it. Add it a little at a time to mixture, and blend in.

6. Serve in warm pastry shell, and garnish with watercress and saffron sprigs.

## Chanterelles with Ham—Cream Style

APPROXIMATE PREPARATION TIME: **30** MINUTES
MAKES **4** SERVINGS

"This is just fabulous with English muffins," Roy Thomas of Monterey Peninsula Winery was telling me as he described this dish. It's a flavor-filled mixture great as a topping for muffins, toast, or croissants.

*½ cup chopped rich, smoked ham*
*2 tablespoons butter*
*½ cup chopped onions*
*1 cup chopped chanterelles*
*½ pint sour cream*

1. Sauté the ham in the butter for 30 seconds, add the onions, and continue cooking until the onions just begin to turn color.

2. Add the mushrooms, and continue to sauté over a medium heat for 2 minutes.

3. Turn off the heat, and add the sour cream (the amount depends on how creamy and sour you would like the dish). Pour over English muffins or over croissants.

## Mushrooms in *Crème Fraîche*

APPROXIMATE PREPARATION TIME: 1 HOUR
USEFUL ADVANCE PREPARATION: PREPARE *CRÈME FRAÎCHE* A DAY IN ADVANCE
        AS INDICATED.
MAKES 4 SERVINGS

Sour cream can be used for this dish as well as *crème fraîche;* the addition of a little sugar cuts some of the acidity. This preparation is best served as a side dish for a larger dinner. We have had it at our house each Thanksgiving since I was a child, and what I find most attractive is the combination of these mushrooms with the turkey stuffing.

*1 tablespoon plain yogurt*
*1 cup heavy whipping cream*
*1½ pounds fresh mushrooms, stems off*
*1 medium onion, chopped*
*4 tablespoons butter or margarine*
*1 teaspoon sugar*
*1 teaspoon salt*
*1 tablespoon soy sauce*
*1 tablespoon chopped parsley*

1. Add the yogurt to the cream, and let stand overnight in a fairly warm spot (72° to 85°). The mixture will be thickened by the next day. (This is only one way of making *crème fraîche.*) It will keep in the refrigerator for over a week.

2. Wash the mushrooms thoroughly, and set aside.

3. In a skillet, sauté the onion in the butter or margarine, until the onions are almost transparent.

4. Add the mushrooms, and sauté over a medium flame for 1 minute, then lower the flame, cover, and cook for 10 minutes.

5. Remove the lid, and continue to cook until most of the liquid has evaporated. Add the sugar, salt, soy sauce, parsley, and *crème fraîche.* Stir until well blended and heated, and serve immediately. This dish can last for up to a week in the refrigerator and can be reheated and used.

# Fried and Grilled Mushrooms

The following recipes are for mushrooms cooked in the quickest way possible. These methods (along with high-heat sautéing, pages 50–51) retain the natural texture of the mushrooms, and are among the best ways to enjoy mushrooms by themselves. A word of caution: Don't overcook!

## Grilled Oyster Mushrooms

Simply grill large caps of oyster mushrooms under a broiler. Mushrooms done this way cool very fast and lose their liquid quickly, so move them around over the fire for better heat control. A little blackening is all right but don't let the mushrooms burn. As the edges begin to toast, add a sprinkle of parmesan cheese to each mushroom, and let it melt. Serve immediately.

# Fried Mushrooms

Besides high-heat sautéing, another way of cooking mushrooms to maintain their natural texture is to deep-fry them. This method takes less than 30 seconds for a golden brown crust to form on the outside with a warm, crunchy texture on the inside. Don't cut the stems for this operation. The following recipe is typical of this sort of preparation.

## Mock Fried Oysters

APPROXIMATE PREPARATION TIME: **45** MINUTES
MAKES **4** SERVINGS

This is made with the oyster mushroom, *Pleurotus ostreatus*, although any type of mushroom can be used, especially those with more delicate caps like *Lepiotas* and *Russulas*. Season the bread crumbs with the spice of your choice, and combine the egg mix with Tabasco or lemon juice to add some zest to the dish. This is finger food at its best.

*8 ounces fresh oyster mushrooms, or any fresh mushrooms*
*1 cup sifted flour*
*2 beaten eggs*
*1 to 2 cups fresh bread crumbs, lightly salted and peppered*
*4 cups cooking oil suitable for frying*

131

1. Clean and dry the oyster mushrooms. The stems can be used for this recipe as well as the caps, because they curve up into the body of the cap and make nice little "handles" for holding while eating.

2. Spread the flour out on a baking dish. Place the eggs in a container so that the mushrooms can easily be dredged in them. Spread the bread crumbs out on another baking dish. The three ingredients, sitting side by side, are now ready for the breading.

3. Start heating the oil in a large skillet. It is ready when a drop of water sizzles when it hits the oil.

4. Begin breading the mushrooms one by one. Start by covering them with the flour and shaking off any excess. Then dredge them in the egg, and finally coat them with the bread crumbs. Press the bread crumbs firmly into the mushrooms until the mushrooms are well covered. Repeat until all the mushrooms are breaded.

5. Drop 2 or 3 of the mushrooms into the hot oil. They should be done in a very short time. Don't move away from the oil while the mushrooms are cooking. If you have to leave, pull the mushrooms out and start over when you return. Repeat the frying process for all the mushrooms, and lay them on a paper towel as they are finished to absorb all the excess oil. Serve with tartar or cocktail sauce. Allow 4 to 6 mushrooms per person.

# Mushroom Canapés

Canapés are tiny canvases against which we draw miniature landscapes of flavor. They are analogous to stocks in a sauce, which, though they do not have much flavor in themselves, lend body and substance to the rest of the dish. The simple canapé is by definition nothing more than a piece of crustless toast with topping, but here it offers the best reason for keeping a quantity of duxelles on hand against the surprise arrival of cocktail guests. The following entries list some ideas for mushrooming up this little canvas.

### Basic Mushroom Canapés

Make canapés by toasting fresh bread and cutting off the crusts. Slice diagonally. The canapés can also be cut out with any shape of cookie cutter. Spread each canapé with warmed Basic Mushroom Duxelles (see page 61), which take about 30 minutes to prepare from scratch. Sprinkle with a few pieces of finely chopped hard-boiled egg.

### Flavored Mushroom Canapés

This is the same thing as the above except that you use the recipe for the Tomato, Garlic, Sweet, Herb, Cream, Cheese, Mixed Vegetable, or any of the Wild Mushroom Duxelles (see pages 62–65). Cover lightly with the finely chopped or crumbled substance, which is mixed with the Duxelles.

### Smoked Salmon Canapés

Spread the canapés with the Smoked Salmon Duxelles (see page 63) and add a small curved sliver of smoked salmon on top.

## Stuffed Mushrooms

Most mushrooms are stuffed before baking. This is one preparation where the common domestic mushroom with its heavy body outperforms most wild mushrooms, because it can afford to lose some water while it sweats in the oven.

I am not going to discuss stuffed mushroom recipes exhaustively here. There are many recipes for them scattered in hundreds of cookbooks. However, I find that one of the best approaches is to stuff a mushroom with a duxelles or stuffing made with a duxelles to reenforce the mushroom's flavor. Cheese and onions are also used to good effect. Covering the stuffed mushrooms with bread crumbs and a little butter gives them a nice browned finish. A few favorites follow.

### Polish-Style Baked Mushrooms

In Poland, this is a typical way to prepare wild mushrooms, especially the *Lactarius deliciosus*. It can also be done with the common domestic mushroom.

133

Wrap a piece of bacon around each mushroom cap (separate the cap from the stem and use only the cap) so that the fat bastes the mushrooms while baking. Use smaller caps so you can roll up the cap in the bacon. Bake in a 350° oven for about 5 minutes or until the bacon is almost, but not quite, crisp. Allow 4 mushrooms per person.

## Stuffed Mushrooms Bonchampi

Fill each large cap with Garlic Duxelles (see page 62), and top with a ¼-inch-thick piece of Bonchampi cheese. Bake in a 350° oven until the cheese melts.

## Stuffed Mushrooms Roquefort

Fill each cap with Cheese Duxelles made from Roquefort as described (see page 64) and coat with salted bread crumbs and a little melted butter. Bake in a 350° oven for 10 minutes or until the crumbs brown.

## Oyster and Snail Stuffed Mushrooms

Fill each cap with some Oyster Duxelles (see page 63). Coat each cap with some oil that has been soaking with minced garlic. Cut some medium-sized snails in half so that they rest flat on top of the stuffing. Bake as in the above recipes.

## Champignon aux Duxelles

APPROXIMATE PREPARATION TIME: 1 HOUR
MAKES 6 SERVINGS

This is another recipe from the Sardine Factory in Monterey, and I think it is one of the best I have seen, because it uses a different kind of shiitake duxelles for the stuffing. Very innovative and very effective. I like a dry Chardonnay like the Vichon from California served with it.

 134

*1 pound shiitake caps, minced*
*1 clove garlic, minced*
*1 shallot, minced*
*¼ pound butter*
*Salt and pepper*
*2 eggs, beaten and lightly salted and peppered*
*6 slices Monterey Jack cheese, cut into 2-by-2-inch slices*
*24 jumbo white mushrooms, washed, with stems removed*
*1 cup white wine*

*Preheat oven to 350°.*

1. Cook the shiitake caps with the garlic and shallot in the butter until all the liquid is evaporated. Season with some salt and pepper.

2. Blend the eggs into the mixture, and fill the white-mushroom caps with it. Top each one with a slice of the Monterey Jack.

3. Bake the white mushrooms in a pan with approximately ¼ inch of white wine for 20 minutes, or until cheese is golden. Serve immediately.

## Stuffed Mushroom Caps Winiarski

APPROXIMATE PREPARATION TIME: 1½ HOURS
MAKES 4 SERVINGS

The following recipes were given to me by Warren and Barbara Winiarski of the Stag's Leap Wine Cellars, one of California's preeminent wineries. Both recipes make fine hors d'oeuvres.

*12 fairly large domestic mushroom caps*
*2 strips bacon, chopped*
*1 tablespoon shallots, chopped fine*
*2 tablespoons melted butter*
*1 cup chopped stems and pieces from domestic mushrooms*
*3 tablespoons softened cream cheese or sour cream*
*¼ cup fine, dry bread crumbs, seasoned with pinch of salt and*
      *pepper*
*¼ teaspoon chopped parsley*
*Salt and pepper to taste*

135

1.  Clean the mushroom caps with a brush.
2.  Sauté the bacon with the shallots until the bacon fat liquefies.
3.  Pour off most of the bacon fat, and replace with a little of the melted butter.
4.  Mix in the chopped stems and pieces, cream cheese or sour cream, bread crumbs, parsley, and salt and pepper.
5.  Place the cleaned mushrooms, stem side up, on a buttered broiler pan, and fill with the mixture, heaping into rounds.
6.  Drizzle a little melted butter on them, and broil until heated through and lightly browned, about 1 to 2 minutes.

## Stuffed Mushroom Caps with Caviar

Stuff white, firm domestic mushrooms about 1½ inches in diameter with a little cream cheese, and top with some golden caviar. Serve with a dry Riesling.

## Piroshki

APPROXIMATE PREPARATION TIME: **6** HOURS
USEFUL ADVANCE PREPARATION: MAKE DOUGH AND FILLING AND ALLOW TO
    CHILL.
MAKES **4** TO **6** SERVINGS

This appetizer is Russian in origin. Store-bought domestic mushrooms are safest, but wild mushrooms give a special and wonderful flavor. Dried wild mushrooms, soaked and chopped, are excellent for use in this recipe, which can easily be adapted to a food processor. The dough can be made in advance and kept in the refrigerator for up to a week.

FOR THE PIROSHKI DOUGH:
*1¼ cups all-purpose flour*
*¼ pound very cold butter*
*3 tablespoons sour cream*

FOR THE FILLING:
*½ pound domestic or wild mushrooms*
*6 tablespoons butter*

*1 large onion peeled and chopped*
*Pinch of savory*
*Salt and pepper*

*Preheat the oven to 400°.*

1. To make the dough, sift the flour into a mixing bowl.
2. Slice the butter into the flour, and cut it in with a pastry blender or fork until the mixture resembles coarse crumbs.
3. Add the sour cream, tossing lightly with a fork just until the mixture holds together enough to form a ball.
4. Wrap the ball of dough in wax paper or plastic, and chill thoroughly, about 3 hours.
5. To prepare the filling, clean the mushrooms, and chop them fine.
6. Heat 3 tablespoons of butter in a skillet. Sauté the mushrooms until they are dry. Transfer to a small bowl.
7. Heat the remaining butter, and sauté the onion until golden brown. Add to the mushrooms. Mix well, and season with the savory, salt, and pepper. Chill for 1 hour.
8. To assemble, begin by pinching off a scant tablespoon of dough, and roll out on a lightly floured surface to a circle 3 inches in diameter.
9. Trim edges with a pastry wheel or cut with a 3-inch cookie cutter. Repeat until all the dough has been used.
10. Paint the edges of the circles with a little water.
11. Put a teaspoonful of filling in the center of each circle.
12. Fold over to make small turnovers, pressing the edges together with the tine of a fork. Pierce the tops with the tines of a fork.
13. Place on a baking sheet, and chill thoroughly for 1 hour.
14. Bake 15 to 20 minutes or until golden brown. Serve immediately. Makes about 24 piroshki.

## Pickled and Marinated Mushrooms

For salads or hors d'oeuvres, this method of preparation is best. The trick to good pickling technique is to allow the flavor of the mushroom to come through. If the pickling solution is too acidic, then the mushroom flavor will be overpowered.

# Joe's Pickled Martini Mushrooms

APPROXIMATE PREPARATION TIME: 1 DAY
USEFUL ADVANCE PREPARATION: ONCE MUSHROOMS ARE MADE, THEY MUST
    MARINATE FOR 24 HOURS. MAKE THIS AT LEAST A DAY IN ADVANCE
    OF USE.
MAKES 2 CUPS MARINADE

At the restaurant, we've been using these marinated or pickled mushrooms in our martinis for the past thirty years. Gasps of shock and delight issue from the most staid executives, who expected the little green eye of an olive to be staring up at them. Try it. These are also excellent as a garnish for a cold appetizer or just on a plate by themselves, sprinkled with some fresh chopped dill. We usually use the canned straw mushrooms found in any Oriental store, but fresh wild mushrooms, boiled, are best. Serve chilled.

> *1½ cups water*
> *½ cup white wine vinegar*
> *¼ cup sugar*
> *1 tablespoon kosher salt*
> *1 tablespoon pickling spices*
> *3 15-ounce cans Chinese straw mushrooms or 20 ounces blanched*
>     *wild mushrooms (see page 53)*

1. To prepare the marinade, combine water, vinegar, sugar, and salt in a pot, and bring to a boil, stirring to dissolve salt and sugar.
2. Let marinade simmer for 5 minutes.
3. Take marinade off heat, and add spices.
4. Add the mushrooms of your choice. Be sure that they are sterilized before marinating. Do this by bringing the mushrooms to a boil in plain water and simmering for 20 minutes. Then drain and rinse the mushrooms. Drain again, and cover with the marinade. Let marinade stand in refrigerator for 24 hours. The finished mushrooms will keep in the refrigerator for about a week.

## Pickled Mushrooms Monterey

APPROXIMATE PREPARATION TIME: 1 DAY
USEFUL ADVANCE PREPARATION: ONCE MUSHROOMS ARE MADE, THEY MUST
      MARINATE FOR 24 HOURS. MAKE THIS AT LEAST A DAY IN ADVANCE
      OF USE.
MAKES 2 CUPS MARINADE

Roy Thomas of the Monterey Peninsula Winery was the first person to show me the rich wild-mushroom harvest that can be gathered on the Monterey Peninsula, including the highly prized cepe. On my last visit to California, he shared with me some of the ways he likes to prepare his mushrooms. He is especially fond of pickling them.

*1 teaspoon crushed allspice*
*1 cup white vinegar*
*¼ teaspoon crushed caraway seed*
*1 medium onion, sliced*
*2 cups fresh mushrooms, sliced*
*Kosher salt*

1. In a medium-size saucepan, heat together the allspice, vinegar, caraway, and onion until the onions just begin to turn color.
2. Add the mushrooms, and cook on a low heat for another 5 minutes. Salt the mixture to taste. Turn off heat, and allow to cool for 1 hour.
3. Place the mixture in a glass jar, and refrigerate for 24 hours. This will last in the refrigerator for at least a week.

## Pickled Mushrooms with Rocket (Arugula)

Arrange some rocket leaves, the pungent Italian salad green also known as arugula, on a small serving platter and place a mixture of pickled mushrooms (using either of the above pickled mushroom recipes, or a combination) in the center. Sprinkle with some ground pepper. Serve with a dill sauce made by blending ½ cup mayonnaise, 1 tablespoon dry sherry, 1 tablespoon Dijon mustard, 1 teaspoon dried ground dill, and 1 teaspoon lemon juice or vinegar. Let the sauce sit for 1 hour before using.

# Special Uses for Mushrooms

## Patti's Pâté

APPROXIMATE PREPARATION TIME: 1 DAY
USEFUL ADVANCE PREPARATION: THIS PÂTÉ MUST BE MADE A DAY IN ADVANCE
      OF USE.
SUGGESTED WINE: BARGETTO CHARDONNAY
MAKES 4 SERVINGS

This recipe for mushroom pâté comes from Patricia Ballard of Bargetto Winery. It is adapted from her book, *Wine in Everyday Cooking,* published by the Wine Appreciation Guild.

> *½ pound butter in 2 quarters*
> *½ pound fresh mushrooms, sliced thin*
> *1 large bunch green onions, sliced thin (use all of white part and*
> *    half of the green part)*
> *4 to 6 medium cloves of garlic, sliced thin*
> *1 pound fresh chicken livers, trimmed of all fat*
> *1 teaspoon salt*
> *½ teaspoon dried rosemary, crumbled*
> *½ teaspoon dillweed*
> *1 teaspoon dry mustard*
> *⅔ cup Chardonnay*

1. Melt ¼ pound (one stick) of butter in a large skillet over low heat. Add mushrooms, onions, and garlic.

2. Sauté for 3 to 5 minutes, stirring constantly. Push vegetables to the side of skillet.

3. Add chicken livers, and cook only until edges turn white; turn at once.

4. Add salt, rosemary, dillweed, and mustard; stir thoroughly, add Chardonnay, stirring again, and cook until liquid is reduced to half.

5. Cut second stick of butter into quarters. Place butter in a blender or food processor fitted with a chopping blade, and add chicken-liver mixture. Blend until smooth. If using a blender, alternate a small amount of cooked ingredients with a small amount of butter and blend. Continue until all ingredients are blended smoothly.

6. Refrigerate, and let flavors blend for 24 hours before serving.

Wonderful on slices of French bread together with ice-cold champagne as a first course. Serves 20 dieters or 10 nondieters.

The pâté will keep up to 10 days in the refrigerator, and freezes well for as long as 3 months.

## Quenelles Sonja

APPROXIMATE PREPARATION TIME: **3** HOURS

USEFUL ADVANCE PREPARATION: THE *PANADE* AND QUENELLES SHOULD BOTH
    BE MADE IN ADVANCE. THE DUXELLES RECIPE HERE IS SLIGHTLY
    DIFFERENT FROM THE ONE IN CHAPTER **4**, ALTHOUGH THE BASIC
    MUSHROOM DUXELLES RECIPE (PAGE **61**) CAN BE USED AS WELL IF YOU
    HAVE SOME.

MAKES **4** SERVINGS

This quenelle dish is made with a sauce derived from mushroom duxelles that adds body and complexity to the normal white sauce. It is named after my daughter Sonja. This dish is best served for a luncheon or as a first course for a formal dinner. The preparation is quite involved and takes a relatively long period of time, but is well worth the effort. Serve with a Chardonnay like Osprey Vineyards.

*1 cup hot milk*
*1 cup fine bread crumbs made with French bread, crusts removed*
*Pinch of salt*
*1 tablespoon butter for buttering dinner plate*
*1 pound fresh white-fleshed fish, cut into small pieces*
*½ pound butter*
*Salt and pepper to taste*
*Pinch of mace or nutmeg, freshly ground*
*2 whole eggs*
*4 egg yolks*
*1 small onion, chopped fine*
*2 tablespoons butter*
*¼ pound fresh mushrooms, chopped (cultivated domestic*
    *mushrooms do very well in this sauce)*
*2 cups fish stock*
*4 tablespoons cornstarch*
*1 cup cream*

1. To make the *panade*, heat the milk in a 1½ quart saucepan.

2. Add dry bread crumbs and salt, and mix to a smooth paste. If not dry enough, return to heat to dry out.

3. While hot, spread *panade* on a buttered dinner plate, and cover with wax paper to avoid dry spots.

4. Prepare the quenelles. Process fish in electric processor until smooth.

5. Cream butter in bowl of mixer.

6. Combine fish and butter, and blend well.

7. Add seasonings and *panade*.

8. Add eggs and egg yolks, one at a time, beating well after each addition.

9. Chill quenelle mixture well.

10. To form quenelles, use a floured board. Form small cylinders of quenelle mixture, 3 inches long by ¾ inches thick. These will puff up during poaching. Return to refrigerator to chill if mixture becomes too soft to work. Chill formed quenelles before poaching.*

11. To make mushroom sauce, in a 10-inch sauté pan, sauté onions in butter until soft.

12. Add mushrooms, and sauté over medium heat until moisture has evaporated, stirring to prevent sticking and burning.

13. Add 2 cups fish stock, and bring to a simmer.

14. Mix cornstarch with cream, and stir until smooth.

15. Add cream mixture to fish stock mixture, stirring all the while until mixture is smooth and thickened.

16. Adjust seasoning off heat.

17. To cook quenelles, bring salted water to a boil in a 10-inch sauté pan.

18. Reduce heat so that water barely simmers.

19. Gently place quenelles, one by one, in the poaching liquid, and cook until they are nicely puffed. Time will vary according to size and number of quenelles in the pan. After poaching a few, you will know when the quenelles are done. Turn gently during poaching to cook thoroughly.

20. Drain on paper towels.

21. Place on a heated plate. Cover with mushroom sauce, and garnish with chopped parsley.

*Note: To freeze quenelles, arrange formed quenelles on a tray lined with wax paper, sprinkled with a little flour. When completely frozen, wrap quenelles in small plastic bags, no more than 4 to a bag. Work quickly so that quenelles do not thaw out and stick together. Label bags, and return to freezer. Do not store over 1 month. Do not freeze sauce.

## Snails *Suillus pictus*

**APPROXIMATE PREPARATION TIME: 2 HOURS**
**MAKES 4 SERVINGS**

This is a cold snail appetizer in which we used dried, reconstituted mushrooms called *Suillus pictus*. Sliced, dried cepes can also be used, since the idea here is to complement the earthy flavor of the snails with the equally concentrated flavors of the mushrooms. Serve with Chenin Blanc.

*1 ounce dried* Suillus pictus *or cepes*
*2 cups water*
*½ teaspoon salt*
*¾ cup mayonnaise*
*1 tablespoon prepared Dijon mustard*
*1 tablespoon dry sherry*
*24 extra large snails, shelled*

1. Place mushrooms, water, and salt in a small saucepan; bring to boil, then let simmer for 20 minutes. The mushrooms will sink to the bottom of the pan when fully reconstituted.
2. Remove mushrooms from water, and save liquid for use in another recipe.
3. In a mixing bowl combine the mushrooms, mayonnaise, mustard, sherry, and snails, and gently fold them together until well mixed. Refrigerate this mixture for 1 hour to combine flavors, then serve on a leaf of romaine, and garnish with a pickled mushroom.

CHAPTER EIGHT

# *Mushrooms with Fish*

## Mushrooms with Fish

The general principles of combining mushrooms with fish and shell-fish are simple. "Of nothing too much" is the best warning. But as with all rules, there are hidden exceptions.

Extracts are almost never used when preparing mushrooms with fish. Shiitake extract can be used, but only in a light sauce. Fresh or canned mushrooms are the most suitable, because they impart a delicate flavor that will not overwhelm the fish. Dried mushrooms are less desirable. Duxelles, once again, are very effective with fish, especially those duxelles that include some sort of fish ingredient, such as oysters or smoked salmon. Cream sauces with mushrooms are excellent, as are some of the lighter sauces. Avoid allowing the mushroom character to become too prominent. The flavor of the mushrooms should stand harmoniously and subtly beside the fish.

The use of salt to bring up the flavors in these recipes is fine, but there is a better alternative. I discovered Chinese fish sauce one Sunday afternoon, during one of my trips to Philadelphia's Chinatown. Never having tasted it before, I purchased some to experiment with. I thought it was awful! Away it went into the far reaches of my kitchen cabinet, where it languished for several months. Then one day, I happened to be working on a recipe for a cream sauce to be used with fish in puff pastry. I tried salting with soy, with salt, then—just for the hell of it—I decided to give the Chinese fish sauce a try. I don't need to tell you that my early misgivings turned into one of the flavor revelations of my life.

By itself, the sauce is strong and unpleasant-tasting, but in sauces, especially the cream variety, it has the peculiar character of giving up its own flavors and enhancing the surrounding ones. It is simply a good example of the principle of sauce making: Flavor is not enough—you must have *body,* too, a canvas against which the primary flavors can express themselves.

### A Staple of Fish Cookery

Quite a few of the following recipes utilize parchment paper for wrapping and baking fish in an oven. I am sure that by now most people are familiar with the method of folding the parchment paper to get that half-moon-shaped result so lovingly described in the technique. I've got a gripe or two about that. One problem is that the classic technique itself—with its tedious folding and refolding—is enough to discourage anyone from using it, and that's a pity since it is truly one of the great ways to prepare fish. It's one of those deliberately intimidating things, I feel—a technique that some cookbook writers include in their books just to remind you that they are experts and you're not. Another reason I don't like the classic method is that it's unnecessarily time-consuming and complicated.

The way to put the paper together the fastest is to fold the top part over the bottom (with the fish inside). Then fold the ends over twice and *staple* them together. Then do the same thing for the two sides. Finished! The end result, which resembles an envelope with three of its sides stapled, takes about 10 seconds, whereas the other method takes about 3 or 4 minutes—if you're already good at it.

### Whole Sea Bass with Mushroom Soy

APPROXIMATE PREPARATION TIME: 1 HOUR
MAKES 4 SERVINGS

This is a Chinese classic, elegantly simple yet amenable to many variations and touches. The principle is steaming to maintain the moisture of the fish while imparting the flavors of the accompanying ingredients. In this recipe a mushroom soy is substituted for the regular thin soy, and mushrooms are used to enhance the effect. This recipe can be used for other delicate, white-fleshed fish such as sole or trout. Serve with stir-fried mixed vegetables, and Sauvignon Blanc or Sancerre.

> *2 small or 1 large fresh whole sea bass, allow about 8 to 10 ounces*
> *per person*
> *½ cup mushrooms, domestic or wild, sliced thin*
> *½ teaspoon fresh ginger, chopped fine*
> *⅓ cup mushroom soy sauce (available in most Oriental grocery*
> *stores)*
> *½ cup scallions, sliced thin*
> *1 tablespoon fresh, chopped parsley*

1. Place fish steamer over medium heat. Steamer is ready to be used for cooking when the water is simmering.*
2. Scale and rinse the fish. Proceed to gut the fish, taking care not to get any of the bile on the flesh. Then rinse again, inside and out.
3. Pat the fish dry, and place on a platter that will fit into a steamer.
4. Cover the fish with the mushrooms, ginger, and mushroom soy and place in the steamer, which should now be producing steam.
5. Steam the fish until done (about 20 minutes for a large fish, 15 minutes for a smaller one). About 1 or 2 minutes before the fish is done, sprinkle with the scallions and parsley. Remove the fish from the steamer, and serve immediately on the dish used for the steaming.

*Note: When steaming fish, keep water at a gentle simmer. Intense boiling will cook the fish too rapidly and result in an overdone dish. One of the advantages of steaming, however, is that even if the fish becomes overcooked, it will still be moist. But keep in mind that the temperature buildup during steaming is higher than that for boiling, so although steaming *seems* to be a less extreme form of cooking, it is actually quicker, temperature-wise, than boiling.

## Poached Sole with Oyster Mushrooms

APPROXIMATE PREPARATION TIME: **30** MINUTES
MAKES **4** SERVINGS

Here is a simple preparation that works well with almost any fish and illustrates the elegant power of using fresh mushrooms with fish. Serve with quick-sautéed string potatoes.

> *½ cup water*
> *1 tablespoon Chinese fish sauce (see pages 144–145)*

*1 tablespoon melted butter*
*1 tablespoon white wine or sherry*
*2 tablespoons sliced scallions*
*2 cups sliced oyster mushrooms, or domestic can be substituted*
*1 tablespoon arrowroot mixed with ¼ cup water*
*4 5-ounce portions of sole filets*

1. Combine in a large skillet all the ingredients except the arrowroot and the fish.

2. Bring ingredients to a simmer, and thicken with the arrowroot-and-water mixture until the thickness is *slightly* more than desired (you may not have to use all of the mixture). Do this because, as the fish cooks later, it will give off its own juices and thin the sauce back to its proper consistency.

3. Add the fish to the skillet, and poach, covered, for about 5 minutes, or until the fish flakes. Fish should never be overdone, and if it is slightly undercooked, that is fine.

4. Remove the fish from the skillet, place on a serving dish, and cover with the skillet sauce.

## Mousse of Sole en Croûte with Watercress and Mushrooms

**APPROXIMATE PREPARATION TIME: 2 HOURS**
**USEFUL ADVANCE PREPARATION: MAKE OR PURCHASE PUFF PASTRY.**
**MAKES 4 SERVINGS**

This recipe uses a *marié,* which is a puree of any herb (in this case watercress) in white vinegar. The acid from the vinegar points up and emphasizes the flavor of whatever herb is used. Again, this recipe works with almost any kind of fish and is especially useful when you have ends, bits, and pieces left over from another dish.

**FOR THE FISH MOUSSE:**
*14 ounces sole filets or pieces*
*1 tablespoon chopped onions*
*1 teaspoon bouquet garni*
*1 tablespoon Chinese fish sauce (see pages 144–145)*
*1 egg*
*1 to 2 cups milk mixed with heavy cream*
*Salt*

**147**

> *4 3-inch squares uncooked puff pastry (see pages 95–96)*
> *1 egg, beaten*

> **FOR THE SAUCE:**
> *1 medium bunch watercress*
> *2 tablespoons vinegar*
> *1½ cups half milk, half cream, or commercial half and half*
> *½ cup fresh sliced mushrooms, sautéed in butter*
> *2 teaspoons Chinese fish sauce (see pages 144–145)*
> *2 teaspoons cornstarch mixed with ¼ cup water*

> *Preheat oven to 450°.*

Roll out each piece of puff pastry to 1/16th-inch thickness and keep refrigerated until ready to use.

1. To make the mousse, in a food processor combine the fish, onions, spice, fish sauce, and egg. Begin to chop in the processor. Slowly add the milk-cream mixture until well blended. The mixture should be moist so that it can be molded easily, but not runny. Force mixture through fine sieve or food mill. Salt to taste. The final consistency should be such that, if a teaspoonful of the mixture is scooped up and held upside down, it will not run off.

2. Divide the mixture into 4 servings.

3. Wrap each of the above portions of fish in the puff pastry. Place each portion in the middle of a square of pastry. Fold two of the opposite diagonal ends over the fish to overlap slightly. Any overlap wider than 2 inches should be trimmed away. Repeat for the other two opposite ends.

4. Cover a baking pan with a double width of aluminum foil or kitchen parchment paper, and place the 4 wrapped portions on it. Refrigerate.

5. After 15 minutes, remove the wrapped fish, and coat the pastry with some beaten egg. Make incisions with a sharp knife in the top of the portions to form a decorative pattern.

6. Place the portions on a double baking sheet. Let the wrapped fish sit for 15 minutes. Place in the oven, and set the timer for 15 minutes.

7. While the fish is baking, make the *marié* by first washing the watercress and then combining it with the vinegar in a blender, and mixing until a puree is formed.

8. Combine the *marié* with the half-and-half, mushrooms, and fish sauce in a pan, and bring to a simmer. Thicken with the cornstarch-and-water mixture. Keep warm.

148

9. Remove the fish from the oven, place on a serving dish, and surround with the sauce.

## Halibut with Dry Wild Mushroom Duxelles

APPROXIMATE PREPARATION TIME: 1 HOUR
USEFUL ADVANCE PREPARATION: PREPARE DRY DUXELLES (SEE PAGE 67).
MAKES 4 SERVINGS

This recipe utilizes dry mushroom duxelles and also illustrates the parchment method of cooking fish, which, along with steaming and poaching, is the best way of maintaining moisture in the fish. This technique can be elaborated by adding almost any kind of herb or vegetable to the parchment during cooking. The following is a simple treatment and emphasizes the flavor of the mushrooms. Serve with zucchini sautéed in garlic and butter, and a Merry's Vintners Chardonnay.

*4 pieces heavy parchment paper*
*2 tablespoons butter, melted, or enough to sprinkle each filet*
  *lightly*
*4 5-ounce halibut filets*
*Wine, enough to sprinkle each filet lightly*
*2 tablespoons Dry Duxelles (from dried cepes)*

*Preheat oven to 450°.*

1. Brush the pieces of parchment with butter.
2. Place each piece of halibut on a piece of the buttered parchment. Sprinkle lightly with some wine and butter, then spoon ½ tablespoon of the duxelles in a single straight line down the center of each filet.
3. Enclose the fish in the parchment by simply folding the edges twice and stapling to seal them.
4. Place the enclosed portions on a double baking sheet, and bake in the oven for 10 minutes.
5. Open the paper and remove the fish for serving.

149

# Salmon in Lobster Sauce with Cepes

APPROXIMATE PREPARATION TIME: **3** HOURS
USEFUL ADVANCE PREPARATION: BOIL LOBSTER, COOL, AND REMOVE MEAT.
      SAVE SHELLS FOR MAKING STOCK.
MAKES **4** SERVINGS

In this dish we are making a lobster sauce using dried cepes. Lobster is strong enough in flavor to stand this sort of treatment and, coupled with salmon, makes an aristocratic dish indeed. Serve with brown rice mixed with pine nuts and parsley, and a Chalone Pinot Blanc.

*1 live 2-pound lobster*
*½ ounce dried cepes*
*1 teaspoon chopped garlic*
*1 tablespoon chopped onion*
*3 tablespoons butter*
*3 tablespoons dry white wine*
*1 teaspoon salt*
*1 teaspoon sugar*
*1 teaspoon soy sauce*
*2 tablespoons tomato paste*
*2 tablespoons arrowroot mixed with ¼ cup water*
*4 portions salmon, 5 ounces each*

1. Boil some water in a large pot. Do *not* salt the water. Add the live lobster and the cepes, and bring back to a boil. Cook the lobster for 20 minutes.

2. Remove the lobster from the water. Cool. Remove all the lobster meat and all innards. Slice and reserve the lobster meat. Put the lobster shells back into the water with the cepes, and boil another hour. The liquid should become a brownish-reddish color and be cooked down to about 2 cups. Strain the liquid. Slice the mushrooms thin, and reserve.

3. Sauté the garlic and onions in the butter in a large skillet until the onions are transparent, and add the sliced mushrooms-and-lobster stock. Reduce this mixture to 1½ cups, and set aside.

4. To the above sauce, add the wine, salt, sugar, soy sauce, and tomato paste. Whisk together to blend. Stir in the arrowroot-and-water mixture until slightly thick.

5. Place the salmon in the skillet with the sauce. Add the sliced mushrooms and lobster. Cover. Poach for about 10 minutes over medium heat. Remove from the skillet, and serve with the rice.

## Shark in Parchment with Oyster Duxelles

APPROXIMATE PREPARATION TIME: 1 HOUR
USEFUL ADVANCE PREPARATION: PREPARE OYSTER DUXELLES (SEE PAGE 63).
MAKES 4 SERVINGS

One of the reasons I am so fond of swordfish and related species like shark is that they have the natural body and character to stand up to the heartier flavors of mushrooms, domestic and wild. This recipe offers the added character of oysters. Serve with *ratatouille niçoise,* and French Chablis.

*4 shark filets, 6 ounces each*
*4 tablespoons Oyster Duxelles*
*4 pieces parchment paper*

*Preheat oven to 450°.*

1. Spread the top of each filet with a tablespoon of the duxelles.
2. Wrap the fish in the parchment by folding over the edges twice and stapling to close, and place on a baking sheet. Place in the oven, and bake for 10 to 15 minutes. Remove from the parchment and serve.

## Red Snapper with Sage Marié

APPROXIMATE PREPARATION TIME: 1 HOUR
MAKES 4 SERVINGS

Here is another recipe utilizing a *marié.* This time it is sage combined with mushrooms to give a rustic edge to this most flavorful fish. Also, the sauce is done béchamel-style to give it greater richness. Serve with wild rice mixed with sautéed leeks, and a Gewürztraminer.

*1 tablespoon fresh sage, or 1 teaspoon dried*
*2 tablespoons lemon juice or vinegar*
*¾ cup fresh wild mushrooms, sliced*
*3 tablespoons melted butter*
*2 tablespoons sifted flour*
*1 cup heavy cream mixed with ½ cup milk*
*1 tablespoon Chinese fish sauce (see pages 144–145) or salt to*
*    taste*
*4 red snapper filets, about 6 ounces each*

1. Prepare the *marié* by grinding together the sage and the lemon juice or vinegar in a blender.

2. In a large skillet, sauté the mushrooms in the butter till they are soft. Sprinkle in the flour, and continue to stir for another minute. Add the half-and-half, fish sauce or salt, and the *marié* and continue to stir until it becomes slightly thick.

3. Add the red snapper filets to this sauce, and cover, leaving the liquid at a simmer. Allow to cook like this for about 10 minutes or until the dish is done. Serve the fish directly from the skillet, and cover with the sauce and mushrooms.


## Stuffed Shad with Cloud-Ears and Five-Spice Sauce

APPROXIMATE PREPARATION TIME: 1 TO 2 HOURS
USEFUL ADVANCE PREPARATION: RECONSTITUTE THE CLOUD-EARS A DAY IN
ADVANCE BY SOAKING IN WARM WATER OR BOILING FOR AN HOUR.
MAKES 4 SERVINGS

When God created shad, He made it impossible to bone the creature without leaving a pocket suitable for stuffing. And so we are blessed with this rich, tasty denizen of the sea that literally begs for filling.

The cloud-ears lend a crunchy counterpoint to the firm, moist texture of the fish, as do the scallions. The five-spice sauce adds an Oriental richness, backed up as it is by the veal stock, which gives the dish real substance. Serve with quick-sautéed julienne carrots and celery, and a full-bodied Chardonnay or Pinot Blanc, like the ones from Monterey Peninsula Winery.

TO PREPARE THE SHAD:
*1 ounce dried cloud-ears (also called tree fungus or Jew's-ear)*
*4 7-ounce portions of boned shad*
*4 tablespoons sliced scallions*
*2 tablespoons white wine*
*2 tablespoons butter*
*Salt*
*4 pieces parchment paper*

FOR THE SAUCE:
*1 cup rich veal stock (see pages 72–73)*
*2 teaspoons Chinese oyster sauce*
*2 teaspoons hoisin sauce*

*¼ teaspoon five-spice powder*
*1 tablespoon arrowroot mixed in ¼ cup water*

*Preheat oven to 450°.*

1. Reconstitute the cloud-ears in water by covering them with plenty of water and bringing to a boil. Simmer for 1 hour. The cloud-ears will expand greatly, and they will be firm and crunchy. Discard the water, and allow the mushrooms to cool. Then slice the cloud-ears into ¼-inch strips.

2. Lay the shad on a covered table, and open the folds for stuffing. Fill the shad with the cloud-ears and scallions, and replace the folds over the center of the fish. Coat the fish lightly with the wine, butter, and pinch of salt.

3. Wrap the fish in the parchment paper by folding over the edges and stapling in place. Repeat for other 3 portions of shad.

4. Place the fish on a double baking sheet and put in the oven for about 14 minutes.

5. While the fish is baking, prepare the sauce by combining the stock, oyster sauce, hoisin sauce, and five-spice in a saucepan. Bring this to a boil, then turn off the heat. Thicken to desired consistency with the arrowroot-and-water mixture and serve over the finished fish.

## Marinated Shad and Mushroom Salad

**APPROXIMATE PREPARATION TIME: 1 DAY**
**MAKES 4 SERVINGS**

This is an excellent pickled salad, using the rich, unctuous shad in combination with the more delicate mushrooms. Although this recipe requires a 24-hour marinating period, the final preparation takes place in less than 5 minutes.

*1 cup lemon or lime juice*
*1 teaspoon sugar*
*1 teaspoon kosher salt*
*½ teaspoon fresh ground pepper*
*½ teaspoon ground, dried basil*
*1 crushed, dried chili pepper*
*2 whole bay leaves*
*2 tablespoons chopped onions*

153

*1 clove garlic, chopped*
*1 pound boned and skinned shad, cut into ½-inch pieces*
*1 cup canned, peeled straw mushrooms*
*1 cup mayonnaise*

1.  Combine all the ingredients except the mayonnaise in a glass jar with a tightly fitting top. Mix well, and let stand overnight in the refrigerator or until the shad is completely "cooked."

2.  Combine mayonnaise with about ⅓ to ½ cup of the liquid from the marinated shad, a little at a time. Blend with a wire whisk until it is smooth. Discard any of the liquid left in the marinated shad.

3.  Mix the shad and mushrooms into the mayonnaise sauce, and refrigerate. This salad will hold in the refrigerator for several weeks. Serve it over a large leaf of romaine.

## Pompano with Smoked Salmon Duxelles

APPROXIMATE PREPARATION TIME: 1 HOUR
USEFUL ADVANCE PREPARATION: PREPARE SMOKED SALMON DUXELLES (SEE
      PAGE 63)
MAKES 4 SERVINGS

Pompano is a rich-textured fish that stands up well to diverse flavors such as salmon and mushrooms. It is also an oily fish and is best served with a salad like tomato, cucumber, and leeks, and a sharp, fruity Chardonnay.

*4 6-ounce pompano filets*
*4 pieces heavy parchment paper*
*Pinch of salt*
*2 tablespoons juice of fresh lemon*
*2 tablespoons white wine*
*4 tablespoons Smoked Salmon Duxelles*

*Preheat oven to 450°.*

1.  Place each filet on a piece of parchment paper, and sprinkle with some salt, lemon juice, and wine, and cover with 1 tablespoon of the duxelles.

2.  Wrap the fish in the paper by folding edges twice and stapling to close, and place in the oven for 10 to 15 minutes.

3.  Open the paper, and remove fish. Serve immediately.

# Trout with Chanterelles

APPROXIMATE PREPARATION TIME: 1 HOUR
MAKES 4 SERVINGS

This dish is redolent of a warm summer day somewhere deep in the woods of Pennsylvania, where a brook runs past a clearing blanketed with chanterelles. Accompaniment: steamed fresh asparagus or steamed fiddlehead ferns with lemon grass, and a dry California Riesling like Raymond.

*½ cup sliced scallions*
*3 tablespoons melted butter*
*½ teaspoon juice of fresh lemon*
*1 cup sliced chanterelles*
*4 medium-sized fresh trout, cleaned and ready to cook*

1. Sauté the scallions over medium heat in 2 tablespoons butter and lemon juice for 1 minute.
2. Add the chanterelles, and sauté for another minute over a medium heat.
3. Add about 1 more tablespoon of butter so that the bottom of the pan is barely covered with some butter liquid. Reduce heat.
4. Place the trout in the skillet, cover with a lid, let cook for 5 minutes over a low flame. Then turn the trout over and finish for another 5 minutes on the other side. Serve the trout on a plate, covered with the chanterelles and scallions blended with the fiddleheads and lemon grass.

# Fresh Trout with Mushroom and Groats Stuffing

APPROXIMATE PREPARATION TIME: 1 HOUR
USEFUL ADVANCE PREPARATION: PREPARE AND COOK BUCKWHEAT GROATS IN
      ADVANCE. FOR METHOD OF PREPARING BUCKWHEAT GROATS SEE PAGE
      247 ( 30 MINUTES).
MAKES 4 SERVINGS

This is a Polish recipe for preparing fresh trout. The delicate flesh of the fish is counterpointed by the gentle crunchiness of the groats stuffing. Serve with warm beet and onion salad.

155

*MUSHROOMS WITH FISH*

> 1 medium onion, chopped
> 4 tablespoons butter
> 1 pound wild or domestic mushrooms, blanched, or blanched
>      home-canned mushrooms of similar texture
> 1 egg, beaten
> 2 cups cooked medium buckwheat groats
> Salt and pepper
> 4 fresh trout, 8 to 12 ounces each
> 2 tablespoons melted butter
> 1 tablespoon white wine
> 4 tablespoons chopped parsley
> Whole fresh herbs for garnish
> 1 lemon
> 2 ounces Pickled Mushrooms (optional) (pages 137–139)

*Preheat oven to 450°.*

1. Sauté onion in butter until transparent.
2. Chop mushrooms.
3. Blend onions, mushrooms, beaten egg, and groats. Salt and pepper to taste for seasoning.
4. Stuff fish cavity, and score.*
5. Brush trout with melted butter, and sprinkle with white wine.
6. Bake trout in the oven for 15 minutes. Garnish trout with parsley, fresh herbs, a wedge of lemon, and a few home-pickled mushrooms.

*Note: To score food, make a series of shallow cuts on the food's surface.

## Tilefish with Black Trumpet Sauce

APPROXIMATE PREPARATION TIME: 1 HOUR
MAKES 4 SERVINGS

Fresh fish should generally be accompanied by light, well-defined sauces that allow the fish to make its own statement. However, heavier-fleshed fish such as tile and swordfish can support more substantial flavors if not overdone. Here is an example that borrows from the Chinese approach to fish—a darkly colored but lightly bodied and full-flavored sauce. Monkfish, striped bass, or sea bass can all be used in this recipe. Serve with sautéed fennel and onions, and a David Bruce Chardonnay.

*1 ounce dried black trumpet mushrooms (dried morels can be*
  *substituted)*
*2 cups water*
*1 teaspoon salt*
*¼ teaspoon sugar*
*1 tablespoon sliced scallions*
*½ teaspoon fresh, crushed ginger*
*1 tablespoon arrowroot mixed with ¼ cup water*
*4 tilefish filets, 6 to 8 ounces each, boned*

1. Combine mushrooms with water, salt, and sugar in saucepan. Bring to boil.

2. Simmer for about 15 minutes, until liquid is down to 1½ cups.

3. Shift mushrooms and liquid to a saucepan with a tight-fitting lid, add scallions and ginger.

4. Thicken this mixture with arrowroot-and-water mixture until liquid is lightly overthickened. Liquid from the fish will bring it around to proper consistency.

5. Add fish, and cover pan with lid. Allow to poach for about 6 to 8 minutes over a low fire until fish flakes.

6. Remove fish from pan, and place on platter. Quickly stir sauce, adding a little water if necessary, and pour around fish, placing some of the mushrooms on top of fish for appearance. Serve.

## Smoked Big Sur Trout with Dried Shiitake Sauce

APPROXIMATE PREPARATION TIME: 1 HOUR
MAKES 4 SERVINGS

Perhaps the finest smoked trout in the world is made in the region of Big Sur, California. Every year my wife, Heidi, and I visit Monterey, and we never neglect to take a ride down the coast to one of the area's fine restaurants. One thing we always order is the smoked trout, which is prepared not more than a few miles from where we are eating.

Several years ago we brought some home to Pennsylvania, and I came up with the following recipe, which combines the smoked fish with the smoky flavor of shiitake. This dish is made from the dried shiitake that can be found in any Oriental grocery store. The smoked trout, weighing from 4 to 8 ounces each, usually can be found in specialty food stores. Choose the slightly larger

157

ones, since they will have a higher percentage of flesh. Serve with an asparagus-leek salad for a luncheon.

> *1 ounce dried shiitake or 5 ounces fresh shiitake*
> *3 cups water*
> *1⅓ teaspoons sugar*
> *1⅓ teaspoons salt*
> *1⅓ teaspoons soy sauce*
> *2 medium-sized smoked trout, preferably the Big Sur variety, but*
>     *any smoked trout will do*
> *1 tablespoon arrowroot mixed with ¼ cup water*

1. Combine shiitake, water, sugar, salt, and soy sauce in a saucepan, and bring to a boil. Let simmer for 30 minutes or until the liquid is reduced to about 1½ cups. Then remove the mushrooms, and slice them thin, removing the stems. Return the mushrooms to the sauce, and keep warm.

2. Place the trout in a 200° oven for about 10 minutes to warm slightly. Just before the trout is ready to be removed from the oven, heat the sauce back to a simmer, and thicken with the arrowroot-and-water mixture. Remove the trout from the oven, and cover with the sauce. Serve.

# Mushrooms with Shellfish

### Baked Lump Crabmeat with Mushrooms

APPROXIMATE PREPARATION TIME: 2 HOURS
MAKES 4 SERVINGS

This has been one of the most popular dishes at our restaurant. Make sure to use large lump crabmeat, since the texture of this dish is as important as the flavor. Serve with sautéed green beans, and a Vouvray or Chenin Blanc.

> *½ cup chopped onions*
> *3 tablespoons melted butter*
> *2 cups sliced mushrooms*
> *Soy sauce to taste*
> *½ teaspoon bouquet garni*
> *2 tablespoons cornstarch mixed with ⅓ cup water*

*1 egg*
*1 tablespoon chopped green pepper*
*1 tablespoon prepared Dijon mustard*
*1 cup prepared mayonnaise*
*1 pound fresh or pasteurized jumbo lump crabmeat*
*¾ cup fresh bread crumbs*
*2 teaspoons paprika*
*4 tablespoons white wine or sherry*

*Preheat oven to 450°.*

1. Sauté the onions in the butter until transparent.
2. Add mushrooms, and sauté over medium heat. Allow the mushrooms to release their water. You do not need to evaporate it.
3. Add the soy sauce and bouquet garni, stir, and thicken with the cornstarch-and-water mixture until the mushrooms are very thick. Remove from heat, and set aside.
4. Blend together the egg, green pepper, and mustard in a blender or food processor.
5. Add the mayonnaise to the egg, pepper, and mustard mixture, blending together with a wire whisk. (Do not use a food processor.)
6. Add the mushrooms to the mayonnaise mixture, blend, then fold the crabmeat very carefully into that mixture.
7. Place in a large ovenproof casserole or in smaller casserole dishes. Sprinkle bread crumbs over the top evenly until completely covered. Dust with paprika, then sprinkle with wine or sherry. This keeps the bread crumbs from burning during the baking.
8. Place crabmeat in the oven, and bake for 15 minutes if the casserole is shallow (2 inches or less), adding 5 minutes for each inch of added casserole depth.

## Soft-Shelled Crabs with Chanterelles

APPROXIMATE PREPARATION TIME: **30** MINUTES
MAKES **4** SERVINGS

This very simple dish is devastatingly delicious, and every year I can hardly wait for the arrival of the first soft-shell crabs of the season, in about the middle of May, to prepare it.

> *8 soft-shell crabs, cleaned*
> *Flour*
> *Salt*
> *⅔ cup melted butter*
> *⅓ cup fresh lemon juice*
> *2 cups sliced chanterelles*

1. Coat the crabs with the lightly salted flour, and set aside.
2. Combine the butter and lemon juice, and add one fourth of it to a nonstick, coated sauté pan.
3. Sauté the chanterelles in the butter-lemon juice for two minutes. Remove, and keep warm. Leave the remaining liquid in the pan.
4. Start sautéing the crabs over a medium heat 2 at a time, in the butter-lemon mixture, replacing any of the lemon butter mixture as is necessary during sautéing. Sauté for 3 minutes on each side. Remove the crabs, and repeat until they are all done, keeping the finished crabs warm.
5. Add back the chanterelles, and serve over the crabs.

## Oysters and Scallops in Sorrel Sauce with Mushrooms

APPROXIMATE PREPARATION TIME: 1 HOUR
MAKES 4 SERVINGS

For those who love a little zest with their mushrooms, this dish will be a treat. It is made with sorrel, which is a tart herb. Also, the musty fragrance of the scallops goes very well with the earthiness of the mushrooms. A critical point to keep in mind when preparing this dish is that you want the oysters and mushrooms to be *just heated,* so that they both retain their raw, firm qualities, while still being warm within. Serve with creamed spinach, and a buttery, slightly aged Chardonnay like a St. Jean, or Batard Montrachet.

> *1 small bunch fresh sorrel, washed*
> *2 tablespoons white wine vinegar*
> *2 tablespoons water*
> *1 cup cream*
> *1 cup whole milk*
> *12 medium-sized opened oysters*
> *2 cups sea scallops, cut into quarters*
> *Chinese fish sauce to taste (see pages 144–145)*

*1 cup quartered mushroom caps, domestic or wild*
*1 tablespoon cornstarch mixed with ¼ cup water*

1. Make a *marié* by combining in a blender the sorrel, vinegar, and water.
2. In a double boiler begin heating the milk and cream after combining.
3. To the cream mixture add about 1½ tablespoons of the *marié*.
4. Add the oysters and scallops to the sauce, and bring to preferred saltiness with the fish sauce.
5. Add the mushrooms, and continue to heat about 5 minutes, or until the oysters have begun to curl at the edges. Both the mushrooms and oysters will be just done by this time. Immediately begin to thicken with the cornstarch-and-water mixture, and serve when desired thickness is attained.

## Sea Scallops with Straw Mushrooms, Szechuan Style

APPROXIMATE PREPARATION TIME: 1 HOUR
MAKES 4 SERVINGS

This is a spicy dish, using either Tabasco or Thai hot sauce. The Thai sauce is much preferable and more flavorful, but the Tabasco is a reasonable substitute. Serve this dish over plain steamed white rice, with a white Zinfandel.

*3 cups sea scallops, cut so that the pieces approximate the size of the*
*    straw mushrooms*
*1 15-ounce can straw mushrooms, drained and peeled*
*¼ cup peanut oil*
*¾ cup sliced scallions, cut into 1-inch pieces*
*1 clove garlic, minced*
*½ teaspoon minced fresh ginger*
*½ cup canned water chestnuts, halved*
*2 tablespoons Chinese oyster sauce*
*1 teaspoon Tabasco or Thai chili sauce*

1. Wash and drain the scallops, and set aside; do the same for the mushrooms.
2. Heat the oil in a wok. Add the scallions, garlic, and ginger, and stir-fry for 1 minute.
3. Add the water chestnuts, and stir-fry for another 30 seconds.

161

4. Add the mushrooms and scallops, and stir-fry for about 2 minutes or until the scallops are white but not broken at the edges.

5. Add the oyster sauce and hot sauce, and stir together for 30 seconds. Serve over white rice.

## Scallops Chardonnay with Basil Duxelles

APPROXIMATE PREPARATION TIME: 1½ HOURS
USEFUL ADVANCE PREPARATION: PREPARE HERB DUXELLES WITH BASIL (SEE
  PAGE 63). ALSO HAVE PUFF PASTRY SHELLS READY.
MAKES 4 SERVINGS

The wine and basil are counterpointed by the earthy mushrooms in this preparation. Serve with sautéed sliced artichoke bottoms with fresh dill, and a Chardonnay.

*1 pound bay scallops*
*1 cup heavy cream*
*⅓ cup Chardonnay, or dry white wine*
*2 tablespoons Herb Duxelles with basil*
*1 teaspoon fresh chopped basil*
*2 tablespoons sifted flour*
*2 tablespoons melted butter*
*4 ready-to-serve puff pastry shells, 2½ inch squares with center cut
    out (see page 96)*
*Chinese fish sauce to taste (see pages 144–145)*

1. Rinse and drain the scallops, and set aside.
2. Place the cream, Chardonnay, and Herb Duxelles in a double boiler, and heat without boiling.
3. Make a roux by mixing the butter and flour, and heating in a sauté pan until the mixture becomes a light golden color.
4. Slowly add the roux to the double boiler mixture, stirring until it begins to thicken. Begin to warm the puff pastry shells.
5. Add the scallops to the sauce. Season the sauce to desired saltiness with the fish sauce. The scallops will cook in the heated sauce without more heat being added. They should be a little underdone in the center.
6. Pour the scallops into the heated puff pastry shells, and serve.

# Poached Oysters Callowhill

APPROXIMATE PREPARATION TIME: 1 HOUR
USEFUL ADVANCE PREPARATION: PREPARE BÉCHAMEL SAUCE (15 MINUTES).
MAKES 4 SERVINGS

This appetizer was named to commemorate the establishment of Reading's first historic district. The story of the dish's conception, however, goes back to a rainy afternoon in New Orleans in 1977. The French Quarter was quite deserted, and I was strolling the streets when a restaurant with the name "Desire" caught my eye. The combination of my love for Tennessee Williams and my now empty stomach led me through its doors. I sat down, and ordered a bottle of Chablis and two dozen fresh raw oysters.

When the waiter brought my lunch, he proceeded to combine the condiments of horseradish, Tabasco, and some fresh lemon juice for me to use on the oysters. This was my first experience with horseradish on oysters, and the taste was memorable. On returning to Reading, I modified the approach by combining a béchamel sauce with a prepared horseradish. The last step was to get the salt component, which I decided to take from a Chinese fish sauce (see pages 144–145), and then to add some fresh mushrooms for texture contrast. It's also important to cook the oysters till the ends *just begin* to curl. Try to buy large plump jumbo oysters, already opened—unless you enjoy opening your own, a pursuit that can be hazardous for a novice. Serve with a Heitz Chablis.

*½ cup béchamel sauce (see pages 126–127)*
*1 tablespoon prepared horseradish*
*Chinese fish sauce to taste (see pages 144–145), or salted fish stock*
*½ cup fresh mushrooms, sliced thin and blanched*
*Water*
*12 half-shells of large oysters, rinsed and scrubbed*
*Chopped parsley*

1. Prepare the sauce first by combining the béchamel, the horseradish, and the fish sauce. Set aside. Add the sliced mushrooms to the sauce.

2. In a shallow saucepan, lightly salt water, and bring to a boil. Reduce to a simmer. Add the oysters. Cook just until the oysters begin to curl at the edges. The oysters should be warm inside but retain the texture of raw oysters. Begin to heat sauce. Remove oysters from water, and pat dry.

3. Place oysters on a half-shell, and cover with the heated sauce. Sprinkle with chopped parsley.

CHAPTER NINE

# Mushrooms with Poultry

As a group poultry can be the easiest or most difficult of meats to cook. From tender, domesticated chickens to farm-grown geese and Muscovy ducks, the books generally assume that the bird you are working with is tender. This is not always the case. Some birds, especially the game variety, are often less than tender, and even domestic turkeys can be quite tough if they are too old or improperly fed. Chicken is generally so popular because it is tender, even though it does not have as interesting flavors as the wild varieties. Methods used in the last century in France describe hanging wild birds for several days until they putrified, so that the natural enzymatic process of decay would break down the muscle fiber responsible for the toughness. Of course, the danger from bacterial infection became so great that this method of tenderizing lost its popularity in this century.

The best method of getting a tender bird is still to know your source of supply, like your butcher, and rely on his judgment. On the other hand, some birds are stubbornly tough in most cases (geese and Muscovy ducks, to name just a couple), and they require special cooking methods to make them tender. In Europe, birds are usually slaughtered when they are quite young, and this increases the chances that they will be tender. The Europeans are accustomed to eating their birds medium rare, as opposed to well done, which is the way Americans are accustomed to eating them. When a bird is not quite cooked through, it is more tender than when cooked to medium or more. A friend of mine who owns and operates a well-known Chinese restaurant in California once told me that duck is excellent when either just barely cooked or cooked to shreds. Anything in between yields a tough bird, and the margin for error is not very great. I recommend that you eat your bird with as little doneness as you can stand (medium rare), and your chances for a tender product will be much greater. You must also understand that some birds are naturally *drier* than other birds (guinea hens, for instance), because they lack the natural fat content of domesticated poultry, and that no amount of care will give the bird more moisture than what it is naturally endowed with. In those instances the practice of larding is useful.

Larding can be used for almost any kind of game birds. Larding adds fat during cooking that you would otherwise get naturally from, for instance, a turkey, which during roasting sweats off its own fat, which is then added back to keep the bird moist (basting). Bacon is often used for larding game birds, but I prefer duck, chicken, or even veal fat. These are rich flavor sources without the smoky flavor of the bacon or pork rind. Cover the bird with the fat, which will baste the bird during roasting and keep it moist, but remember to remove it 15 minutes before the end of the cooking time, or the bird will not brown. Also, remember to cover the tips of the wings and drumsticks with foil or fat to prevent scorching them.

Using mushrooms with poultry can lead to interesting flavor combinations. Birds are paired with more types of sauces than you can imagine. Fruit sauces are common, as are sauces made with honey and other sweet ingredients. Chanterelles come into their own here, and I believe they are better with poultry than with anything else, because their fruity, apricotlike flavor fits perfectly with the richer sauces used on birds. Also, the flavor of morels and cepes are well expressed with poultry, because the flavor of the flesh does not compete with the mushrooms as much as the stronger tasting meats do.

Birds have another characteristic: the cavity left when the insides are removed literally begs to be filled with some rich, ample substance. Here again, mushrooms are very useful and can provide an opportunity for another flavor contrast to the bird. The fillings described here are mostly offshoots of duxelles recipes and are very easy to prepare, especially because you have so much leeway in the amount of liquid you leave in the duxelles. I make the duxelles, but instead of evaporating all of the liquid, I add bread crumbs to soak it up and then an egg to bind bread crumbs and duxelles. Remember to readjust the seasoning because the bread crumbs will dilute the flavor of the duxelles. In some instances I have used the duxelles by itself, and that's explained in the specific recipes.

# Mushrooms with Chicken and Turkey

## Roast Chicken with Bread and Mushroom Stuffing

**APPROXIMATE PREPARATION TIME: 4 TO 5 HOURS**
**USEFUL ADVANCE PREPARATION: CUT OFF CRUSTS OF BREAD, CUT BREAD INTO**
**CUBES, AND SPREAD ON A COOKIE SHEET TO DRY THE NIGHT BEFORE.**
**MAKES 4 SERVINGS**

This recipe has delighted our family for three generations and continues to be a holiday favorite. Traditional holiday side dishes are called for here, but Sauerkraut with Dried Mushrooms and Peas (see pages 255–256) is also excellent. Mushrooms in *Crème Fraîche* (see page 130) is excellent too.

*1 pound loaf of white bread, sliced and cubed*
*1 4-to-6-pound roasting chicken*
*Salt*
*Celery leaves*
*1 medium onion, whole*
*2 handfuls parsley, stems removed*
*1 medium onion, chopped*
*¼ pound butter*
*½ pound mushrooms, chopped (choose a flavorful gill variety such*
*    as fresh chanterelles or shiitake)*
*3 ribs celery*
*3 eggs*
*Salt to taste and freshly ground pepper*
*1 medium onion, sliced*
*1 cup dry sherry wine*
*4 teaspoons cornstarch and ½ cup water*

*Preheat oven to 350°.*

1. The day before, cut the crusts off the bread, cut into cubes, and spread on a cookie sheet to dry.
2. The following day, rinse chicken. Dry well with paper towels inside and out. Set aside.
3. Place neck, heart, gizzard, and wing tips of chicken in a 3-quart pot. Cover with cold water and bring to a simmer. Skim off the solids, which will

float to the top. Add salt, the leaves from the celery, 1 whole onion, and a few sprigs of the parsley. Simmer until meat is tender.

4. Sauté chopped onion in ¼ pound butter until soft.

5. Add mushrooms, and sauté until most of moisture has evaporated.

6. While mushrooms are cooking, cut celery into small pieces, and put into a blender or food processor with 3 eggs and parsley. Process for a nice puree.

7. Add egg mixture to bread cubes in a large bowl, and toss lightly until well mixed.

8. Add onions and mushrooms. Mix well, and add salt to taste.

9. Remove giblets from pot, reserving broth.

10. Stuff the chicken loosely. (If all the filling does not fit, place remainder in a separate ovenproof dish. Cover with aluminum foil, and bake with the chicken during last 30 to 45 minutes of roasting.)

11. Fasten openings securely with needle and thread or small cooking skewers.

12. Place chicken on a rack in a baking pan. Sprinkle with salt and freshly ground pepper. Put sliced onion on top of chicken, and place pan in the oven.

13. Baste with dry sherry wine, ¼ cup at a time, at ½-hour intervals, and roast until the bird is a nice golden brown or when the thigh bone can be easily moved at the body of the chicken. This may take 2 to 2½ hours, or a bit longer.

14. When chicken is done, remove it from the pan, place on a heated platter, cover with aluminum foil and kitchen towel to keep warm.

15. Add 1 cup of broth to drippings in roasting pan. Put pan on direct heat (medium), and scrape up the particles that adhere to the pan. If there is too much fat in the pan, take it off the fire, tilt the pan, and skim off the fat.

16. Add 2 more cups of broth to the pan. (If there is not enough broth, add water to make 2 cups.) Simmer for a few minutes.

17. Mix the cornstarch in ½ cup water, stir well, and add to sauce, stirring until the sauce is smooth and thickened.

18. Adjust salt to taste. Strain into a heated sauce boat, and serve with a garnish of your choice.

**167**

## Chicken Rosenthal

APPROXIMATE PREPARATION TIME: 1 HOUR
USEFUL ADVANCE PREPARATION: PREPARE MOREL SAUCE ROSENTHAL (SEE
   PAGES 82–83).
MAKES 4 SERVINGS

In addition to the basic Morel Sauce Rosenthal, cultivated mushrooms can be sautéed with butter and onion, and added to this dish without masking the flavor of the morels. Use about 3 to 6 ounces of mushrooms and sauté (see pages 50–51). Serve with new potatoes sprinkled with dill and coated with butter. Accompany with a Stag's Leap Merlot.

*Salt and pepper to taste*
*1 3-to-4-pound chicken, cut into serving pieces and lightly coated*
   *with flour*
*5 tablespoons peanut, vegetable, or corn oil*
*2½ cups Morel Sauce Rosenthal*

1. Salt and pepper the chicken pieces.
2. Begin to heat a heavy skillet for 1 minute, then add enough cooking oil to make a depth of ⅛ inch in the skillet. When the oil is lightly bubbling, add the chicken pieces, and cook until brown on both sides. This will take about 4 to 5 minutes. Drain off excess oil, and reduce heat.
3. Pour sauce over chicken, and continue to cook, covered, until the chicken is done.

## Chicken with Oyster Mushrooms

APPROXIMATE PREPARATION TIME: 20 TO 30 MINUTES
USEFUL ADVANCE PREPARATION: THIS RECIPE UTILIZES LEFTOVER, COOKED
   CHICKEN MEAT.
MAKES 4 SERVINGS

This recipe is for leftover chicken or turkey meat. Any part of the cooked carcass can be used, white or dark meat. It is very quick and satisfying. Serve over toast triangles, and with a Chablis.

*1½ cups heavy cream*
*½ cup chicken stock*

*1 tablespoon cream sherry*
*1 teaspoon fresh, crushed garlic*
*1 tablespoon prosciutto or Westphalian ham, chopped fine*
*1 tablespoon onion, chopped fine*
*12 ounces cooked chicken or turkey meat from breast, cut into 2-
    inch strips*
*8 ounces fresh oyster mushrooms, sliced into 2-inch strips*
*Salt and pepper to taste*
*2 tablespoons cornstarch mixed with ⅓ cup water*

1. Combine all the ingredients except the cornstarch mixture in a heavy skillet. You may also want to save the salting until the dish is slightly heated.

2. Heat until simmering over a medium flame, then continue simmering over a low flame for 5 minutes.

3. Thicken with the cornstarch-and-water mixture, and adjust for salt as necessary. Serve.

## Chicken with Cepes and Pine Nuts

**APPROXIMATE PREPARATION TIME: 1 HOUR**
**MAKES 4 SERVINGS**

This is a very straightforward dish made magnificent by the addition of *Boletus edulis* (cepes). Accompany with mashed potatoes, and Cabernet Sauvignon Blanc or any white Bordeaux.

*¼ cup vegetable oil*
*Thighs and drumsticks of two 5-pound chickens, separated from
    each other*
*1 medium onion, sliced thin*
*2 cups water*
*1 ounce dried cepes*
*1 teaspoon sugar*
*1 teaspoon salt*
*1 tablespoon soy sauce*
*1 tablespoon cornstarch mixed with ⅓ cup water*
*1 small clove garlic, crushed*
*⅓ cup pine nuts*

1. Place a heavy skillet over a medium flame, and heat for 1 minute.

**169**

2. Add the vegetable oil, and heat for 1 minute.

3. When the oil is heated, add chicken pieces, and brown them on each side for about 1 minute per side. Make sure that the chicken is slightly browned before removing from the pan. You may have to do this operation twice if all the chicken pieces do not fit into the pan in the first browning. If this becomes necessary, use more vegetable oil as needed.

4. Remove chicken from pan, and place on a plate that has been covered with a paper towel to absorb any excess fat or oil. Reduce heat to low flame.

5. Drain all but 1 tablespoon of oil and fat remaining in pan. Scrape any hardened fat or grease out of the pan, and discard. Make sure to retain 1 tablespoon of liquid in pan.

6. Add onions, and sauté in the fat-oil for 1 minute. Add water, cepes, sugar, salt, and soy sauce and bring to a boil. Reduce quickly to a simmer, and allow to simmer for 15 minutes, uncovered. While stirring, slowly add the cornstarch-and-water mixture to thicken. Add crushed garlic and pine nuts. Add chicken, and resume simmering. Cover, and let simmer for about 20 to 30 minutes, or until the chicken is done. Stir occasionally to prevent any of the solids from sticking to the skillet. Remove chicken from skillet, place on a serving dish, and cover with the cepes and remaining liquid. Correct for salt if necessary.

## Chicken with Chanterelles My Father's Way

APPROXIMATE PREPARATION TIME: **2** HOURS
USEFUL ADVANCE PREPARATION: PREPARE CHANTERELLE DUXELLES (SEE PAGE **66**).
MAKES **4** SERVINGS

This was one of the first dishes I learned to make under my father's tutelage. The flavor of the chanterelles is very subtle and exists only in the filling. Serve with rice tossed with more of the Chanterelle Duxelles.

*2 double sets of boneless chicken breasts, skin removed*
*Salt and pepper*
*1 cup Chanterelle Duxelles*
*1 cup chicken broth*
*1 cup heavy cream*
*½ teaspoon bouquet garni, dried*
*1 small onion, chopped*

*3 tablespoons butter*
*3 tablespoons flour*
*Paprika*

*Preheat oven to 450°.*

1.  Split each set of breasts so that you have 4 single breasts. Pound each breast until it is ⅛ inch thick, and sprinkle with salt and pepper.

2.  Place ¼ cup of the duxelles on one side of each pounded breast and roll it up into a roulade. Pat dry and set aside. Repeat with other 3 breasts.

3.  Combine the chicken broth, cream, and bouquet garni in a saucepan, and gradually bring up the heat without boiling. Season with salt and pepper. Do not allow the liquid to evaporate. Remove from heat.

4.  In a sauté pan, gently toss the onions in the butter for about 2 minutes, then sprinkle with the flour, and stir over a low heat for about 3 minutes. Add the creamed chicken broth mixture, and stir until it becomes thick.

5.  Place the chicken pieces in an ovenproof dish that will hold them all, and cover with the sauce. Sprinkle with paprika. Cover, place in the oven, and cook for 15 minutes. Remove from oven, and place over a bed of the rice.

## Apricoted Cornish Hens with Chanterelles

**APPROXIMATE PREPARATION TIME: 2 HOURS**
**USEFUL ADVANCE PREPARATION: PREPARE STUFFING BREAD, OR PURCHASE**
        **MIX. IF MAKING OWN STUFFING, CUT BREAD INTO VERY SMALL ( ⅛-**
        **INCH) CHUNKS.**
**MAKES 6 SERVINGS**

This is another of the recipes given to me by Patti Ballard of Bargetto Winery in Soquel, California. She has the dubious distinction of having made the world's only chanterelle wine. By Patti's own admission it was not one of her most successful efforts. As she said to me, "Have you ever seen gray wine?" Fortunately, the following combination, served with wild rice, is much more satisfying. It comes from her *Everyday Cooking with Wine,* published by the Wine Appreciation Guild.

*4 cups sliced chanterelles*
*1 large white onion, diced*
*3 stalks celery with leaves, diced*

**171**

*1 clove garlic, crushed*
*3 tablespoons butter*
*6 cups commercial stuffing mix (plain)*
*2½ cups dried apricots, snipped in half*
*2 cups Bargetto apricot wine*
*6 Cornish game hens, viscerated, rinsed, and patted dry*
*8 tablespoons butter*

*Preheat oven to 375°.*

1. Sauté chanterelles, onion, celery, and garlic in butter until onions are transparent.

2. Add mixture to stuffing mix, and toss until well blended. Add the dried apricots, and toss again. Sprinkle with 1 cup apricot wine, mix well.

3. Stuff hens lightly to allow expansion of dressing during baking. Baste with butter.

4. Roast in preheated oven for 45 minutes to an hour, basting every 15 minutes with the remaining apricot wine.

## Turkey with Belon Oyster and Duxelles Stuffing

APPROXIMATE PREPARATION TIME: **6 TO 7 HOURS**
USEFUL ADVANCE PREPARATION: **PREPARE OYSTER DUXELLES (PAGE 63), AND DRY BREAD CRUMBS IN ADVANCE.**
MAKES **8 TO 10** SERVINGS

The strong metallic, flavor of Belon oysters comes across more forcefully than the blue-point type we are accustomed to buying, but blue-points are suitable if the Belons are unobtainable. The idea in this recipe is to contrast the rich oyster flavor with the flavor of mushrooms. Accompany with traditional Thanksgiving side dishes such as beet and cranberry salad.

*6 cups Oyster Duxelles, using Belon oysters*
*4 to 5 cups dried bread crumbs*
*3 whole eggs*
*½ cup chopped celery*
*2 tablespoons salt*
*1 whole 12-to-15-pound turkey, ready to roast*

*1 ounce lard or butter*
*¼ cup wine (optional)*

*Preheat oven to 325°.*

1. Combine the duxelles with the bread crumbs. Use enough bread crumbs to absorb the liquid left in the duxelles. Adjust this mixture for salt.

2. In a blender, combine the eggs and celery. Work this into the duxelles-bread crumb mix.

3. If you have a microwave oven, test a small amount (about 1 teaspoon) of this mixture for 30 seconds to see how it sets. If it is too runny, add some bread crumbs. If it is too stiff, add some water (or oyster juice, if you have it) to the mix, and try it again. If you do not have a microwave oven, simply fry the mix in some butter and see how it sets.

4. Salt the turkey inside and out, and fill loosely with the stuffing. Spread the exposed surface with lard or butter. Place the turkey in the oven, and roast uncovered for about 5½ hours, basting every ½ hour with wine and the bird's own juices. The turkey is done when the drumsticks move easily when bent. Also, it can be tested by placing a meat thermometer inside it. A reading of 190° indicates doneness.

# Mushrooms with Duck

Duckling may be the most versatile meat available. Rich, stock-based sauces go with it as well as fruit does. I like using chanterelles with duck because the richness of the meat matches the fruitiness of the mushrooms.

Although whole-roasting is the most popular way to prepare duck, I prefer it boned. I dislike fighting with the breast and thigh bones to get to the meat. Therefore, the succeeding recipes include several in which the duck is fully boned. Learning the technique for boning takes more patience than skill, but it can be mastered.

### A Note on Boning Duck

To bone a duck, remove the bag of organs from the cavity and reserve for making sauce another time. Begin by making an incision through the skin and fat, down the middle of the back and (on the other side) down the middle of the breastbone—running your knife along the length of the bird. (The knife you use should be as narrow and as sharp as possible. This operation is best carried out on a solid, nonslip surface, like a wooden table.) The incision should be down to the flesh but not cutting into it.

Remove the wings from the body. Next remove the drumsticks, using this method: Take the end of the drumstick and bend it so that the bone snaps off the thigh bone. You will hear it snap when this happens. Cut the skin away from the outer tip of the drumstick, and pull the drumstick bone out as far as you can. Slip the blade of your knife between the flesh and the bone to where the thighbone joins the drumstick, and sever the connecting tissue holding the thigh to the drumstick. Cut the remaining drumstick flesh from the drumstick bone, and pull away the bone until it is free of the flesh. Repeat for the other side of the bird.

Begin removing the skin from the duck by running your knife between the skin, with its layer of fat, and the flesh, keeping the skin portion in one piece on either side of the duck. When you are finished, you should have two pieces of fat-skin, and the thigh meat and bone and breast still attached to the body. Set the fat-skin aside. Remove the breast meat from the carcass. Then with your hands break the thigh from the body and sever the bone. Keep the meat as intact as possible. Repeat for the other side. You should now have completely boneless meat.

Save the leg bones and carcass for stock. Try to save the fat-skin in one piece for wrapping other birds during roasting. To do so, lay it on a flat surface and begin removing the fat from the skin. This should be done with a long, sharp fish knife, keeping the knife parallel to the table as you are skinning to minimize breaking or tearing the skin. You can safely freeze the skin for up to 2 months.

## Duck with Apricots and Chanterelles

APPROXIMATE PREPARATION TIME: **2 TO 3 HOURS**
USEFUL ADVANCE PREPARATION: **PREPARE CHANTERELLE SAUCE (SEE PAGES 89–90) AND CHANTERELLE DUXELLES (SEE PAGE 66).**
MAKES **4** SERVINGS

Apricots have the most affinity with the flavor of chanterelles, simply because they are the most alike. This recipe uses the combination twice—once, with tendered dried apricots in the duxelles, and again with apricot liqueur in the sauce. Serve with wild rice, and a Mosel or Rheingau.

*1 cup Chanterelle Duxelles, using the dried, reconstituted*
*    mushrooms from the sauce (instead of adding them to the*
*    sauce mixture as directed on page 66). If more chanterelles*
*    are required to make 1 cup, then reconstitute dried*
*    chanterelles as needed.*
*2 cups Chanterelle Sauce*
*2 4-to-5-pound whole ducks, preferably young Long Island*
*    ducklings*

*Preheat oven to 450°.*

1. Prepare the Chanterelles Duxelles and the Chanterelle Sauce. Keep sauce warm, and set aside.

2. Remove the ducks from their wrapping, and pat them dry. Remove the bag of organs from the cavities, and bone each bird, as described on pages 173–174. Retain defatted skin.

3. Place ¼ cup of the duxelles on top of each breast-thigh meat portion. Wrap the defatted skin tightly around the duxelles-duck meat, using just enough to cover the top of the meat and overlap slightly underneath. The thigh and the breast meat should be wrapped together, touching end-to-end so that the final product is about 6 to 8 inches long from the end of the breast to the end of the thigh. Repeat for the other portions.

4. Place the duck portions smooth side up in a roasting pan with a rack. Roast in the oven for 30 minutes. When finished, the duck should be about medium rare with a crispy skin. Cover with the sauce.

## Duck with Oyster Mushrooms and Cassis-Zinfandel Sauce

APPROXIMATE PREPARATION TIME: 1 HOUR FOR BONED DUCK; 2 HOURS FOR
    WHOLE ROAST DUCK
MAKES 4 SERVINGS

The fruit sauce in this recipe is not quite as sweet as what you may be used to. The presence of the Zinfandel makes the flavor drier and also adds to the fruity quality. Use black-currant vinegar for this recipe if you can, but red-wine vinegar will do if it is of a good quality. Serve with risotto cooked in poultry stock, and Ridge Zinfandel.

*2 4-pound ducklings*
*1 cup Zinfandel*
*4 teaspoons soy sauce*
*1 teaspoon black-currant vinegar, or red-wine vinegar*
*2 teaspoons crème de cassis*
*2 teaspoons sugar*
*1 teaspoon lemon juice*
*2 cups oyster mushrooms, sliced*
*2 teaspoons butter*
*1 tablespoon arrowroot mixed with 1/3 cup water*

*Preheat oven to 350°.*

1. Bone the duck as described (pages 173–174) or prepare for whole roasting. For whole roasting, pat the ducks dry, and place on an oven rack in a roasting pan. Roast in the oven for 1½ hours or until tender.

2. Combine the wine, soy sauce, vinegar, cassis, sugar, and lemon juice in a saucepan, and bring to a simmer.

3. While the sauce simmers, sauté the mushrooms in the butter in a sauté pan. Add the mushrooms to the sauce.

4. Thicken the sauce with arrowroot-and-water mixture, and serve with the duck.

VARIATION
## Duck with Jaegermeister and Steinpilze

APPROXIMATE PREPARATION TIME: 1 HOUR FOR BONED DUCK; 2 HOURS FOR
        WHOLE ROAST DUCK
MAKES 4 SERVINGS

This recipe is prepared the same way as in Duck with Oyster Mushrooms (pages 175–176) except that you replace the crème de cassis with Jaegermeister, which is a German herbal liqueur. Also, replace the oyster mushrooms with *Steinpilze*, which are the same as cepes, or *Boletus edulis*. Serve with buttered egg noodles spiced with fresh savory.

# Duck Steaks with Cepes

APPROXIMATE PREPARATION TIME: 1 HOUR
MAKES 4 SERVINGS

This is one of the most elegant ways to enjoy duck. The method of serving the duck in this fashion is utilized both in China and in France. The raw power of the cepes gives the normally delicate duckling flavors some zing. If fresh cepes are not available, you can use domestic mushrooms for the presentation part, but you must have the dried cepes for the sauce. Accompany this dish with salsify sprinkled with ground fenugreek, a Middle Eastern herb available in most specialty food stores. Serve with Pinot Noir from Chalone or Acacia.

*4 single duck breasts*
*½ cup cooking oil*
*1 ounce dried cepes*
*2 cups duck or chicken stock*
*1 teaspoon salt*
*1 teaspoon sugar*
*1 tablespoon soy sauce*
*1 tablespoon arrowroot mixed with ⅓ cup water (optional)*
*4 large caps cepes or domestic mushrooms*
*¼ cup chopped onions*
*2 tablespoons butter*
*Salt*

1. Pat the duck breasts dry. Heat the oil in a sauté pan, and begin cooking the duck breasts over a medium flame in the oil, making sure to brown the breasts about 2 minutes on all sides. When the ducks are finished (they should be medium rare), set them aside and keep them warm.

2. Make the sauce by combining the cepes, stock, salt, sugar, and soy sauce in a saucepan and bringing to a boil. Let simmer for 20 minutes, making sure to replace any of the evaporated stock with water. The sauce may be thickened with a little arrowroot-and-water mixture or left in its juicy state.

3. Slice the mushroom caps about ¼-inch thick. Over a medium heat, sauté the onions in the butter till transparent. Lower the heat, and add the mushrooms, and cook slowly for 10 minutes, covered, salting to season. Add remaining saucepan-mixture liquid to the sauce.

4. Slice the duck. To serve, alternate pieces of duck with slices of mushroom. Do this for all four portions, and pour the sauce over them.

177

# Mushrooms with Game Birds

## Quail with Chanterelles, Truffles, and Pine Nuts

APPROXIMATE PREPARATION TIME: 1 HOUR
USEFUL ADVANCE PREPARATION: PREPARE CHANTERELLE DUXELLES (SEE PAGE
    66), AND TRUFFLE CREAM SAUCE (SEE PAGES 85–86)
MAKES 4 SERVINGS

For formal dining, serve as a game course (1 bird per person). As a main course, serve with quick-sautéed snap peas in lemon butter and California Gamay.

> *8 quail, ready to roast*
> *Salt*
> *2 cups Chanterelle Duxelles*
> *⅓ cup pine nuts, toasted*
> *8 pieces of duck fat or pork fat, or 16 strips of bacon*
> *2 cups Truffle Cream Sauce*

*Preheat oven to 450°.*

1. Remove the gizzards and kidneys from the quail. Salt the cavity and the outer surface of the bird.
2. Heat the Chanterelle Duxelles, and add the pine nuts to it.
3. Stuff the mixture into birds, and cover them with the fat, or 2 pieces each of the bacon, making sure that the wing tips are covered with foil.
4. Roast the bird on a rack fitted into a roasting pan for 15 minutes. Remove the remaining fat and continue to roast for 10 more minutes. The bird should be done by this time. Cover with the heated sauce. Allow 2 birds per person.

# Quail with Crayfish and Morels in Cream

**APPROXIMATE PREPARATION TIME: 1 HOUR**
**USEFUL ADVANCE PREPARATION: PREPARE MOREL CREAM SAUCE (SEE PAGE 84)**
**MAKES 4 SERVINGS**

Embed these birds on a warm mattress of brown rice. Serve with a rich Chardonnay.

*8 quail, ready to roast*
*Salt to taste*
*½ cup onions, chopped*
*3 cloves garlic, minced*
*¼ cup butter, melted*
*¾ cup (3 ounces) crayfish meat, peeled, deveined, and cooked\**
*1½ cups fresh wild mushrooms*
*1 teaspoon lemon juice*
*½ teaspoon Tabasco sauce*
*½ teaspoon salt, or to taste*
*8 pieces of duck fat or pork fat, or 16 strips of bacon*
*2 cups Morel Cream Sauce*

*Preheat oven to 450°.*

1. Prepare the quail by removing the insides, and salting them inside and out.
2. Sauté the onions and garlic in the butter for 2 minutes, or until the onions become transparent.
3. Add the crayfish, mushrooms, lemon juice, Tabasco, and salt, and continue to sauté for another 3 minutes. Adjust for salt, and cook until all the liquid has evaporated.
4. Stuff the quail with crayfish-mushroom mixture. Cover the bird with the fat or 2 pieces each of the bacon, and roast on a rack fitted into a roasting pan 15 minutes. Remove the fat, and continue to roast for another 10 minutes. Serve, covered with the sauce.

*Note: Outside Louisiana, crayfish tails or meat are almost always purchased cooked.

**179**

## Squab with Savory-Mushroom Stuffing

APPROXIMATE PREPARATION TIME: 1 HOUR
USEFUL ADVANCE PREPARATION: PREPARE BASIC MUSHROOM DUXELLES (SEE
    PAGE 61 ) AND SAUCE BONCHAMPI (SEE PAGE 80).
MAKES 4 SERVINGS

Young pigeon is one of the most delectable game birds available. This version is stuffed with a duxelles filling highlighted by savory, which is a natural complement to the flavor of domestic mushrooms. It is not as necessary to cover 2 squabs with fat as in the recipes for quail, because these birds have more fat than quail does. You may consider this an optional step. Serve with Stir-Fried Mushrooms (see pages 120–121) and Pinot Noir.

*2 cups Basic Mushroom Duxelles recipe*
*½ teaspoon crushed savory, dried, or 1 teaspoon fresh chopped*
    *savory*
*1 cup bread crumbs, mixed with ½ teaspoon salt*
*Salt to taste*
*1 beaten egg*
*¼ cup chopped celery*
*4 fresh squab*
*4 pieces duck fat large enough to cover squab while roasting*
    *(optional)*
*2 cups Sauce Bonchampi*

*Preheat oven to 450°.*

1. Heat the duxelles, and blend with the savory and bread crumbs. Adjust for salt.

2. Blend together the egg and the celery in a blender until a puree is formed, and mix with the stuffing.

3. Stuff the birds with the stuffing, and tie the legs together. Cover with the fat (optional), and place on a roasting pan.

4. Roast the birds for 15 minutes. Then remove them from the oven, and move the fat so that only the wing tips are covered. Leave the rest of the bird uncovered so that it will brown, and roast 10 minutes. Begin heating the sauce.

5. Remove the birds from the oven, and serve with the sauce.

*The forms of wild mushrooms*

*Joe's Wild Mushroom Soup (pages 96–97)*

*Shiitake and Sausage Sauté (page 121)*

*Morel Croissant (page 113)*

*Duck with Oyster Mushrooms and Cassis-Zinfandel Sauce*
*(pages 175–176)*

*Piroshki (pages 136–137)*

*Salmon in Lobster Sauce with Cepes*
*(page 150)*

*Chicken with Oyster Mushrooms*
*(pages 168–169)*

*Strip Steaks with Sirloin Mushrooms*
*(pages 185–186)*

*Jack's Spicy Beef Casserole (page 189)*

*Scotch Roebuck Casserole (pages 223–224)*

*Veal Rosenthal (page 196)*

*Domestic Mushrooms with Rice (page 244)*

*Monterey Lemon Torte (pages 278–279) and Raspberry Pear Stefan*
*(pages 286–287) with Meringue Mushrooms (page 294)*

# Partridge in Hominy with Morels and Caraway

**APPROXIMATE PREPARATION TIME: 2 HOURS**
**MAKES 4 SERVINGS**

These tiny birds are paired and combined with caraway and morels, then set on a bed of hominy cooked in the mushroom-caraway extract.

*1 ounce dried morels*
*3 cups water*
*2 teaspoons salt*
*1 teaspoon sugar*
*1 tablespoon soy sauce*
*½ teaspoon caraway seeds*
*¾ cup hominy grits*
*2 tablespoons butter*
*8 partridges*
*2 tablespoons green pepper, chopped fine*
*8 pieces duck fat large enough to cover a bird while roasting or 8*
*    strips bacon (1 strip per bird)*
*Salt and pepper*

*Preheat oven to 450°.*

1. Combine the morels with the water, salt, sugar, and soy sauce in a saucepan, and bring to a boil. Let simmer uncovered for 20 minutes.

2. Remove the morels from the saucepan, and set aside to cool. When cool, chop them fine, and set aside.

3. Bring morels mixture back to a simmer, and add the caraway seeds. Let simmer for another 10 minutes, adding back any liquid that evaporates. With a strainer, remove the caraway seeds.

4. To the simmering liquid, slowly add the hominy grits and butter, while stirring. The mixture will begin to thicken. Lower the heat, and continue to cook the grits, uncovered, for about 1 hour, stirring often.

5. While the grits are cooking, stuff the partridges with the chopped morels and green pepper, season birds to taste, and roast them in the oven for 20 minutes. Remember to cover the partridge with some bacon or fat before roasting and to remove the fat 10 minutes before finishing, to insure that the birds brown.

6. When finished roasting, remove the partridges from the oven, and place them on a serving dish that has been covered with the hominy grits.

**181**

## Roast Pheasant True and False

APPROXIMATE PREPARATION TIME: 1½ HOURS
ADVANCE PREPARATION: SOAK SLICED TRUFFLE IN PORT FOR 2 HOURS.
MAKES 4 SERVINGS

Fresh or canned truffles can be used in this recipe. It also utilizes the *Totentrompete,* or champignon de mort, or black trumpet mushroom, also called the false truffle—hence the name of this dish. The truffles add earthiness to the dish, and the black trumpets have a very buttery characteristic unlike any mushroom I know. The procedure for making the sauce is the usual for dried mushrooms, e.g., Cepe Sauce (pages 76–77). If the mushrooms you get are fresh, then boil these until the liquid from the boiling is black, about 20 minutes. If it doesn't get black, you have to add more mushrooms. Then proceed with the rest of the recipe as if you were using dried mushrooms. Or, you can dry your mushrooms (pages 309–311) and proceed as directed. Serve with potatoes whipped with coarse ground black pepper and crushed fresh garlic.

*2 2½-pound pheasants ready-to-cook*
*½ ounce dried black trumpet mushrooms*
*3 cups water*
*1 tablespoon soy sauce*
*1 teaspoon salt*
*1 teaspoon sugar*
*1 tablespoon port*
*1 small truffle, sliced thin, that has soaked in port wine at least 2*
*  hours*
*1 tablespoon arrowroot mixed with ¼ cup water*

*Preheat oven to 450°.*

1. Remove the breast, leg, and thigh from the breastbone in one piece. Repeat for the other side and for the other bird. Discard the carcass.

2. Place the four pieces, skin side up, on a rack and set in a roasting pan. Roast in the oven for ½ hour, or until the meat is medium rare.

3. While the pheasant is roasting, make the sauce by combining the rest of the ingredients, except the arrowroot. Bring to a boil, and simmer for 20 minutes. Let the liquid reduce to 1½ cups liquid.

4. Thicken the sauce with the arrowroot-and-water mixture, and keep warm until the pheasant is done.

## Pheasant with Pommery Mustard and Truffles

**APPROXIMATE PREPARATION TIME:** 1½ HOURS
**MAKES 4 SERVINGS**

Accompany this with pasta tossed with fine-chopped truffles, onions, and butter, and a dry Bordeaux or Sauvignon Blanc.

*2 2½-pound ready-to-cook pheasants*
*1 cup strong chicken, pheasant, or veal stock (see pages 72–73)*
*2 ounces Pommery mustard*
*2 ounces soy sauce*
*1 tablespoon garlic oil or granulated garlic, or minced fresh garlic*
*1 tablespoon honey*
*1 small truffle, sliced thin, which has been soaked in port*
*1 tablespoon cornstarch mixed with ¼ cup water*

*Preheat oven to 450°.*

1. Remove the breast, leg, and thigh from the breastbone in one piece. Repeat for the other side and for the other bird. Discard the carcasses.
2. Place the 4 pieces, skin side up, on a roasting rack and set in a roasting pan. Roast in the oven for ½ hour, or until the meat is medium rare.
3. Make the sauce by combining the rest of the ingredients, except the cornstarch. Simmer for 5 minutes, and thicken with the cornstarch-and-water mixture.

183

CHAPTER TEN

# Mushrooms with Meat

## Mushrooms with Beef

Americans eat more beef than any other nationality. There are two main reasons for that:

The first reason has to do with the difference in available raw materials between this country and Europe. Europeans have never eaten beef with anything like the relish of their American cousins. Therefore the raising and marketing of first-rate beef has become an American specialty.

The second reason is that the majority of early settlers in this country were from the United Kingdom, and their habits of meat eating were much different from their continental neighbors'. In England, for example, a simple "joint" or "saddle" or "baron" is considered the noblest of dining center-pieces. This is generally true in America as well, although our favorites seem to be precut versions such as sirloin strip steak and filet mignon. Still, most American meat eaters enjoy the pleasures of a properly cooked piece of beef unadorned and, contrary to the Continental approach, serve it dry, rarely accompanied by liquid embellishments.

Happily, one of the frequent exceptions to this is the use of mushrooms directly on beef or in sauces, and the combinations are both legion and intriguing. The following recipes use some basic cuts with mushrooms and related sauces. They are followed by some recipes that utilize more traditional

European methods of cooking beef as well as some Chinese ideas. As far as Chinese concepts are concerned, I confess that one flavoring agent that has always been a favorite of mine with beef is oyster sauce. The union of beef, oyster sauce, and wild mushrooms is one of the truly great eating combinations I can think of, and I use it several times in the following recipes.

The successful combination of beef with mushrooms is due to the fact that mushrooms, with their straightforward qualities, can stand next to the flavor of beef and add to the enjoyment of it. Needless to say, to do this requires some of the more robust mushroom flavors such as cepes, since beef itself is big-bodied on the palate and goes well only with distinctive sauces. For this reason morels and chanterelles do not go well with beef.

## Strip Steaks with Sirloin Mushrooms

APPROXIMATE PREPARATION TIME: 1 HOUR
USEFUL ADVANCE PREPARATION: MUSHROOMS MAY BE PREPARED IN ADVANCE.
MAKES 4 SERVINGS

This popular cut of meat is also called New York strip. The meat can be broiled or sautéed, with the mushrooms added at the end. Serve with baked potato topped with mushrooms, and a Petite Sirah or Rhone wine.

> *½ cup melted butter*
> *1 medium onion, sliced*
> *1½ pounds mushrooms, domestic or wild; use small, whole caps*
> *Soy sauce to taste*
> *¼ teaspoon dried savory or 2 tablespoons fresh savory*
> *Water*
> *2 tablespoons cornstarch mixed with ⅓ cup water*
> *4 half-pound sirloin strip steaks, trimmed of fat and gristle*

1. Pour the butter in a pan, and add the onions. Sauté until the onions are transparent.

2. Add the mushrooms, and cover with a lid. Turn the heat down to a low flame, and let simmer for about 20 minutes. This method for preparing mushrooms requires that the mushrooms sweat and give off their water, which adds flavor to the sauce.

3. Add the soy sauce and savory. If dried savory is used, this mixture must sit for half an hour while the herb permeates the liquid.

185

4. Add back enough water to make 3 cups of mushrooms.

5. Thicken with cornstarch-and-water mixture to desired consistency while stirring. This must be done while the mushrooms are simmering.

6. In the meantime, broil or sauté the steaks to the desired doneness, and serve the mushrooms over or beside the steaks, reserving some for the potatoes.

## Sirloin Steaks with Cheese Duxelles and Anchovies

APPROXIMATE PREPARATION TIME: **45** MINUTES
USEFUL ADVANCE PREPARATION: MAKE CHEESE DUXELLES (PAGE **64**).
MAKES **4** SERVINGS

Here's an interesting way to do sirloins, combining some seemingly strange bedfellows to create a steak lover's fantasy. Serve with Lyonnaise potatoes made with a little Roquefort cheese, and a Cabernet Sauvignon or Bordeaux.

*4 8-to-10-ounce sirloin steaks, trimmed of fat and gristle*
*3 tablespoons lard or vegetable oil for sautéing*
*1 cup Cheese Duxelles (using Roquefort or other blue cheese)*
*24 anchovies*

1. To cook steaks, heat a heavy skillet over a medium flame. Add lard or vegetable oil, and heat for 15 seconds.

2. Begin sautéing steaks in skillet (a medium rare steak will take about 3 minutes per side over a medium flame). When steak is done on one side, turn over, and sauté.

3. When 1 minute remains on the cooking time, remove the steaks from the heat, and spread each one with the duxelles. Cover in a crosswise fashion with the anchovies, and return the steaks to the skillet.

4. Cover, and let cook for another minute. Remove from skillet and serve.

# Filet Mignon with Wild Mushrooms and Szechuan Pepper

APPROXIMATE PREPARATION TIME: **2** HOURS
USEFUL ADVANCE PREPARATION: SOAK PEPPERCORNS (IF DRIED) OVERNIGHT
      IN VINEGAR.
MAKES **4** SERVINGS

The sauce for this dish has a well-defined edge to complement the beef. Green Madagascar peppercorns can also be used and will require less treatment if they are canned rather than dried, since they will already be soft, unlike the dried Chinese peppercorns. The important step here is combining the peppercorns with the vinegar to give a distinct, acidic character to the sauce. Serve with Truffled Rice (see pages 245–246), and a hearty Cabernet like a Heitz Martha's Vineyard.

*10 Szechuan peppercorns*
*3 tablespoons white wine vinegar*
*1½ ounces dried cepes*
*3 cups water*
*2 ounces onions, chopped*
*2 tablespoons clarified butter (see page 51)*
*1 teaspoon sugar*
*1 teaspoon salt*
*1 tablespoon soy sauce*
*1 ounce cream sherry or Madeira*
*1½ tablespoons arrowroot mixed in ¼ cup water*
*4 filets mignon, 10 ounces each, well-trimmed*

1. Start by soaking the peppercorns in the vinegar overnight. These will be slightly softened the next day but still fairly hard. Grind together the peppercorns and the vinegar in a blender, to make a mixture that is primarily liquid. Set aside.

2. Add the cepes to the water, and bring to a boil, then let simmer for 10 minutes. Allow ½ hour if the caps are whole. Set aside and cool before slicing whole caps.

3. Sauté the onions in the butter until they are transparent.

4. Add to the onions the mushrooms with their liquid, sugar, salt, and soy sauce. Simmer until the volume of the liquid is 2 cups.

5. Add the cream sherry or Madeira and about 2 teaspoons of the peppercorn mixture (more if you prefer a very sharp sauce) to the above liquid. Let simmer for 1 more minute.

6. Strain the liquid through a fine sieve. Heat again, and thicken with the arrowroot-and-water mixture. Add the mushrooms left in the sieve back to the sauce, and keep warm.

7. Broil or roast the filets, and serve with the sauce.


## Prime Rib with Cepe Juice

APPROXIMATE PREPARATION TIME: 1½ HOURS
MAKES 4 SERVINGS

This beef dish is a variation on an American classic. Instead of the *jus* being a thin beef stock, it has been enriched here by the addition of dried cepes, which add immeasurably to the complexity of the dish without detracting from the flavor of the beef. Serve with Polenta with Porcini (see pages 249–250), and a red Hermitage Rhone wine.

*A rib roast of beef, well-trimmed, cut for 4 people*
*5 pounds beef fat (obtainable from a butcher)*
*1½ cups strong veal or beef stock (pages 72–73)*
*½ ounce dried cepes* (Boletus edulis)
*1 teaspoon salt*
*1 teaspoon sugar*
*1 teaspoon soy sauce*

*Preheat oven to 500°.*

1. Strip roast of all fat and gristle. Place the rib roast on an oven pan on a rack. Cover flesh-exposed parts with the fat.

2. Place in oven with the curved side up. Brown for 15 minutes.

3. Reduce heat and continue to cook at 350° for 12 minutes per pound for a rare doneness.

4. While the meat is cooking, make the sauce by combining the stock, mushrooms, salt, sugar, and soy sauce in a saucepan. Bring to a boil, then let simmer for 20 minutes.

5. After removing the rib from the oven, let stand for ½ hour before carving. Cut slices, and cover with the cepe-beef juice just before serving.

## Jack's Spicy Beef Casserole

APPROXIMATE PREPARATION TIME: ½ HOUR
MAKES **4** SERVINGS

This dish is great for odds and ends of beef, veal, or lamb that have been trimmed from the primary cuts. It can be finished in 10 minutes. A top-quality hot sauce makes this a success because the spiciness comes through as a counterpoint to the flavor of the beef. Try to get some chili sauce from Thailand, which is available in most Oriental food stores. Fresh domestic or fresh wild mushrooms can be used. This is a one-pan dish. Partially cooked vegetables like carrots or broccoli can be added. Serve with a spicy Pinot Noir like a David Bruce.

> *5 ounces Polish sausage, sliced thin*
> *1 cup strong beef or veal stock (pages 72–73)*
> *6 tablespoons Chinese oyster sauce*
> *1 cup red wine*
> *1 teaspoon Thai hot sauce (preferable) or Tabasco*
> *2 scallions sliced*
> *12 mushroom caps, wild or domestic, sliced*
> *1½ pounds tenderloin tips or odd parts of tender meat, trimmed*
> *of all fat and gristle, and cut into 1-inch pieces*
> *1½ tablespoons arrowroot mixed with ¼ cup water*

1. In a saucepan, combine the sausage, stock, oyster sauce, wine, hot sauce, scallions, and mushrooms. Bring to a boil, and stir to combine. Let simmer for 5 minutes.

2. Add the beef, and continue to simmer for just another 2 minutes. Try to cook the meat so that it is still rare inside.

3. Thicken the dish with the arrowroot-and-water mixture, and serve immediately.

## Steak Kew

APPROXIMATE PREPARATION TIME: 1 HOUR
MAKES **4** SERVINGS

This is the classic Chinese dish that first aroused my interest in oyster sauce. The flavor of oyster sauce seems to be a lost cousin of the flavor of beef.

**189**

Its most important attribute is that it lends body to any dish, and where beef is concerned, this is essential, because the flavor of beef can easily overpower less sturdy suitors to our palates. The strength of the shiitake also shows up well here. A wok is highly recommended for this preparation although a good Teflon skillet will do. Serve with white rice tossed with whole, tenderized black beans.

> *1 teaspoon peanut oil*
> *1 clove garlic, minced*
> *½ ounce ginger, minced*
> *15 caps mushrooms, preferably shiitake*
> *1½ pounds tenderloin or sirloin, well-trimmed and cubed into*
> *    1-inch pieces*
> *3 tablespoons scallions, cut coarse*
> *½ pound snow peas*
> *3 tablespoons oyster sauce*
> *½ teaspoon sugar*

1. Heat the wok until it starts to smoke. Add the peanut oil, and heat for 15 seconds.

2. Stir-fry the garlic and ginger for 30 seconds.

3. Add the mushrooms, beef, scallions, and snow peas, and continue stir-frying for about 2 minutes or until the meat is medium rare.

4. Add the oyster sauce and sugar, and continue to stir for another minute. Serve next to the rice.


## Potted Beef with Wild Mushrooms

**APPROXIMATE PREPARATION TIME: 2 HOURS**
**MAKES 4 SERVINGS**

Here is a beef stew with the added complexity of mushrooms to give it some extra body and flavor. Neither the type of meat nor the choice of vegetables is vitally important, because this dish is as flexible as the leftovers from Sunday dinner.

> *2 pounds beef, trimmed of all fat and gristle, cut into 1-inch pieces*
> *    (or 1½ pounds meat cooked)*
> *1 ounce lard or ¼ cup cooking oil*
> *Onions*

*Carrots*
*Celery*
*Potatoes*
*Sausage (optional)*
*Beef stock*
*Red wine*
*Bay leaf*
*1 ounce dried* Boletus edulis *(cepes)*
*Salt*
*Soy sauce*
*Cornstarch in water*

1. In a skillet, brown the beef in melted lard or cooking oil, about 2 minutes over a high heat, turning frequently.

2. Cut the onions, carrots, celery, and potatoes (and the sausage, if you have some) to approximately the same size as the beef cubes. Keep the celery cubes separate. The relative amounts of vegetables are not important. Remember, this is a leftover dish.

3. Place beef and remaining ingredients, except the cornstarch and celery, in a pot, and bring to a boil. Stock and red wine should be in equal proportions and be enough to cover the solid ingredients. The dried mushrooms should be completely submerged. Use about equal portions of salt and soy sauce to taste.

4. Bring everything to a boil, then cover, and let simmer for 1 hour, stirring occasionally and adding back water when necessary.

5. When the potatoes are almost soft, add the celery, and continue cooking for about 10 minutes. Thicken with the cornstarch-and-water mixture and serve in soup bowls.

## Beef Roulades with Oyster Duxelles

APPROXIMATE PREPARATION TIME: 1 HOUR
USEFUL ADVANCE PREPARATION: MAKE OYSTER DUXELLES (SEE PAGE 63)
MAKES 4 SERVINGS

The trick to this dish is not to overcook the roulades. Choose the tenderest beef available, because if cheaper cuts are used, the beef must be cooked well in order for it to be tender. Even with tenderloin it is a good idea to tenderize the meat by pounding with a mallet. Serve with *Spaetzle* accompanied by some of the sauce, and Burgundy.

*8 pieces of beef, each 2½ ounces, trimmed*
*½ cup Oyster Duxelles*
*2 cups water*
*¼ cup soy sauce*
*½ teaspoon garlic powder, or crushed garlic*
*½ teaspoon salt*
*1 teaspoon sugar*
*3 tablespoons cream sherry or Madeira*
*1 tablespoon onion, chopped*
*¼ teaspoon bouquet garni*
*3 tablespoons melted butter*
*3 tablespoons sifted flour*

*Preheat oven to 350°.*

1. With a mallet, roll and flatten each piece of beef into a round, about 6 inches in diameter.

2. Place ⅛th of the oyster duxelles on one end of each piece of pounded meat, and roll up into a roulade. Do this for all the pieces.

3. In a saucepan, combine the rest of the ingredients, except the butter and flour, and simmer for about 15 minutes. Cook this down to about 2 cups liquid.

4. Strain the liquid, and set aside.

5. Make the roux by blending the flour and butter, cooking until it becomes golden brown. Add the liquid, and stir until thickened. Keep warm.

6. Place the roulades on a rack over a baking pan, and cook for 15 minutes in the oven. Remove from oven, and serve with the sauce.

## Filet Mignon en Croûte with Tarragon Butter

APPROXIMATE PREPARATION TIME: **2** HOURS
USEFUL ADVANCE PREPARATION: MAKE BASIC MUSHROOM DUXELLES RECIPE
    (SEE PAGE **61**), HAVE PUFF PASTRY READY, AND PREPARE TARRAGON
    BUTTER.
MAKES **4** SERVINGS

This preparation has become almost commonplace in the eastern United States. The predecessor of this dish, however, was Beef Wellington, which is an entire tenderloin of beef wrapped in puffy pastry and baked. The idea of wrapping smaller cuts (filets) in puff pastry individually and serving them with tarragon butter and mushroom duxelles was originated by my mother and father in 1960. Its popularity quickly spread, and by the late seventies the dish had appeared on menus from Miami to New York. The classic Wellington uses pâté de foie gras on the beef whereas we substituted duxelles, because of its earthy qualities. The tarragon butter is to be spread on top of the finished and wrapped filet. Serve with Mushrooms with Vegetables Polonaise Style (see pages 254–255), and a good bottle of Cabernet.

> *¼ cup cooking oil or lard*
> *4 filets of beef, 7 to 8 ounces each, well-trimmed*
> *4 tablespoons Basic Mushroom Duxelles*
> *4 4-inch squares puff pastry (see pages 95–96)*
> *1 egg, beaten*

> **FOR THE TARRAGON BUTTER:**
> *1 teaspoon dried tarragon*
> *⅓ cup white wine vinegar*
> *2 egg yolks*
> *⅓ cup softened butter*

*Preheat oven to 450°.*

1. Heat a sauté pan, and add the oil or lard.
2. When oil or lard is smoking, place the filets in the pan, and braise for 2 minutes on each side until lightly browned. Remove from heat, and pat dry.
3. Coat the top of each filet with 1 tablespoon of Basic Mushroom Duxelles.
4. Roll the puff pastry squares thin, one at a time. Take the squares of puff pastry from the refrigerator one at a time, or they will get warm and become difficult to handle.
5. Place 1 filet on 1 piece of puff pastry, duxelles side down (touching the pastry).
6. Fold the 4 corners of the puff pastry over the meat, so that they overlap and cover the meat completely.
7. Place the 4 wrapped filets on a double baking sheet, which has been covered with aluminum foil or baking paper. Coat the pastry with a little beaten egg to give a nice browned appearance when done. Cut a decorative series of incisions on the top side of the wrapped filets.
8. Place the filets in the oven for 15 minutes.
9. While filets are baking, make the tarragon butter by adding tarragon to the vinegar (or you can use ready-made tarragon vinegar).

**193**

10. With a hand or an electric blender, whip the egg yolks until they have the appearance of whipped butter. Add the butter to the yolks until blended.

11. Add the tarragon vinegar to the yolks and butter. (You may not have to use all the vinegar indicated; stop adding it when the mixture is acidic enough for you.) Blend until well mixed. Portion the tarragon butter into 4 small cups to be served with the finished steaks. It can be refrigerated if not used immediately.

12. Remove filets, and serve with the tarragon butter.


## Tenderloin en Brochette

APPROXIMATE PREPARATION TIME: 1 HOUR
USEFUL ADVANCE PREPARATION: PREPARE SIRLOIN MUSHROOMS (SEE PAGES
     185 – 186).
MAKES 4 SERVINGS

This is a good recipe for using extra ends and pieces from a tenderloin of beef. Pieces of sirloin can also be used. Serve with stir-fried snow peas, and Pinot Noir.

*1½ cups Sirloin Mushrooms*
*2 tablespoons cornstarch mixed in ⅓ cup water*
*1 tablespoon sour cream or* crème fraîche
*2 pounds trimmed tenderloin or sirloin, cut into approximately 20*
     *equal size cubes*
*4 puff pastry shells, moderately warmed (see page 96)*

*Preheat broiler.*

1. Heat the Sirloin Mushrooms. Blend in the sour cream or *crème fraîche.* Keep warm.

2. Place 5 pieces of tenderloin on each of 4 metal skewers.

3. Broil the meat to desired doneness.

4. De-skewer the meat onto four plates, so that each group of cubes lines up on one side of the plate. Place a puff pastry shell on the other side of the plate, across from the meat, and fill each of the pastry shells with the mushrooms. Serve either from a large platter or on individual plates.

# Mushrooms with Veal

Of all the types of meat that go best with mushrooms, veal is certainly one of the choicest. Food lovers often rave over the delicate flavors and texture of veal. A cynic might comment that veal really has no flavor at all. I suspect that the truth lies somewhere in between. To my mind, the flavor of veal is definitely mild but very clean tasting, and this is what makes it so popular with preparations that utilize a rich or complex sauce: Its subtlety can come through without being overwhelmed by the meat. For these reasons, veal is one of the few main-course meats that act as a background for its complements.

When buying veal, always choose meats with the lightest, whitest color and never more than a blush of pink. This indicates that the animal from which it came was milk-fed and will yield the tenderest flesh. This degree of tenderness is what can make veal expensive. The loin is always the tenderest part, and it is unsurpassed for presentation purposes. Whether served as chops or whole, tenderloin is the most elegant cut to come from the calf. Meat from the leg portion of a quality calf is also excellent and cheaper than loin meat, but leg meat almost always has to be cut into scallops or into cubes for casseroles. The other parts of the calf are also good for casseroles but take longer to cook. Veal variety meats (organs and other parts of animals that are not classified as regular cuts, but are rich in important nutrients), such as sweetbreads or kidneys, are considered to be the choicest because of their light color and absence of strong, beefy flavors.

Veal is ideal for use with most kinds of wild mushrooms, except chanterelles, whose slightly fruity character does not work with it; save chanterelles for the poultry dishes. Shiitake are good with veal, as are oyster mushrooms and cepes; they have defined, robust flavors, which act as worthy embellishments to the delicate calf meat. But the best combination of all is veal with morels; in few other dishes is the flavor of morels so elegantly described as with veal.

# Veal Rosenthal

APPROXIMATE PREPARATION TIME: 1 HOUR
USEFUL ADVANCE PREPARATION: PREPARE MOREL SAUCE ROSENTHAL (SEE
    PAGES 82–83).
MAKES 4 SERVINGS

This veal dish uses morels with green peppers and onions. Like the sauce with which it is served, it is named after Jack Rosenthal, founder of the Culinary Institute of America. Serve with braised winter radish in parsley butter, and a good Burgundy.

*4 milk-fed veal chops, about 1 inch thick*
*1 1/2 cups Morel Sauce Rosenthal*

*Preheat oven to 450°.*

1. Place the chops on a roasting rack and then into a roasting pan.
2. Put the veal into the oven, and roast for 15 minutes.
3. Prepare the sauce while the chops are cooking, and pour over them when they are ready. The meat should be slightly pink inside.

# Veal in Morel Juice

APPROXIMATE PREPARATION TIME: 30 MINUTES
MAKES 4 SERVINGS

This dish uses the *jus* method for making a mushroom sauce—that is, blending a mushroom extract with a veal stock. Serve with spinach braised in some of the stock, and a Stag's Leap Chardonnay.

*4 milk-fed veal chops about 1 inch thick*
*1 1/2 cups strong veal stock (pages 72–73)*
*1/2 ounce dried morels*
*1 teaspoon salt*
*1 teaspoon sugar*
*1 teaspoon soy sauce*
*1 tablespoon chopped green pepper*

*Preheat oven to 450°.*

1. Place the four chops on a roasting rack in a roasting pan.

2. Combine the rest of the ingredients in a saucepan, and bring to a boil. Let simmer for ½ hour. Add back water as needed to retain 1½ cup yield.

3. Roast the chops, and when they are finished (about 15 minutes), cover with the thin sauce.

## Scallops of Veal in Creamed Morel Sauce

APPROXIMATE PREPARATION TIME: 1 to 2 HOURS
MAKES 4 SERVINGS

The actual cooking time for the veal here is very brief. Making the sauce takes little longer. Serve with steamed broccoli coated with onion butter, and a rich Chardonnay.

*12 2-ounce pieces veal loin or leg, flattened with a cleaver*
*Flour, sifted*
*1 ounce dried morels*
*1 cup strong veal stock (pages 72–73)*
*1 tablespoon chopped red pepper*
*1 tablespoon chopped onion*
*1 teaspoon salt*
*½ teaspoon garlic powder*
*1 teaspoon sugar*
*1 teaspoon soy sauce*
*½ cup heavy cream*
*1 tablespoon sour cream or* crème fraîche
*1 tablespoon Madeira*
*2 tablespoons cornstarch mixed with ⅓ cup water*
*¼ cup butter, melted*

1. Dredge the veal lightly with the flour, and set aside.

2. Combine all ingredients from the morels to the soy sauce in a saucepan, stir together, and bring to a boil. Let simmer for 20 minutes. Maintain a 2-cup quantity with water.

3. Add the cream, sour cream or *crème fraîche,* and Madeira to the liquid, and stir while simmering for another minute.

4. Thicken this sauce with the cornstarch-and-water mixture, and keep warm.

5. Sauté the veal in the butter for 4 minutes on each side, or until it is golden, and cover with the sauce. Serve 3 scallops per person.

**197**

# Veal with Morels and Caraway

**APPROXIMATE PREPARATION TIME: 1 HOUR**
**MAKES 4 SERVINGS**

Caraway is a natural flavor complement to morels. Here, it is paired with green pepper to bring out the morel flavor to the fullest. This sauce is light but full-flavored—and low-calorie too! Serve with a puree of leeks and shaved broccoli stalks, and a white Pinot Noir.

*1½ cups water*
*½ ounce dried morels*
*¼ teaspoon caraway seeds*
*1 teaspoon salt*
*1 teaspoon sugar*
*1½ teaspoons soy sauce*
*½ teaspoon chopped onion*
*½ teaspoon chopped green pepper*
*1 tablespoon melted butter*
*8 medallions of veal cut from the loin or tenderloin, 2 to 3 ounces*
 *each, slightly flattened.*
*1 tablespoon arrowroot mixed with ⅓ cup water (optional)*

*Preheat oven to 450°.*

1. Combine all the ingredients except the medallions of veal and the arrowroot, and bring to a boil in a saucepan. Let simmer for ½ hour, maintaining liquid level with water.

2. Strain the mixture, remove the morels from the solid residue, and add to the liquid. Set aside.

3. Place the medallions on a wire rack in a roasting pan, and roast for 6 minutes.

4. Remove the veal, place on serving dish, and cover with the sauce. The sauce may be thickened with the arrowroot-and-water mixture to add body, but this sauce is meant to be delicate and subtle, so be careful with the thickening!

## Veal Copernicus

APPROXIMATE PREPARATION TIME: **2** HOURS
MAKES **4** SERVINGS

Copernicus, as we all know, was a famous Polish astronomer whose questions about our universe led to a better understanding of our solar system. This small tribute honors him. Serve with a trio of sautéed vegetables, carrots, green beans, and cauliflower, sprinkled with dill and butter, and Chardonnay.

*1½ pounds veal (leg or loin meat preferably), trimmed of excess*
    *fat and cubed into ½-inch pieces*
*3 cups strong veal stock (pages 72–73)*
*Water*
*1 ounce dried cepes*
*¼ cup dry sherry*
*2 teaspoons sugar*
*1 teaspoon fresh crushed garlic*
*1 cup cepes, or domestic mushrooms, quartered*
*1 teaspoon salt*
*2 teaspoons soy sauce*
*Bouquet garni*
*2 tablespoons* crème fraîche *or sour cream*
*1½ cups heavy cream*
*4 4-inch squares puff pastry, baked and ready to use (see pages*
    *95–96)*
*5 egg yolks*

1. In a large saucepan, combine all the ingredients through the soy sauce, making sure that the veal is covered by adding water, and blend.
2. Bring the stew to a boil, and let simmer until the veal is tender, about 45 minutes. The liquid total should be about 2 cups. Keep stew on a low simmer.
3. Add to the stew the bouquet garni, *crème fraîche* or sour cream, and 1 cup of the heavy cream, stir together. In the meantime, warm the puff pastry shells by putting them in an oven toaster.
4. Add the egg yolks to the other ½ cup of cream, and whisk together.
5. While the stew is simmering, thicken with the liaison of cream and egg yolks. This mixture must be added slowly, while stirring, and taken off the heat immediately after it becomes thick. Serve in the warmed puff pastry shells.

## Shiitake Veal with Sausage

**APPROXIMATE PREPARATION TIME: 1½ HOURS**
**MAKES 4 SERVINGS**

The recipe below calls for the use of both dried and fresh shiitake, and directs the cook to remove the dried caps from the dish when finished. This is optional. You can use either the dried or the fresh shiitake or include them both. The reason for using the dried product along with the fresh is to intensify the flavor of the mushroom, as the dried gives off more flavor during the simmering period. But you do not have to have both to make this a successful dish. Make this a one-dish meal by adding some fresh vegetables like carrots and onions while cooking.

*1 pound veal from leg or loin, trimmed of excess fat and cubed
    into ½-inch pieces*
*½ pound good Polish sausage, cubed into ½-inch pieces*
*Water*
*1 ounce dried shiitake caps*
*2 cups fresh shiitake, caps quartered*
*2 teaspoons chopped onion*
*1½ teaspoons salt*
*1½ teaspoons sugar*
*1½ teaspoons soy sauce*
*Salt to taste*
*1½ tablespoons arrowroot mixed with ⅓ cup water*

1. In a large saucepan, combine all ingredients through the soy sauce, and bring to a boil, making sure that the veal is covered with enough liquid.
2. Simmer the mixture until the veal is tender. Remove the reconstituted shiitake from the stew. The liquid volume should be about 2 cups.
3. Adjust for salt if necessary, and simmer for 5 minutes, then thicken with the arrowroot-and-water mixture. Serve.

# Whole Veal Loin with Morels and Cepes

APPROXIMATE PREPARATION TIME: **2** HOURS
MAKES **4** SERVINGS

Whole veal loin served like this with a first-rate California cabernet like the Cask 23 from Stag's Leap Wine Cellars, or a Martha's Vineyard cabernet from Joe Heitz, is the epitome of formal dining. Serve with a spinach soufflé.

*1 whole veal loin, about 3 to 4 pounds, trimmed of all fat, bone,*
*  and gristle*
*½ ounce dried morels*
*½ ounce dried cepes*
*3 cups veal stock or water*
*1 teaspoon salt*
*1 teaspoon sugar*
*1 teaspoon soy sauce*
*1 teaspoon chopped onions*
*1 teaspoon chopped green pepper*
*1 tablespoon clarified butter (page 51)*
*1 tablespoon arrowroot mixed with ⅓ cup water*

*Preheat oven to 400°.*

1. Place the loin on a wire rack in a roasting pan and roast for 30 minutes. It should be pink inside.

2. While the veal is roasting, combine the mushrooms with the veal stock or water, salt, sugar, and soy sauce. Bring to a boil, and let simmer for 20 minutes.

3. While the mushrooms are simmering, sauté the onions and peppers in the butter.

4. Add the mushroom mixture to the onions and peppers, and bring back to a simmer for 10 minutes. Reduce the liquid to 1½ cups.

5. If the veal is done before you finish the sauce, reduce the oven temperature, and keep the veal warm. Open the oven door for a few minutes to keep the veal from a further high concentration of heat. Strain the sauce, adding back the mushrooms, and thicken with the arrowroot-and-water mixture. When the veal is ready for serving, slice it into ½-inch thick pieces, and cover with the sauce.

# Osso Bucco with Porcini

**APPROXIMATE PREPARATION TIME: 3 TO 4 HOURS**
**MAKES 4 SERVINGS**

*Osso bucco* is an Italian favorite, thought to have originated near Milan. This variation pairs the veal with porcini, which is the Italian word for cepes, or *Boletus edulis*. Serve with a Grignolino from Heitz Vineyards.

> *4 veal shanks cut into 2-inch pieces, with all meat left on*
> *Flour*
> *2 tablespoons olive oil*
> *3 tablespoons butter*
> *1 carrot, sliced*
> *1 celery stalk, sliced*
> *½ cup chopped onion*
> *1 clove garlic, chopped*
> *½ cup tomato puree*
> *½ cup dry white wine*
> *½ ounce dried porcini (equivalent to cepes)*
> *3 cups strong veal stock (pages 72–73)*
> *2 tablespoons chopped parsley*
> *1 teaspoon lemon zest*
> *½ pound fresh mushrooms, domestic or wild*
> *Salt and pepper to taste*
> *3 tablespoons cornstarch mixed with ⅓ cup water*

1. Coat the veal shanks lightly with some flour, and shake off any excess. Put the oil and butter in a skillet. Heat the oil, and brown the veal on all sides in it.

2. Transfer the veal to a deep, wide saucepan (6-to-8-quart capacity) with the remaining oil, and add to it the rest of the ingredients, except the cornstarch.

3. Place the veal over low to medium heat, and cook covered for about 2 hours, stirring occasionally.

4. Thicken with the cornstarch-and-water mixture, and serve over fresh pasta.

# Sweetbreads with Curry and Mushrooms

APPROXIMATE PREPARATION TIME: **2** HOURS
USEFUL ADVANCE PREPARATION: COOK AND COOL SWEETBREADS IN ADVANCE.
MAKES **4** SERVINGS

Fine, pure white sweetbreads should be used for this preparation, because they contrast sharply with the dark, spicy sauce around them. Serve with simple brown rice.

*1½ pounds veal sweetbreads*
*10 cups water and 1 tablespoon vinegar*
*½ cup chopped onions*
*¼ cup melted butter*
*1½ pounds domestic mushrooms, sliced*
*½ cup rich, red wine*
*3 tablespoons soy sauce*
*1 teaspoon bouquet garni*
*2 teaspoons curry powder (see page 204)*
*1 teaspoon sugar*
*Salt to taste*
*2 tablespoons cornstarch mixed with ⅓ cup water*

1. Soak the sweetbreads in water for 1 hour, and rinse until no more blood comes from the drained liquid. Remove all fat and sinews from the sweetbreads. Place the sweetbreads in a 4-to-6-quart pot, and cover with water, to which 1 tablespoon of vinegar has been added. This will maintain the color of the sweetbreads. Bring the sweetbreads to a boil, and let simmer for 20 minutes. Remove from the water and rinse with cold water. Place in refrigerator, and let cool for several hours. When the sweetbreads are cool, slice them about ¼ inch thick and set aside.

2. In a large skillet, sauté the onions in the butter until they are transparent.

3. Add the mushrooms, and continue cooking over a low heat for about ½ hour. Keep a lid on the skillet during cooking, and do not let the liquid evaporate.

4. Add the rest of the ingredients except the cornstarch and sweetbreads, and continue cooking over a low heat for another 10 minutes, adjusting for salt.

5. Thicken the mushrooms and liquid lightly with the cornstarch-and-water mixture.

6.  Spread the sweetbreads out in the sauce, but do not cover them with the sauce, or this will discolor them. Return this to the heat, and keep over a low flame, covered, for 5 minutes to heat the sweetbreads. Serve over brown rice.

Note: Curry can of course be obtained in any store but you might try making your own just for once. Hundreds of variations exist, so the following recipe is merely a general guide.

*1 tablespoon coriander*
*½ teaspoon fenugreek*
*½ teaspoon turmeric*
*1 teaspoon cumin*
*1 teaspoon black pepper*
*2 bay leaves*
*1 tablespoon celery seeds*
*½ teaspoon nutmeg, ground*
*½ teaspoon cloves*
*1 tablespoon dehydrated onion*
*1 teaspoon crushed red pepper*
*½ teaspoon ground ginger*
*1 teaspoon cayenne pepper*

Place all of the above ingredients in a blender, and grind together until powdered. Store in a jar with a tight-fitting lid. This spice will last for a long time if kept covered. The above ingredients are all obtainable in the supermarket with the exception of fenugreek, which is carried in most specialty food stores.

## Baked Calf's Liver with Wild Mushrooms

APPROXIMATE PREPARATION TIME: 1½ HOURS
ADVANCE PREPARATION: PREPARE MUSHROOMS IN BÉCHAMEL SAUCE I or II
     (PAGES 126 – 127)
MAKES 4 SERVINGS

Prepare with any gilled wild mushroom, such as *Russula* or *Pleurotus*, but the common domestic *Agaricus* can be substituted. Serve with tiny cubed sautéed potatoes.

*1½ pounds fresh calf's liver sliced into four 6-ounce pieces*
*1 cup milk*
*3 tablespoons cooking oil*
*1 ounce chopped onion*
*2 cups Mushrooms in Béchamel Sauce*
*Salt and pepper*
*Fresh bread crumbs*

*Preheat oven to 425°.*

1. Remove any membranes from liver by slicing out with a sharp knife. Soak liver in milk for ½ hour.
2. Heat oil in an 8-inch skillet, and lightly sauté onion. Begin to heat mushrooms in a 4-quart saucepan.
3. Cut liver into bite-size pieces. Pat dry, add to skillet with onion, and sauté for about 3 minutes. Salt lightly.
4. To finish dish, put liver into a heated ovenproof dish, and cover with the Mushrooms in Béchamel Sauce.
5. Cover all with fresh bread crumbs, and bake in the oven until the crumbs are lightly browned, about 10 minutes.

## Veal Brains with Eggs and Morels

APPROXIMATE PREPARATION TIME: **30** MINUTES
MAKES **4** SERVINGS

The brains-and-egg combination is elaborated upon here with the addition of morels. Fresh morels are best for this dish, but dried ones can be used (in which case see pages 47–48). Remember to save the reconstitution liquid for a sauce!

*1 pound veal brains, cleaned and sliced*
*¼ cup sliced onions*
*¼ cup green pepper, sliced thin*
*3 tablespoons butter*
*1 pound fresh morels, sliced, or reconstituted dried morels (see*
*above)*
*10 eggs, beaten*
*Salt and pepper*

1. Clean the brains by thorough rinsing. Pat dry, then slice.
2. Sauté the onions and green pepper in the butter until they are almost limp.
3. Add the morels, and continue to sauté. The morels will draw water. Continue cooking until all of the liquid is evaporated.
4. Add the brains, and sauté, using a higher heat, for 3 minutes.
5. Add the beaten eggs, and scramble until done. Season with salt and pepper.

## Kidneys with Cepes and Almonds

APPROXIMATE PREPARATION TIME: 1 HOUR
USEFUL ADVANCE PREPARATION: PREPARE CEPE VELOUTÉ SAUCE (SEE PAGES
 77–78).
MAKES 4 SERVINGS

This is a kidney dish that utilizes an extract of cepes for the counterpoint to the kidneys. You may use domestic mushrooms in the dish itself, because the flavor of wild mushrooms comes through in the sauce. The almonds add textural contrast. Serve with wild rice mixed with chopped almonds.

*1½ pounds fresh veal kidneys cleaned and sliced, about ½-inch*
 *thick\**
*2 tablespoons clarified butter (see page 51)*
*1 cup Cepe Velouté Sauce*
*½ cup fresh domestic or wild mushrooms, sliced. (The mushrooms*
 *used in making the sauce may also be used, but these are not*
 *as good as the fresh types for this dish.)*
*¼ cup sliced, toasted almonds*

1. Sauté the kidneys in the butter over high heat till lightly browned, about 1 minute on each side.
2. Add the sauce, the mushrooms, and the almonds, and bring to a simmer. Let simmer for 3 minutes. Serve immediately. The kidneys should be done no more than medium rare.

\*Note: If kidneys are bought whole, clean them by placing them, fat side up, on a wooden cutting board. Remove fat by cutting around the edges of the wedge of fat, into the kidney, so that the fat wedge can be lifted out clean. Finish by peeling off any outer membrane.

# Mushrooms with Lamb

Lamb, curiously, is generally perceived in two distinct lights. On one hand, it has been accepted by many beef eaters in this country as a satisfying alternative to filet mignon or sirloin, which accounts for the popularity of rack of lamb and broiled lamb chops. On the other hand, from China to the Middle East and from Europe to America, no other meat can better stake its claim to international use than lamb. Thus it combines the sober reputation of beef with the wild-eyed notoriety of pork. Mushrooms blend exceedingly well into this versatile milieu of perceptions and can complement lamb on both levels.

## Rack of Lamb with Marjoram, Savory, and Morels

**APPROXIMATE PREPARATION TIME: 1 HOUR**
**MAKES 4 SERVINGS**

This is a rack of lamb with a light sauce. It is flavorful, but more delicate than many of the others. Serve with batter-fried sliced zucchini, and a medium-bodied Cabernet.

> *2 half-racks of lamb, about 2 pounds each, trimmed and ready for use; allow 3 chops per person.*
> *1 ounce dried morels*
> *3 cups water*
> *1½ tablespoons chopped onions*
> *1½ tablespoons chopped green peppers*
> *2 tablespoons clarified butter (page 51)*
> *1 teaspoon salt*
> *1 teaspoon sugar*
> *1 tablespoon soy sauce*
> *¼ teaspoon marjoram*
> *¼ teaspoon savory (use half these amounts for the herbs if they are dried)*
> *1½ tablespoons arrowroot mixed with ⅓ cup water*

*Preheat oven to 400°.*

1. Place the racks of lamb on a wire rack in a roasting pan, and roast in the oven. They should take about 45 minutes for a medium-rare doneness.

Test this by piercing the flesh with a knife or small skewer. The juice should be brownish-red.

2. Add the morels to the water, and bring to a boil. Let simmer for 30 minutes.

3. Sauté the onions and green peppers in the butter until the onions are transparent.

4. Add the mushroom-and-liquid mixture to the onions and peppers. Add the salt, sugar, and soy. Strain the combined liquid, reserve, and add back the morels from the solid remains.

5. Cook the mushroom mixture down to 2 cups liquid, then add the marjoram and savory, and let the sauce sit for 5 minutes. Thicken with the arrowroot-and-water mixture.

6. Remove the racks from the oven, cut into chops (each rack should yield 6 chops) and pour the sauce around them.

## Broiled Lamb Chops with Parsnips and Mushrooms

APPROXIMATE PREPARATION TIME: 1 HOUR
MAKES 4 SERVINGS

You can prepare this recipe with fresh domestic or wild mushrooms. The mushrooms will give off their juice while cooking and will make their own sauce. Generally speaking, chops cut 1½ inches thick will take about 4 minutes on each side to achieve medium doneness. You can subtract or add time accordingly to adjust doneness. As with all meat, it is important that the chops be at room temperature before broiling, because cold meat can yield burned outsides and raw insides. The recipes that follow can also be made by sautéing the chops. You may find this preparation more convenient, since good broiling facilities are not common in most homes. To sauté the chops, melt 1 tablespoon of butter in a pan, and add 1 tablespoon of cooking oil. Cook on each side for 3 minutes for medium doneness. Serve with a Burgundy or Pinot Noir.

*6 parsnips, peeled*
*1 pound fresh, cleaned mushrooms, sliced*
*1 medium onion, chopped*
*⅓ cup melted butter*
*2 tablespoons flour*
*½ teaspoon sugar*
*1 tablespoon soy sauce*

*¹/₂ teaspoon salt*
*12 lamb chops 1¹/₂ inches thick, trimmed of fat and gristle*

1.  Boil the parsnips in water for 30 minutes, or until tender. Remove and slice.

2.  Sweat the mushrooms by placing them in a small saucepan with a little water at the bottom. Cover tightly, and cook over a low flame for 20 minutes. Do this while the parsnips are cooking.

3.  When the mushrooms are cooked, add in enough water to make about 1 cup. Add the parsnips to the mushrooms and water.

4.  Sauté the onions in the butter until transparent, and add the flour. Cook for another minute.

5.  Add the mushrooms, water, parsnips, sugar, soy, and salt to the saucepan, and cook while stirring for 2 minutes. This mixture will thicken.

6.  Prepare the chops as indicated above, and serve on the same plate as the mushrooms and parsnips.

## Roast Leg of Lamb with Cumin and Wild Mushrooms

APPROXIMATE PREPARATION TIME: **2 HOURS**
MAKES **4** SERVINGS

This dish can be made with any kind of wild mushroom, fresh or dried. In any case, dried mushrooms are also used to enrich the sauce. Serve with vermicelli cooked in mushroom extract (see pages 73–74, 238), and Cabernet or Bordeaux.

*1 ounce dried forest mushrooms*
*2 cups rich meat stock (pages 72–73)*
*1 5-to-6-pound leg of lamb*
*2 cloves garlic*
*1 teaspoon salt*
*1 teaspoon sugar*
*1 tablespoon soy sauce*
*1 teaspoon crushed cumin*
*2 tablespoons tomato paste*
*¹/₄ teaspoon Tabasco or Thai hot sauce*
*1 cup fresh wild mushrooms, sliced, or use dried ones above*
*2 tablespoons chopped onions*
*3 tablespoons melted butter*
*3 tablespoons sifted flour*

209

*Preheat oven to 450°.*

1. Add the dried mushrooms to the stock, and bring to a boil. Let simmer for 30 minutes.

2. Trim lamb of excess fat and tough outer skin, leaving a thin layer of fat. Cut the garlic into small pieces. Cut slits in the lamb, and insert the garlic into these slits.

3. Place the leg in a shallow roasting pan with some water, and set in the oven for 20 minutes to brown. Cut the heat to 350°, and let roast for another hour. The meat is done when the center is just warm. Test by inserting a skewer or fork into the center of the thickest part of the leg. Do not touch the bone with the probe.

4. To the dried mushrooms in the water, add the salt, sugar, soy sauce, cumin, tomato paste, Tabasco or Thai hot sauce, and the sliced mushrooms. Let simmer for 5 minutes, stirring well.

5. In a skillet, sauté the onions in the butter until they are transparent. Sprinkle in the flour, and stir for 2 minutes. Add to this the liquid from the mushroom liquid, and stir in until it thickens. Slice lamb thin, place over vermicelli, and cover with some of the sauce.

## Lamb Curry with Morels and Turmeric Rice

APPROXIMATE PREPARATION TIME: **2 HOURS**
MAKES **4** SERVINGS

Many of the commercial morels we find in specialty food stores come from India and Pakistan. These mushrooms have been eaten there for hundreds of years, especially in the region of Kashmir. Turmeric rice is a colorful golden yellow, which matches the hue of the curry. Turmeric is available in most grocery stores in the spice section. Serve with a spicy, herbaceous Sauvignon Blanc or Semillon.

*1½ ounces dried morels*
*3 cups water*
*¾ cup heavy cream*
*½ teaspoon curry powder*
*½ teaspoon fresh crushed garlic*
*1 teaspoon salt*
*1 teaspoon sugar*
*1 tablespoon soy sauce*
*2 pounds lamb, well-trimmed and cubed into ½-inch pieces*

*1½ cups long-grain rice*
*1 cup water for rice*
*½ teaspoon turmeric*
*2 tablespoons cornstarch mixed with ⅓ cup water*

1. Add the mushrooms to the water, and bring to a boil. Let simmer for 30 minutes.

2. Set morels aside, and bring the mushroom liquid volume back up to 3 cups. Save half of the liquid for the rice, and cook down the other half to ¾ cup.

3. To the cooked-down ¾ cup, add the cream, curry, garlic, salt, sugar, soy sauce, and lamb. Add back the morels. Cover, and cook 45 minutes, or until the lamb is tender.

4. To make the rice, place the liquid reserved for the rice in a pot with a tight-fitting lid. Add the rice, the additional water, and the turmeric, and mix. Bring to a boil.

5. Let the rice cook for 20 minutes, covered, until all the water is evaporated. Let stand while you finish the casserole.

6. Thicken the curried lamb mixture with the cornstarch-and-water mixture while it simmers, and serve over the rice.

## Lamb with Cabernet, Cepes, and Basil

APPROXIMATE PREPARATION TIME: 1 HOUR
MAKES 4 SERVINGS

This is another quick, one-pan dish that can be made in minutes once the lamb is cooked. This is typical of a stewed dish made with dried mushrooms. Serve with rice mixed with warmed raisins, and Cabernet.

*1 pound lean lamb, cut into ½-inch pieces*
*2 cups meat stock (pages 72–73)*
*1½ cups Cabernet Sauvignon (Bordeaux red will do), young*
    *wine preferable*
*1 ounce dried cepes*
*1 teaspoon salt*
*1 teaspoon sugar*
*1 tablespoon soy sauce*
*1 teaspoon dried basil, or 1 tablespoon fresh chopped*
*Water*
*2 tablespoons arrowroot mixed with ⅓ cup water*

*MUSHROOMS WITH MEAT*

1. Place all the ingredients except the arrowroot in a large skillet, making sure the meat is covered completely; add more water if necessary. Bring to a boil, and simmer 45 minutes, uncovered, or until the meat is tender.

2. Thicken with the arrowroot-and-water mixture, and serve.

## Lamb with Sausage, Potatoes, and Mushrooms

APPROXIMATE PREPARATION TIME: 1½ HOURS
MAKES 4 SERVINGS

This is the kind of dish that's better the day after it's made, so you can prepare it in large quantities, and eat it for a week. It's also a one-pot dish.

> *2 tablespoons cooking oil*
> *2 tablespoons butter*
> *2 pounds lean lamb, cubed into ½-inch pieces*
> *1 medium onion, chopped*
> *1 clove garlic, chopped*
> *3 cups meat stock (pages 72–73)*
> *3 cups water*
> *1 teaspoon salt*
> *1 teaspoon sugar*
> *1 tablespoon soy sauce*
> *1 pound Polish sausage, cubed*
> *1 large potato, cubed*
> *½ ounce dried mushrooms, such as morels or cepes (optional)*
> *1 pound fresh wild or domestic mushrooms, quartered*
> *3 tablespoons cornstarch mixed with ⅓ cup water*
> *Salt to taste*

1. In a large sauté pan, combine the cooking oil and butter, and heat. Add the lamb, and brown the meat on all sides.

2. Add the onions and garlic, and continue to sauté on a medium fire with the meat.

3. When the onions are clear, add the stock, water, salt, sugar, soy, sausage, and potatoes. (At this point, you can also add about ½ ounce dried mushrooms, and it will greatly enhance the flavor of the broth. But this step is optional.) Bring the whole thing to a boil, then lower to a simmer.

4. Let the stew cook for about 30 minutes, or until the meat is tender. The potatoes should also be done by this time. Add the quartered mushrooms, and cook another 5 minutes.

 **212**

5. Thicken the stew with the cornstarch-and-water mixture. Adjust for salt, and serve.

## Lamb Javanese
## (And Why the Phillies Won the World Series in 1980)

APPROXIMATE PREPARATION TIME: 1 HOUR
MAKES 4 SERVINGS

This is a spicy dish done in the kabob style and is ideal for outdoor grilling. I think the marinade used is one of the best I've ever come across.

We ate Javanese Lamb one afternoon in August of 1980, a time when the Phillies were rolling along in what looked to be another so-so season. I'm a big Philadelphia Phillies fan, and that afternoon we had invited ballplayers Steve Carlton, Tug McGraw, and Tim McCarver and their wives and some friends for a day of serious wine tasting, swimming, and food. We ate, drank, told stories, and otherwise had a good time eating Lamb Javanese, lobster, and wineberries.

The following weekend, the Phillies swept four games from the Pittsburgh Pirates, and that ignited the spark that ultimately sent them to the world championship two months later—the first World Series the Phillies have ever won. Now I don't intend to take credit for the Phillies' triumph that year, but if anyone notices the connection, well . . .

*20 pieces well-trimmed lamb loin, cubed into 1-inch pieces*
*12 medium fresh domestic mushrooms*
*1 large green pepper, cut into 1-inch squares*
*3 ounces Brazil nuts, chopped fine*
*2 teaspoons coriander, ground*
*2 teaspoons chili powder*
*2 teaspoons garlic, chopped fine*
*2 tablespoons lemon juice*
*1 tablespoon brown sugar*
*1/4 teaspoon fresh ground pepper*
*5 tablespoons soy sauce*
*3 tablespoons salt*
*1 large onion, chopped fine*
*1/2 cup red wine*
*2 tablespoons vinegar*

*Preheat broiler or charcoal grill.*

213

1.  Place the lamb, mushrooms, and peppers on a skewer, alternating the three until everything is used up.

2.  Combine the rest of the ingredients, and blend well.

3.  Pour the marinade into a wide, shallow pan, and place the skewers of meat and mushrooms in the marinade. Turn frequently to cover completely. Let the meat sit at room temperature in the marinade for 30 minutes.

4.  Broil the meat for 3 minutes on each side, adding more marinade as needed. Serve over rice.

# Mushrooms with Pork

Whereas beef dishes imply serious consideration, pork dishes imply fun. A primal cut, whose formal presentation is interrupted only by the complementary flavor of mushrooms, is replaced by a ne'er-do-well, free-wheeling type of meat that has virtually limitless possibilities. Indeed, no two types of meat are so different from one another as beef and pork—and for good reason. Beef can be eaten at any stage of doneness, from raw tartare to well-done. Pork, on the other hand, must always be thoroughly cooked because of the danger of trichinosis. Other obvious differences are the contrasting flavors and textures. But the biggest difference between beef and pork is the way these two meats are perceived by potential consumers. For some reason, the idea has gotten around that, although one must be somewhat reverent when approaching beef, one can do anything with pork, and it will taste fine. I'm not going to attempt to alter this impression; on the contrary, I intend to exploit it, because it makes cooking with pork all the more intriguing.

## Roast Pork with Shiitake

APPROXIMATE PREPARATION TIME: 1 HOUR
USEFUL ADVANCE PREPARATION: MAKE SHIITAKE DUXELLES (SEE PAGE 67).
MAKES 4 SERVINGS

Here's a quick dish that's flavorful and fun. The duxelles are made from shiitake mushrooms but domestic duxelles or almost any of the variations will do just fine. Serve with Buckwheat Groats (kasha) Kraców Style (see page 248) and Zinfandel.

*4 pork chops, ¾ inch thick, trimmed of excess fat, lightly salted on*
    *each side*
*1 clove garlic, sliced into thin slivers*
*Flour*
*4 tablespoons Shiitake Duxelles*

*Preheat oven to 450°.*

1. Make small cuts in the chops, and insert the garlic into these slits. You should have enough garlic for all the chops. If not, cut some more.

2. Flour the chops, and roast them in the oven for 20 minutes. Check the temperature of the chops at this point. They should be 180° at the center.

3. Coat the top of each chop with 1 tablespoon of the duxelles. Return to the oven, and continue to roast for another 5 to 10 minutes. Serve immediately.

## Twice-Cooked Pork with Straw Mushrooms

APPROXIMATE PREPARATION TIME: **2** HOURS
USEFUL ADVANCE PREPARATION: COOK PORK IN ADVANCE.
MAKES **4** SERVINGS

Double-cooking is done here so that the pork can be finished by stir-frying. Pork cannot be stir-fried from the raw like other meats; it has to be pre-cooked by boiling. I have elaborated on this method a bit by doing what I call a hot marinade. Instead of being boiled in plain water, the pork is boiled in a liquid that consists of wine, stock, and other components, which imparts its flavors to the meat. Additionally, the broth left over is used as the basis of the sauce for this dish, or any other you wish to use it for. Serve with fried rice and cold beer.

*1½ pounds pork, from the butt or tenderloin, well-trimmed and*
    *cut into three long strips*
*2 cups meat stock (pages 72–73)*
*2 cups water*
*2 cups red wine*
*1 clove garlic, chopped*
*1 medium onion, chopped*

**215**

*2 tablespoons hoisin sauce*
*2 tablespoons oyster sauce*
*2 tablespoons sugar*
*1 tablespoon soy sauce*
*1 tablespoon cornstarch*
*2 tablespoons peanut oil*
*3 small green peppers, cut into 1-inch squares and deseeded*
*2 tablespoons scallions, sliced into 1-inch pieces*
*1 15-ounce can straw mushrooms, drained*

1. In a pot, covered, cook the pork strips in the stock, water, wine, garlic, onion, hoisin, oyster sauce, and sugar, for 1 hour.

2. Remove the pork from the liquid, and let cool. Then cut the pork into 1-inch cubes. Be certain that the pork has been thoroughly cooked. There should be no pink in the meat.*

3. Strain the liquid that was used for cooking the pork. Cook this liquid down to about 1 cup. Check for salt; this sauce should be pretty intense, and you may want to add water to desalt it. Use only half of the sauce for the stir-fry, putting it aside to let it cool.

4. When the sauce is cool, add soy sauce and cornstarch, and stir thoroughly. The sauce is now ready for adding to the stir-fry.

5. Heat the oil in a wok until it begins to smoke. Add the peppers and scallions, and stir-fry for 1 minute. Then add the pork, and stir-fry for another 2 minutes.

6. Add the mushrooms, and stir-fry for another 30 seconds. Slowly add to the wok the sauce mixed well with the cornstarch while stirring the pork mixture. Add liquid to desired thickness.

*Note: This dish can also be made casserole-style in a single pot. After the pork is done cooking in the marinade, add the peppers, scallions, and mushrooms, and bring to a boil. Then thicken with some arrowroot or cornstarch. Adjust for salt.

## Pork with Bonchampi

APPROXIMATE PREPARATION TIME: 1½ HOURS
USEFUL ADVANCE PREPARATION: MAKE MUSHROOM CREAM SAUCE I (SEE PAGES 78–79)
MAKES 4 SERVINGS

Bonchampi is a cheese from France made with mushrooms. Its rich, milky flavor combined with pork gives this dish a unique status among pork roulades. Serve with a combination of buttered diced carrots and turnips, and Pinot Blanc.

> *8 ounces Bonchampi, sliced lengthwise, rind removed*
> *8 3-ounce pieces pork tenderloin, pounded thin into rounds 5*
> *    inches in diameter*
> *8 romaine lettuce leaves*
> *½ cup dry sherry*
> *1½ cups Mushroom Cream Sauce*

1. Place 1 piece of cheese in each piece of pork, and roll the pork into a roulade with the cheese in the middle.

2. Wrap a leaf of romaine around each roulade, and place the roulades in a flameproof casserole that will accommodate all 8 of them.

3. Place a little sherry in the bottom of the pot (about ½ cup), and cover with a tight-fitting lid. Place over a low flame, and cook for 1 hour.

4. Remove roulades from pot, and cover with heated sauce. Serve immediately.


## Pork with Sesame and Cloud-Ears

APPROXIMATE PREPARATION TIME: **2** HOURS
USEFUL ADVANCE PREPARATION: RECONSTITUTE CLOUD-EARS.
MAKES **4** SERVINGS

The cloud-ears provide a nice, crunchy counterpoint to the pork in this recipe. Serve with Orzo Marco Polo (see pages 239–240) and Gewürz-traminer.

> *2 cups meat stock (pages 72–73)*
> *1 teaspoon salt*
> *1 teaspoon Chinese five-spice*
> *1 teaspoon hoisin sauce*
> *1 ounce dried cloud-ears (also called tree fungus)*
> *½ teaspoon Chinese fish sauce*
> *½ teaspoon garlic, powdered or granulated*
> *1 tablespoon sliced scallions*
> *1½ pounds lean pork, boiled until done in lightly salted water*
> *    and sliced thin*
> *1½ tablespoons arrowroot mixed with ⅓ cup water*

217

*MUSHROOMS WITH MEAT*

1. Combine the ingredients up to and including garlic in a saucepan, and bring to a boil. Let simmer for 1 hour, covered, or until the cloud-ears are soft through. They will feel crunchy when bitten.

2. Add the pork and scallions, and continue to simmer for another 10 minutes. Then begin thickening with the arrowroot-and-water mixture. Serve immediately.

## Pork 'n Port

APPROXIMATE PREPARATION TIME: 1 HOUR
MAKES 4 SERVINGS

This sauce can be made from dried *Boletus edulis* (cepes) or dried forest mushrooms or even from morels, although the morels will make a lighter sauce. Serve with potatoes whipped with butter, cream, and a pinch of cayenne pepper, along with a good Merlot.

> *1 ounce dried mushrooms*
> *3 cups water*
> *1 teaspoon salt*
> *1 teaspoon sugar*
> *1 tablespoon soy sauce*
> *2 tablespoons port*
> *¼ teaspoon dried basil*
> *4 pork chops, about 1 inch thick, trimmed and lightly salted on
>     each side*
> *3 tablespoons flour*
> *3 tablespoons butter*

*Preheat oven to 450°.*

1. In a saucepan, bring the mushrooms and the water to a boil, and let simmer for 30 minutes.

2. Add salt, sugar, soy sauce, port, and basil, and simmer for another 5 minutes. Remove the mushrooms from the liquid, and reserve them. The volume of the liquid should now be about 2 cups.

3. Slice the mushrooms, and set aside.

4. Begin roasting the chops in the oven until done, about 30 to 45 minutes.

 218

5. While the meat is roasting, make the roux by combining the flour with the butter in a saucepan and stirring over a medium heat till golden. Add the liquid from the mushrooms, and stir until thickened. Add back the mushrooms to the sauce.

6. Remove the chops from the oven, pour the sauce over them, and serve.


## Pork with Red Peppers and Morels

APPROXIMATE PREPARATION TIME: 1 HOUR
MAKES 4 SERVINGS

This is another one-pot dish that can benefit from adding more vegetables to the stew. Pour everything over plain rice. Serve with a Heitz Brut.

*3 cups water*
*1½ ounces dried morels*
*1½ pounds pork butt or tenderloin, well-trimmed and cut into*
*    1-inch squares*
*1 teaspoon salt*
*1 teaspoon sugar*
*1 tablespoon soy sauce*
*1 tablespoon cream sherry*
*2 large sweet red peppers, cut into 1-inch squares*
*1½ tablespoons arrowroot or cornstarch mixed with water*

1. In a large saucepan, bring the water and the dried morels to a boil, and simmer, uncovered, for ½ hour.

2. Add the rest of the ingredients except the arrowroot, bring to a rapid boil, and let simmer for another 30 minutes. Adjust for salt, if necessary. The liquid content should be about 2 cups.

3. Thicken the casserole with the arrowroot- or cornstarch-and-water mixture, and serve on a bed of rice.

**219**

# Pork with Thyme and Mushrooms

APPROXIMATE PREPARATION TIME: 1 HOUR
MAKES 4 SERVINGS

Thyme is one of the stronger herbs, and you must be careful how much of it you use in this recipe. Fresh thyme is best, but the dried will do just fine. Serve with potatoes with butter and peppercorn sauce, and a Beaujolais.

*1½ cups water*
*1 pound domestic mushrooms, sliced*
*1 teaspoon sugar*
*½ teaspoon salt*
*1 tablespoon soy sauce*
*1 tablespoon onions, chopped*
*1 tablespoon butter, melted*
*4 pork chops, trimmed, cut about 1-inch thick, and lightly salted*
    *on each side*
*1 tablespoon cornstarch or arrowroot mixed with ⅓ cup water*
*½ teaspoon fresh thyme or ¼ teaspoon dried thyme*

*Preheat oven to 450°.*

1. Put the water and the mushrooms in a saucepan, and "sweat" the mushrooms by turning the heat on high for 3 minutes, then to low for another 20 minutes. Cover tightly. This will extract the liquid from the mushrooms and make a richer sauce. Add the sugar, salt, and soy sauce.
2. In another saucepan, sauté the onions in the butter for 1 minute, then add the liquid from the mushrooms, and bring back to a simmer. Your volume of liquid at this point should be about 2 cups. Add back the mushrooms, and keep on a low flame.
3. Roast the chops in the oven for 30 to 45 minutes.
4. Just before the chops are done, thicken the mushroom sauce with the cornstarch- or arrowroot-and-water mixture, add the thyme, stir for 30 seconds, and serve over the chops.

## Pork with Mustard and Mushrooms

APPROXIMATE PREPARATION TIME: 1 HOUR
USEFUL ADVANCE PREPARATION: COOK PORK ACCORDING TO STEPS 1 AND 2
        OF TWICE-COOKED PORK RECIPE, (SEE PAGES 215–216).
MAKES 4 SERVINGS

This dish is prepared in much the same manner as Pork with Thyme and Mushrooms, but with entirely different results. The creamed sauce is the essence of domestic mushrooms. Serve with asparagus sautéed with toasted almonds, and Riesling.

*1 cup water*
*1 pound domestic mushrooms, sliced*
*1 teaspoon sugar*
*½ teaspoon salt*
*1 tablespoon soy sauce*
*1 tablespoon onions, chopped*
*1 tablespoon butter, melted*
*1 cup heavy whipping cream*
*1 tablespoon prepared Dijon mustard*
*1½ pounds pork butt or tenderloin, trimmed of excess fat, cooked,*
    *and sliced*
*3 egg yolks, slightly beaten*

1. Put ⅓ cup of water and the mushrooms in a saucepan, and "sweat" the mushrooms by turning the heat on high for 1 minute, then to low for another 20 minutes. Cover tightly. This will extract the liquid from the mushrooms and make a richer sauce. Add the sugar, salt, and soy sauce.

2. In another saucepan, sauté the onions in the butter for 1 minute, then add the liquid from the mushrooms and bring back to a simmer. Add back the mushrooms, and keep on a low flame. Add ¾ cup of the heavy whipping cream and the mustard, and blend well.

3. Add the cooked pork to the mushroom mixture, and in a separate cup whisk together the remaining ¼ cup cream with the egg yolks.

4. Bring the mixture back up to a simmer, and thicken it by slowly adding, while stirring, the cream-egg mixture. When the sauce is thick enough, remove it from the heat, and serve immediately.

**221**

**CHAPTER ELEVEN**

# *Furred Game with Wild Mushrooms*

Nothing matches the combination of wild mushrooms with game. Game cookery can be tricky, though. Here are a few generalizations that can be made about furred wild animals.

First, nowadays some "game" animals such as rabbits, hares, deer, and buffalo are, in fact, being raised in less than wild environments. Preserves have sprung up across the country, from which we can now obtain such diversified specimens as lion, llama, and wild boar. The implication of this is that these animals are fed far better than they can feed themselves in their natural habitat, and the quality of the meat is generally quite good. Most "real game" is apt to be stringy and tough beyond edibility. Game from a preserve can be fairly tough too, but at least the quantity of meat gives the chef something to work with.

Second, because the meat of most game animals is quite lean, cooking beyond the medium-rare point causes it to become firm and tough. Therefore, with "safe" game meat like buffalo, venison, or rabbit, it is better to serve the entree rare or medium rare. But it is not always possible to eat game rare, since some types, such as wild boar and bear, are potential hosts for the parasite that causes trichinosis. (Consult a reliable book on meats to determine which game meats are safe to eat rare and which ones are not.)

Third, how does one eat game beyond medium rare and still have a tender dish? Prepare game by boiling the meat. But don't boil it in plain water or stock. The classic method for tenderizing game is to marinate it for several days before cooking; that way the muscle fiber is broken down by the acids in the marinade. I suggest that, instead of using a cold marinade, you boil the meat in this marinade. The method for doing this is described, when appropriate, in the recipes that follow. The idea is to tenderize the meat while at the same time permeating it with the flavors of the marinade ingredients. Also, it takes a fraction of the time to prepare that the classic cold-marinating method does.

Using mushrooms with game affords many possibilities. Virtually all the recipes already described for pork apply to comparable cuts of game. Remember, though, that the game always needs longer cooking for tenderness. Chanterelles and cepes go particularly well with game, as do domestic mushrooms. Sweet and rich sauces pair nicely with venison and bear. Buffalo strip sirloin can be made like sirloin strips according to the method described for that cut of beef (see pages 185–186).

## Scotch Roebuck Casserole

APPROXIMATE PREPARATION TIME: **2** HOURS
MAKES **4** SERVINGS

This is one of the signature dishes developed at Joe's utilizing hoisin sauce, which is used in Chinese cooking. The rich, sweet taste of the hoisin is a natural complement to the gaminess of the roebuck and consistent with the philosophy of venison cookery of Middle Europe. Serve with kasha (buckwheat groats). Late Harvest Zinfandel is the best wine to serve with this dish.

> *2 pounds venison from a Scotch roebuck or any venison meat,*
> *  boned and cut into ½-inch cubes*
> *3 cups red wine*
> *2 cups water or (preferably) veal stock (see pages 72–73)*
> *2 cloves crushed garlic*
> *½ cup chopped onions*
> *1 teaspoon salt*
> *2 tablespoons hoisin sauce*
> *Salt to taste*
> *16 medium caps fresh shiitake*
> *2 tablespoons arrowroot mixed with ⅓ cup water*

**223**

1. Combine in a pot the venison, wine, water or veal stock, 1 clove of the garlic, the onions, salt, and 1 tablespoon hoisin sauce. Bring to a boil, cover, and simmer together until the venison is tender, about 1 to 2 hours. This allows the flavor of the marinade to penetrate the meat.

2. Remove the meat from the liquid, and transfer the liquid to a saucepan. Add to this liquid the remaining garlic and hoisin sauce, and bring to a boil, reducing by ⅓. Salt to taste.

3. Add to the liquid the shiitake and the roebuck or venison, bring to a boil, and heat for 5 minutes. Thicken with the arrowroot-and-water mixture. Serve with brown rice.

## Venison Steaks with Mushroom Game Sauce

APPROXIMATE PREPARATION TIME: 1 HOUR
USEFUL ADVANCE PREPARATION: PREPARE WILD MUSHROOM GAME SAUCE (SEE
    PAGES 80–81).
MAKES 4 SERVINGS

Do not overcook the venison here. It should be done no more than medium rare in the center. This preparation does not require marinading, because of the tenderness of the loin meat. Serve with quick-sautéed potatoes with dill sauce, and Stag's Leap Cabernet.

*4 venison steaks cut from loin, 6 to 8 ounces each*
*Ground juniper berries*
*2 teaspoons salt*
*⅓ cup melted butter*
*2 cups Wild Mushroom Game Sauce*

1. Pound the steaks to ½-inch thickness. Sprinkle lightly with the juniper berries and salt.

2. Sauté the steaks with the butter for about 3 minutes on each side. The meat should be done no more than medium rare.

3. Heat the Wild Mushroom Game Sauce, adjust for salt, pour over the steaks, and serve.

## Venison with Currants and Chanterelles

APPROXIMATE PREPARATION TIME: 1½ HOURS
MAKES 4 SERVINGS

Currants are a favorite in European cooking because they combine fruitiness with acidity. Chanterelles are the best mushrooms to use with game because of their almost fruitlike flavor. Serve with apricot rice and a Sterling Vineyards Merlot.

*2 pounds venison meat, boned and cubed or sliced*
*2 cups water or (preferably) veal stock (pages 72–73)*
*3 cups red wine*
*1 tablespoon crushed dried onion*
*2 cloves crushed garlic*
*1 teaspoon salt*
*1 pound fresh currants or 1 cup currant jelly*
*4 ounces fresh chanterelles or 2 ounces canned*
*2 tablespoons arrowroot mixed with ⅓ cup water*
*Salt to taste*

1. "Hot-marinade" the venison by combining it with the water or stock, wine, onion, garlic, and salt, and bring all these ingredients to a boil. Let them simmer, covered, for 1 hour, or until the venison is tender.
2. Add currants or currant jelly and chanterelles, and bring back to a boil. Thicken with the arrowroot-and-water mixture. The use of currant jelly instead of fresh currants will make a slightly sweeter sauce. Adjust for salt, and serve with rice.

## Stuffed Venison Rymanów

APPROXIMATE PREPARATION TIME: 1½ HOURS
USEFUL ADVANCE PREPARATION: MAKE GARLIC DUXELLES (SEE PAGE 62) AND
　　　　MUSHROOM CREAM SAUCE III (SEE PAGE 79).
MAKES 4 SERVINGS

Rymanów style is a method of preparation in which meat is pounded very thin and then stuffed with a duxelles. It bears a generic resemblance to roulade, which is stuffed, then rolled. Rymanów preparation, on the other hand, leaves the meat flat, then utilizes breading before finishing. The thinness

**225**

of the pieces and shortness of cooking time obviate the need for marinading. The name is that of a Polish town about a hundred miles southeast of Kraków and the birthplace of my grandmother Magdalena. Serve with kasha tossed with walnuts and Polish sausage, cut fine. Accompany with a woody, big Chardonnay or white Burgundy.

> *8 3-ounce pieces venison loin*
> *1 tablespoon finely crushed juniper berries*
> *2 teaspoons salt*
> *4 tablespoons Garlic Duxelles*
> *1 egg, beaten*
> *1 cup milk*
> *2 eggs*
> *Flour*
> *Bread crumbs, seasoned lightly with salt and pepper*
> *Salt (optional)*
> *Cayenne pepper (optional)*
> *¼ cup clarified butter (see page 51), or cooking oil*
> *1½ cups Mushroom Cream Sauce III*

1. Pound the pieces of venison flat with a mallet. These cutlets should be very thin.

2. Sprinkle the venison on one side with the juniper berries. Add salt.

3. Place 1 piece of the venison down on a surface with the berry-coated side up. Place 1 tablespoonful of the duxelles in the middle, and spread evenly over the venison to a point about ½ inch from the edge of the cutlet. Paint the edge of the cutlet with some beaten egg. Place another piece of the flattened venison berry-coated side down on top of the first. Do this until you have 4 individual portions.

4. Beat together the milk and the eggs. Place flour in a shallow dish that will fit the venison cutlets. Place the bread crumbs in another shallow dish of the same size.

5. Dredge the venison in the flour first, coating well, then dredge in the milk-egg mixture (this mixture can be salted and made interesting with a little cayenne pepper). Then coat the venison with the bread crumbs, making sure to cover completely.

6. Add the butter or oil to a sauté pan, and heat till bubbling. Add the venison cutlets, and cook over a moderate heat until golden brown. This will take about 3 minutes on each side.

7. Remove the venison to a serving dish, and serve surrounded by the Mushroom Cream Sauce.

226

## Wild Suckling Boar with Whiskey and Juniper Berries

APPROXIMATE PREPARATION TIME: **8** HOURS
USEFUL ADVANCE PREPARATION: MAKE KASHA-MUSHROOM STUFFING FOR
      BOAR (SEE PAGES **247–248**) AND WHISKEY AND JUNIPER BERRY SAUCE
      WITH SHIITAKE (SEE PAGES **87–88**).
MAKES **4** SERVINGS

This is a dish for those extra special occasions when we entertain in an outpouring of cheer and celebration of life.

> *1 whole suckling wild boar pig, about 10 pounds (Have your*
>     *butcher prepare it.)*
> *⅓ cup olive oil*
> *1½ tablespoons sesame oil*
> *Salt*
> *Pepper*
> *1 tablespoon fresh ginger, minced*
> *4 cups Kasha-Mushroom Stuffing*
> *2 cups water or veal stock (see pages 72–73)*
> *1 apple*
> *2 cherries*
> *1½ cups Whiskey and Juniper Berry Sauce*

*Preheat oven to 325°.*

1. Coat outside of boar with the olive oil and the sesame oil.
2. Coat inside of boar with salt, pepper, and ginger to coat lightly.
3. Stuff boar with Kasha-Mushroom Stuffing. Close opening with skewers, and lace with kitchen twine.
4. Place boar on rack in roasting pan, and add 2 cups water or stock to the pan.
5. Place a block of wood in boar's mouth for opening for apple, and cover meat with aluminum foil. Place in oven.
6. Baste boar every ½ hour while roasting in the oven for 5 to 6 hours.
7. Remove boar from pan, and insert an apple in the mouth and cherries in the eyes. Let stand for 10 minutes before carving and serving.
8. Surround the boar with the sauce.

# Wild Boar with Shiitake, Apples, and Strawberry Liqueur

APPROXIMATE PREPARATION TIME: **3** HOURS
USEFUL ADVANCE PREPARATION: MAKE MUSHROOM CREAM SAUCE II,
UNTHICKENED (SEE PAGE **79**).
MAKES **4** SERVINGS

This dish is prepared casserole-style, using boar that has been pre-cooked in the Chinese manner. The purpose of this is to ensure that the meat is done and to penetrate the flesh with some flavors that it will carry to the casserole. Serve with braised cabbage and onions, and German Riesling.

*3 pounds boar loin, cut into chunks 2 inches in diameter and
    about 6 inches long.*
*2 cups veal or beef stock*
*Water*
*1 cup white wine*
*1 small onion, sliced*
*4 tablespoons soy sauce*
*2 tablespoons brown sugar*
*2½ cups Mushroom Cream Sauce II, unthickened*
*12 caps shiitake, oyster mushrooms, or domestic mushrooms*
*1 teaspoon strawberry liqueur or strawberry syrup*
*Several medium-sized apples peeled and sliced*
*1 tablespoon* crème fraîche *(optional)*
*2 tablespoons cornstarch in ⅓ cup water*

1. Put the boar, stock, water (enough to cover the boar), wine, onion, soy sauce, and sugar in a large pot, and simmer until done, about 1 hour. The boar should have no pink in the center. Remove the boar, and cool it in the refrigerator.

2. Slice the boar into thin pieces to approximate the size of the apple slices.

3. Place the Mushroom Cream Sauce, boar, and mushrooms in a saucepan, and bring to a simmer.

4. Add the liqueur and apples, and continue to simmer for another 10 minutes. At this point, you may also wish to add some *crème fraîche* to give the dish a bit of an acid edge. Thicken with cornstarch-and-water mixture.

5. Place immediately on a serving platter.

## Wild Boar with Cepes

APPROXIMATE PREPARATION TIME: 2 HOURS
USEFUL ADVANCE PREPARATION: PREPARE BOAR AS IN WILD BOAR WITH
    SHIITAKE (SEE PAGE 228), AND MAKE MUSHROOM CREAM SAUCE III
    (SEE PAGE 79).
MAKES 4 SERVINGS

This is a very full-flavored dish, typical of an eastern European treatment of game and wild mushrooms. The magic is in the sauce, which is made with an extract from the cepes (see recipe for Mushroom Cream Sauce III). Because of this you can substitute domestic mushrooms in the dish itself. Serve with wild rice and chopped pistachios, and a big Chardonnay.

> *3 pounds wild boar, precooked and sliced as in steps 1 and 2 of*
>     *Wild Boar with Shiitake*
> *½ pound fresh or 4 ounces canned cepes (or ½ pound domestic*
>     *mushrooms)*
> *1½ cups Mushroom Cream Sauce III, unthickened*
> *2 tablespoons cornstarch mixed with ⅓ cup water*

Combine the boar, the mushrooms, and the sauce in a pan, and heat to a simmer for 10 minutes. Thicken with cornstarch-and-water mixture, and serve.

## Wild Boar Zrazy with Morels

APPROXIMATE PREPARATION TIME: 2 HOURS
USEFUL ADVANCE PREPARATION: PREPARE WILD MUSHROOM DUXELLES OF
    CHOICE (SEE PAGES 65–67), AND PREPARE MOREL VELOUTÉ SAUCE
    (SEE PAGE 83).
MAKES 4 SERVINGS

This is one of the favorites of old Polish cookery. *Zrazy* are similar to roulades, being a meat dish that is pounded, then stuffed and rolled. They are stuffed with any number of different farcis, or in this case a duxelles. Wild boar is wonderful for *zrazy*, because of its distinctive flavors and adaptability to different sauces. Serve with steamed spinach mixed with ham, chopped eggs, and cream.

**229**

> *8 2-ounce pieces wild boar loin (or ham)*
> *2 teaspoons crushed juniper berries*
> *4 tablespoons Wild Mushroom Duxelles*
> *4 tablespoons butter*
> *4 leaves romaine lettuce*
> *1 cup beef or veal stock*
> *Salt*
> *2 cups Morel Velouté Sauce*

1. Pound the boar pieces with a French cleaver or mallet till very thin. Rub the juniper berries into the meat.

2. Spread the boar with ½ tablespoon each of the duxelles.

3. Roll each piece of meat into a tight form. These pieces are called the *zrazy*.

4. Melt butter in a saucepan, and brown the *zrazy* on 2 sides for about 2 minutes each.

5. Place the romaine leaves on the bottom of a medium-size saucepan with a tight-fitting lid.

6. Place the *zrazy* on the romaine leaves to keep it from burning, and add the stock. Lightly salt the *zrazy,* and cover the pan. Bring the liquid to a simmer, and continue cooking until the *zrazy* are tender, about 1 hour. Add more stock or water if necessary to the pan while cooking.

7. Place *zrazy* on a serving dish, discard romaine leaves, and cover with the heated sauce and serve immediately.

## Buffalo with Game Sauce

APPROXIMATE PREPARATION TIME: 1 HOUR
USEFUL ADVANCE PREPARATION: PREPARE WILD MUSHROOM GAME SAUCE (SEE PAGES 80–81).
MAKES 4 SERVINGS

Buffalo are not unique to the American plains. European bison, called the wisent or *żubr* in Polish, has roamed the forests of central Europe for millennia. There is even a vodka called *żubrowka,* which is made from a special type of grass called bison grass, growing today in the only forests where these bison still exist.

In this country, there has been a renewed interest in buffalo meat, and thus it is not particularly difficult to obtain. It tastes quite beefy, but cannot be cooked past medium rare, or it will toughen very quickly. This is a very old recipe that goes back to the seventeenth century. Serve with Sauerkraut with Dried Mushrooms and Peas (see pages 255–256), and a David Bruce Pinot Noir.

> *4 buffalo sirloin steaks, cut 1½ inches thick*
> *¼ cup melted butter*
> *2 cups Wild Mushroom Game Sauce*

1. Sauté each steak with the butter over a high heat for 3 minutes. The steak should be medium rare.
2. Place steak on platter, and add heated sauce, using ½ cup sauce per steak.

## Buffalo Sirloins with Cepes

APPROXIMATE PREPARATION TIME: 1 HOUR
MAKES 4 SERVINGS

The one thing to keep in mind about cooking buffalo is that, if the meat is cooked past medium rare, it begins to toughen. This is especially important with cuts that are to be broiled, as in this case, so be careful not to overdo the meat. Buffalo, when prepared right, tastes more meaty than beef. Serve with Morel Rice (see page 245) and Monterey Peninsula Cabernet.

> *1 large onion, sliced into thin rounds*
> *3 tablespoons butter*
> *2 cups fresh cepes (Other wild mushrooms can be substituted.)*
> *4 buffalo sirloin steaks ¾-inch thick*
> *Salt*

> *Preheat broiler.*

1. Sauté the onions in the butter until transparent.
2. Add mushrooms, and continue to sauté with the onions over a medium heat. The liquid should be mostly evaporated. Set aside.
3. Lightly salt the steaks, then broil until they are done medium rare, about 2 minutes per side, turning frequently.
4. Top the steaks with the mushrooms and onions, and serve.

## Buffalo Burgers

**APPROXIMATE PREPARATION TIME:** **1** **HOUR**
**USEFUL ADVANCE PREPARATION: PREPARE TOMATO DUXELLES (SEE PAGE 62).**
**MAKES 4 SERVINGS**

There are times when it is much easier to get ground buffalo than the better cuts of domestic meat. The rich flavor of this animal lends itself extremely well to one of our American classics.

*½ cup Tomato Duxelles*
*2 pounds ground buffalo meat*
*4 slices Bonchampi*
*Salt to taste*
*4 hamburger rolls, toasted*

1. Blend the duxelles with the ground buffalo meat.
2. Form the mixture into patties about ⅓ to ½ inch thick and cook over outdoor fire or in pan over the stove. Cook approximately 3 minutes per side to medium rare.
3. Top each patty with a slice of the cheese, and cover until the cheese is melted.
4. Salt these cheeseburgers lightly, and serve in buns.

**VARIATION**

This burger is also good with mushrooms and onions sautéed in butter for a "triple" mushroom-buffalo burger.

# Wild Hare Kabobs

APPROXIMATE PREPARATION TIME: **3** HOURS
USEFUL ADVANCE PREPARATION: PRECOOK SADDLE OF HARE.
MAKES **4** SERVINGS

For this recipe it is necessary to precook a saddle of wild hare (or the less gamier-tasting rabbit), before preparing the final steps. The dish should be taken off the skewers before serving so that the laid-down look is of the shiitake alternating with the hare and green pepper. A good Zinfandel is a nice accompaniment.

> *1 ready-to-cook saddle of a 2-to-4-pound wild hare or rabbit*
> *12 caps medium-sized shiitake*
> *1 large green pepper, cut into 1-inch skewering cubes, seeds*
> *removed*
> *2 tablespoons hoisin sauce*
> *2 tablespoons oyster sauce*
> *1 tablespoon melted butter*
> *1 teaspoon white wine or sherry*

*Preheat oven to 400°.*

1. To prepare the saddle of hare, clean the meat, put it on a wire rack in a roasting pan, and roast in the oven for about 1½ hours, or until tender. Cool this roasted saddle in the refrigerator.

2. When the saddle is cooled, remove the tenderloin and rib meat running along the bone. Take this meat out carefully because you want to keep the cylindrical-shaped piece of meat on either side of the body intact, so that you can make uniform, even pieces when slicing.

3. Slice the saddle into ½-inch pieces.

4. Place these pieces on a skewer, alternating with the shiitake and green pepper. (You may want to precook the green pepper for 1 to 2 minutes, by simply steaming in a covered saucepan with ½ inch of water.)

5. Broil the kabobs (these may be done barbecue-style also) for 1 minute on each side.

6. Combine the hoisin, oyster sauce, butter, and white wine or sherry, coat the meat with this mixture, and broil for 1 more minute. De-skewer, and serve immediately.

233

## Hare-in-the-Woods

APPROXIMATE PREPARATION TIME: 1½ HOURS
USEFUL ADVANCE PREPARATION: PREPARE CHANTERELLE SAUCE (SEE PAGES
**89–90**).
MAKES **4** SERVINGS

This hare (or rabbit) dish uses ingredients that a hare or rabbit might feed on in July in the Pennsylvania woods. Serve with gently steamed fiddleheads, lightly salted, and a good Chenin Blanc like a Grand Cru.

*1 tablespoon onion, chopped fine*
*1 clove garlic, minced*
*1 tablespoon butter*
*2 cups Chanterelle Sauce, unthickened*
*1 wild hare, about 6 pounds, cut into bite-sized pieces,*
        *or 1 6-pound rabbit*
*¾ cup sliced chanterelles*
*½ cup fresh blueberries*
*1 tablespoon pine nuts, toasted*
*1½ tablespoons arrowroot dissolved in ⅓ cup water*

1. In a saucepan, sauté the onion and garlic in the butter for 1 minute.
2. Add the unthickened Chanterelle Sauce to the pan, and bring to a simmer.
3. Add the hare to the sauce, cover, and cook until the hare is tender (about 20 minutes).
4. Add the chanterelles, and simmer for 5 more minutes.
5. Add the blueberries and pine nuts, and thicken immediately with the arrowroot-and-water mixture.

## Bear Sobieski with Croissants

APPROXIMATE PREPARATION TIME: 2½ HOURS
MAKES **4** SERVINGS

This dish bears the name of King Jan III Sobieski (1629–1696), the savior of Vienna and the greatest king in Poland's history. There are two reasons for the name. One is that King Jan was, indeed, a bear of a man, being large of girth and fierce of temper. The second reason is that the principal flavor ingredient here is cumin, a spice used throughout the former Ottoman Empire, whose expansion King Jan halted at Vienna (1683). Another famous food invented to celebrate that event, the croissant, is used to finish off eating the sauce in this dish. Serve with a good Cabernet Sauvignon.

*2 pounds bear meat, cubed*
*1 quart dry red wine*
*1 quart strong meat stock, veal preferred (see pages 72–73)*
*3 cloves garlic, crushed*
*3 large onions, cut coarse*
*1 cup honey*
*1/3 ounce dried cepes*
*1 tablespoon crushed cumin*
*3 tablespoons butter*
*3 tablespoons sifted flour*
*2 teaspoons salt*
*2 tablespoons soy sauce*
*1 1/2 cups fresh wild or domestic mushrooms*
*4 croissants*

1. Place the bear, wine, stock, garlic, onions, honey, cepes, and cumin in a pot that will accommodate them. The liquid should cover the meat; if it does not, then add water to cover. Bring to a boil. Let simmer until the bear meat is tender (about 1½ hours).

2. Remove the bear from the liquid, and set aside. Strain the liquid, and cook down to 3 cups.

3. Make a roux by combining the butter and flour, and cook until the roux is very dark. This will take about 15 minutes. Be careful not to burn the roux.

4. Add to the roux the liquid, salt, and soy sauce. Stir until thickened. Warm the croissants.

5. Add the bear and the mushrooms, and continue to cook for another 5 minutes. Serve with the croissants.

CHAPTER TWELVE

# Mushrooms with Pasta and as Side Dishes

## Mushrooms with Pasta

Pasta, rice, cereals, potatoes, and vegetables are more easily permeated with the flavor of mushrooms than almost any other foods. Since many of them are bought dried, a basic method of preparation is to cook them in a mushroom broth rather than in water. Fresh pasta is even more amenable than dried to absorbing the mushroom flavor because the dough can incorporate powder, extracts, or purees during the kneading process. The following list gives you an idea of how these flavors can interact.

### Methods of Combining Mushrooms with Pasta

SAUTÉ AND TOSS. This is the most widely used means of combining mushrooms with noodles, etc. You simply sauté mushrooms with any complementary ingredients, and then toss them with the pasta. Chinese stir-frying is a good example of this method. Stir-Fried Mushrooms (see pages 120–121) can be put over any pasta or grain.

SAUCE METHOD. Just make a sauce, and pour it over. This is only slightly different from the first method, and the two are more often than not combined. Spaghetti and meatballs with mushrooms is a well-known example.

**PASTA TOSSED WITH OIL.** This is a classic Italian method occasionally seen in better restaurants. In mushroom cookery the method is to toss the pasta with a mushroom butter, a relatively low-calorie means of enjoying vermicelli and similar pasta dishes.

**PASTA COOKED IN ENRICHED WATER.** Whether you make your own pasta or not, you can increase the mushroom character of the dish by cooking the pasta in water to which dried mushrooms have been added. How many mushrooms to add can become an economical rather than a practical question, considering the cost of some dried mushrooms, but the water you are using should change to a perceptibly dark color for it to make a difference. You may salt the water with a mixture of salt, sugar, and soy sauce (see pages 57–58). Be aware, however, that pasta cooked in salted water will be a bit softer than when cooked without salt.

**FILLED PASTA.** This is an old method of intertwining flavors, the means whereby we incorporate mushroom duxelles into tortellini, ravioli, *uszka,* and other filled noodle products.

## Making Pasta with Mushroom Flavorings

If you are interested in making your own pasta, there are several ways to get the mushroom flavor right into the dough of the pasta itself. But these methods are for the experienced pasta maker, who knows the right texture for the finished dough.

**PASTA WITH MUSHROOM PUREE.** In this method the pasta dough is made by blending the flour with a mushroom purée. (See instructions on making a mushroom purée, pages 67–70, for details.) If you use this method, you will not need any additional water for the pasta making. For ¾ cup puree of wild mushroom from *Boletus edulis* (cepes), you will need 1½ pounds flour, or even a bit more. Proceed with the rolling and cutting from this point. When the pasta is cooked, be sure to cook·it in a broth that has been enriched with more dried mushrooms; if plain water is used, the flavor you put into the dough will be diluted again.

**PASTA FROM MUSHROOM EXTRACT.** Here, the liquid used for preparing the pasta dough is a concentrated liquid extract made from dried mushrooms. You simply substitute a rich mushroom extract for the water while making the dough. You may salt the extract if you wish by the salt, sugar, and soy sauce method described on pages 57–58. When cooking the pasta make sure to enrich the water with some dried mushrooms.

**PASTA FROM MUSHROOM POWDER.** A preparation popularized by Jacques Pepin, this method calls for replacing about one quarter of the flour you would normally use to prepare the dough with mushroom powder (see pages 71–72). Again, cook the finished rolled dough in water enriched with some dried mushrooms.

## Combined Methods

A mushroom sauce poured over a pasta that has been made with mushroom powder, extract, or purée (or all three) and cooked in a mushroom-enriched broth provides the ideal expression of the sensuous flavor of mushrooms. Don't worry about overdoing the mushroom flavor. Do remember, though, that when you incorporate mushroom flavor into a dish like this, you will have some color changes. Your pasta with mushroom powder will be speckled with brown spots, and your white rice won't be white anymore. Take this into account for aesthetic appeal before you begin.

## Pork and Shiitake with Cellophane Noodles

**APPROXIMATE PREPARATION TIME: 3 HOURS**
**MAKES 4 SERVINGS, FOR A LUNCH OR AS PART OF A MULTICOURSE ORIENTAL DINNER**

These clear noodles, often dismissed with a cursory glance in our jaunts through Oriental grocery store, are a nice change from pasta and rice. They require little cooking; in fact, soaking them in hot water for an hour is sufficient.

> *Water for cooking noodles*
> *1 small package cellophane noodles*
> *1 teaspoon soy sauce*
> *½ pork butt, about 2 pounds*
> *Water for cooking pork*
> *1 cup dry red wine*

*6 large shiitake caps, sliced*
*3 scallions, sliced*
*2 tablespoons peanut oil*
*¼ cup hoisin sauce*
*¼ cup Chinese oyster sauce*

1. Boil the water for cooking noodles, then turn off the heat. Add a little soy sauce to the water. Place the noodles in the water, and let them sit for an hour.

2. Trim the pork butt of any fat and cut into about 3 or 4 strips, 6 inches long. Place the pork in the water for cooking pork, to which the wine has been added. Bring to a boil, and then let simmer, covered, for 45 minutes. The pork should be thoroughly cooked.

3. Remove the pork from the water, and let cool. Then cut the pork into thin slices, and set aside for stir-frying.

4. Prepare the mushrooms and scallions for stir-frying.

5. Heat the oil in a wok until it just starts to smoke.

6. Stir-fry the scallions for 30 seconds. Add the mushrooms and pork, and stir-fry for another 2 minutes. Add the hoisin and oyster sauce, and mix with the scallions, pork, and mushrooms.

7. Drain the noodles. Dish the pork and mushrooms over the noodles, and serve immediately.

## Orzo Marco Polo

APPROXIMATE PREPARATION TIME: 1 HOUR
MAKES 4 SERVINGS

Orzo has become one of the more popular pastas or noodles, because it is so quickly prepared. Chinese sausage is available in most Oriental grocery stores. It can be fairly fatty, and as it sautés, it will shrink considerably. Reserve this fat for the dish.

*Water for cooking orzo*
*1 cup orzo*
*1 Chinese sausage, sliced thin*
*1 15-ounce can straw mushrooms, drained and sliced into 3 pieces*
   *each*

1. Bring water to a boil. Add orzo to begin cooking. Orzo is finished when tender, about 5 to 7 minutes.

2. While orzo is cooking, add the sausage to a sauté pan, and begin to heat over a very slow fire. The fat from the sausage will immediately begin to melt into the sauté pan.

3. When the sausage begins to brown on the edges, add the mushrooms, and stir for about a minute.

4. Remove the orzo from the water, and drain. Place on a serving dish.

5. Toss the sausage and mushrooms into the orzo, and serve immediately.

## Vermicelli with Morels and Garlic

APPROXIMATE PREPARATION TIME: 1 HOUR
MAKES 4 SERVINGS

This dish is useful as a side dish or as a course on its own.

*1½ pounds vermicelli (if used as a main course; ½ pound*
*    vermicelli if used as an accompaniment)*
*2 to 3 quarts water for cooking vermicelli*
*1 teaspoon salt*
*½ ounce dried morels*
*1 cup water*
*¼ teaspoon sugar*
*¼ teaspoon salt*
*½ teaspoon soy sauce*
*1 cup heavy (whipping) cream*
*1 teaspoon minced garlic*
*1 tablespoon butter*
*1 tablespoon cream sherry*
*2 tablespoons cornstarch mixed with ⅓ cup water*

1. Begin cooking the vermicelli in the water to which salt has been added.

2. While vermicelli is cooking, combine the morels, water, sugar, salt, and soy sauce in a saucepan, and begin to boil. Let simmer for 10 minutes. Remove from heat, add the heavy cream, and blend.

3. Place the minced garlic in a sauté pan with the butter, and begin to

sauté the garlic for 1 minute, then add the morel-cream mixture along with the sherry. Thicken with cornstarch-and-water mixture.

4. Remove the vermicelli from the water, and drain. Serve the morel sauce over the vermicelli.

## Ziti with Mushroom Butter

APPROXIMATE PREPARATION TIME: **30** MINUTES
USEFUL ADVANCE PREPARATION: MUSHROOM BUTTER (SEE PAGE **71**).
MAKES **4** SERVINGS

This is a quick preparation, using Mushroom Butter. Use hardened butter, which is then cut into small, coarse pieces, or even "shaved" with a knife. This will facilitate the melting and coating process. Melted mushroom butter cannot be used because of possible separation *but* the butter can be softened at room temperature and then added.

> *1 small package ziti*
> *Salted water for cooking ziti*
> *½ cup Mushroom Butter, domestic or wild, roughly cut into tiny*
> *(½ inch) chunks or slivers*
> *¼ cup chopped fresh parsley*

1. Cook the ziti in the salted water.
2. Drain the ziti, and add the Mushroom Butter. Toss the Mushroom Butter with the pasta as it melts. Sprinkle with parsley, and serve.

## Fettucine Czarnecki

APPROXIMATE PREPARATION TIME: **45** MINUTES
MAKES **4** SERVINGS

The sauce for this dish is really a Mornay sauce (béchamel sauce with cheese), using Bonchampi. Italian Gorgonzola with porcini can also be used, but remember that this is a stronger cheese than Bonchampi. You may want to use less.

> *1½ pound fettucine (if used as a main course; ½ pound fettucine*
> *if used as an accompaniment)*

241

*2 to 3 quarts water for cooking pasta*
*1 cup heavy whipping cream*
*1 cup milk*
*3 tablespoons butter*
*3 tablespoons sifted flour*
*½ pound Bonchampi cheese, rind removed, cheese cut into small*
*    pieces (Italian mushroom cheese can be substituted.)*
*Salt to taste*
*¼ cup chopped parsley*

1. Begin to cook the pasta in the water.
2. Combine the cream and milk in a double boiler, and begin to heat.
3. In a sauté pan, blend the butter and flour in a roux, and cook for 2 minutes but do not let it brown.
4. When the milk and cream are hot but not boiling, add the cheese, and stir until it is blended with the milk-cream mixture.
5. While stirring, add the roux to the mixture, and continue to stir until it thickens. Add salt if necessary.
6. Drain the pasta when it is done, pour the sauce over it, and toss. Sprinkle with chopped parsley.

## Spaghetti with Truffles

APPROXIMATE PREPARATION TIME: 1 HOUR
SUGGESTED WINE: HEITZ GRIGNOLINO
MAKES 4 SERVINGS

White Italian truffles from Piedmont are best for this recipe; simply scrub the truffle with a coarse brush to remove any dirt.

*1½ pound spaghetti (if used as a main course; ½ pound spaghetti*
*    if used as an accompaniment)*
*2 to 3 quarts salted water for cooking spaghetti*
*3 tablespoons butter*
*3 tablespoons flour*
*1 cup heavy cream*
*1 cup milk*
*Salt*
*Dash cayenne pepper*
*1 whole white truffle, skinned*

1. Begin to cook the spaghetti in the water.
2. Combine the butter and flour in a sauté pan, and stir together over a medium heat for 5 minutes.
3. While stirring, add the cream and milk. Stir until it becomes thick. Add some salt and the cayenne pepper.
4. Pour the sauce over the spaghetti, and toss together. Grate the fresh truffle directly over the pasta. Toss again, and serve.

## Mushroom Dumplings

APPROXIMATE PREPARATION TIME: 1½ HOURS
MAKES 4 SERVINGS

These dumplings can be served as a side dish for 6 to 8 people or as a main course for 4, covered with one of the mushroom cream sauces or with polonaise sauce; or, they can be used as an ingredient in a broth-type soup by being added to boiling broth and cooked.

*1 ounce dried* Boletus edulis
*2 cups water*
*2 tablespoons butter*
*2 eggs, separated*
*3 tablespoons sifted flour*
*Salt and pepper to taste*

1. Combine the mushrooms and water in a saucepan, and bring to a boil. Turn down the heat, and let simmer, covered, for 20 minutes. Remove the mushrooms from the liquor, and rinse them thoroughly.
2. Chop the mushrooms fine. Rinse again.
3. In a medium-sized earthenware bowl, cream the butter, and combine it with the yolks of the eggs and the chopped mushrooms.
4. Beat the whites of the eggs until they are stiff, and add them to the creamed butter and egg mixture, stirring lightly.
5. Sprinkle flour into the mixture, and blend to make the dumpling mix. Season to taste.
6. Drop the dumplings into boiling water. They are finished when they rise to the top. If you are going to use these dumplings in a soup, then drop them directly into the boiling soup.

# Mushrooms with Rice, Cereals, and Beans

## Domestic Mushrooms with Rice

**APPROXIMATE PREPARATION TIME: 1 HOUR**
**MAKES 4 SERVINGS**

"Mushroomed" rice, like pasta, can be made several ways (see pages 236–237). Here, the rice is simply tossed with sautéed mushrooms. This recipe makes an ideal side dish for broiled or grilled beef.

> *2 tablespoons melted butter*
> *½ cup chopped onions*
> *½ pound sliced mushrooms*
> *1½ cups water*
> *1 cup uncooked rice*
> *1 teaspoon salt*
> *1 teaspoon sugar*
> *1 tablespoon soy sauce*
> *1 tablespoon corn oil*
> *2 tablespoons chopped parsley*

1. Put the butter in a sauté pan, and add the onions. Sauté until the onions are just transparent.
2. Add the mushrooms, cover, and sauté them over a low heat. You want the mushrooms to release as much water as possible without causing it to evaporate.
3. Add 1½ cups water to the pan. Bring to a boil, and add the rice. Add the rest of the ingredients, bring back to a boil, and stir. Reduce to a simmer and cover. The rice should be done in about 20 minutes. Toss with the oil and parsley and serve.

# Morel Rice

APPROXIMATE PREPARATION TIME: 1 HOUR
MAKES 4 SERVINGS

This method illustrates the method of cooking the rice in a mushroom extract. The same method can be used for cooking rice with cepes (below). Cover this with a Morel Velouté Sauce (see page 83), and serve as part of a main meal.

*1 ounce dried morels*
*⅓ cup chopped green peppers*
*3 cups water*
*1 teaspoon salt*
*1 teaspoon sugar*
*1 tablespoon soy sauce*
*1 cup uncooked rice*

1. Combine all the ingredients except the rice in a saucepan, and bring to a boil. Reduce the heat, and simmer for ½ hour. The liquid should reduce to 2 cups.
2. Add the rice, and stir briefly. Return to a boil, then reduce to a simmer. Cover the pan with a lid. This rice should be done in 20 minutes. Toss, and serve.

VARIATION 1
# Cepe Rice

Substitute dried cepes for dried morels; use ⅓ cup chopped onions in place of green peppers.

VARIATION 2
# Truffled Rice

The classic way to send a truffle as a gift is to embed it in rice. If you are the fortunate recipient of such a gift, then you can then cook this rice, and it will be redolent of the flavor of the truffle. Prepare the rice in the usual manner for cooking. Grate the truffle into the rice if you wish to maximize

245

the flavor, but don't do this until you are ready to make the rice, because the truffle character is very fleeting. To the water you use to cook the truffled rice, add about 1 tablespoon of cognac.

## Wild Rice with Chanterelles and Apricots

APPROXIMATE PREPARATION TIME: 1 HOUR
USEFUL ADVANCE PREPARATION: COOK WILD RICE.
MAKES 4 SERVINGS

This preparation goes best with game birds. It can also be used to stuff small birds like quail. Just be sure to close the open end of the bird.

*1 cup raw wild rice*
*Water to cover*
*3 cups water*
*1 teaspoon salt*
*⅓ cup chopped onions*
*3 tablespoons butter*
*1½ cups fresh chanterelles, sliced, or ½ cup canned chanterelles,*
*    drained and sliced*
*2 tablespoons chopped dried apricots*
*½ teaspoon salt*

1. Wash the rice, then cover with water; soak for 30 minutes. Drain off water, and rinse in cold water.
2. Bring water, salt, and butter to boil in a saucepan. Add rice. Cover and cook until rice grains are just tender, about 30 minutes. Pour off excess water. Keep warm.
3. When rice is about half-cooked, sauté the onions in 2 tablespoons of butter, until they just turn transparent.
4. Add the chanterelles and apricots, and continue to sauté for another 2 minutes.
5. Add the salt and the remaining butter, and stir-fry for 1 minute.
6. Stir in the wild rice, and blend until the rice is warmed and well-mixed with the mushrooms and apricots. Serve with duck or any game dish.

# Mushrooms with Kasha and Other Grains

Buckwheat groats, or kasha, is a staple food of European peasants. It can be prepared in two ways: first, by cooking without first separating the grains, in which case the end product resembles a porridge; and second, by carefully tossing and frying the kasha with an egg, which separates and coats each of the grains and yields an elegant and flavorful side dish.

The porridge method of preparing kasha is very useful in making stuffings. The kasha is so dense that you won't even require an egg to bind the whole together. It is excellent for poultry of all kinds, especially the fattier types like duck. Combining mushrooms with this kasha stuffing is best done with duxelles or purees of mushrooms. The other type of kasha should have a fine and gentle texture when finished.

For the latter type of kasha most recipes call for 2 cups of water for each cup of kasha, but I prefer to call for about a quarter cup less water for perfect kasha. I also recommend the fine rather than the coarse kasha for aesthetic appeal. Finally, kasha is prepared best in a double boiler rather than over direct heat.

### Kasha-Mushroom Stuffing for Boar

APPROXIMATE PREPARATION TIME: 1 HOUR
USEFUL ADVANCE PREPARATION: PREPARE PURÉE OR DUXELLES OF CHOICE
    (PAGES 61 – 70).
MAKES 4 SERVINGS

This stuffing is also appropriate for game birds like pheasant or squab.

*1¾ cups chicken or duck stock with some fat (see pages 72–73)*
*1 teaspoon salt*
*1 teaspoon sugar*
*1 cup kasha*
*½ cup mushroom puree or ½ cup duxelles with herbs*

1. Boil the stock, salt, and sugar in a saucepan, and transfer it to a double boiler. Add the kasha, and cover. The heat should stay at about medium high under the double boiler.

247

2. When the kasha is done, it will look like a hot cereal. Stir in the puree or duxelles. Allow to cool before using for stuffing.

## Buckwheat Groats Kraców Style with Wild Mushrooms

APPROXIMATE PREPARATION TIME: 2 HOURS
MAKES 4 SERVINGS

This is my father's recipe for making perfect kasha with wild mushrooms.

*1½ ounces dried* Boletus edulis *mushrooms*
*1¾ cups water*
*1 cup fine buckwheat groats*
*1 raw egg, lightly beaten*
*1¾ cups water*
*1 teaspoon salt*
*1 small onion, chopped*
*2 tablespoons butter*
*Salt to taste*
*5 tablespoons flour*
*⅛ cup chopped fresh parsley*
*⅛ cup chopped fresh dill*

1. Combine dried mushrooms and water. Bring to boil and simmer for 30 minutes. Set aside to cool.
2. Put groats in a 10-inch skillet, and add the eggs. Blend thoroughly to coat each grain.
3. Heat the skillet over a low fire, and stir groats until they are thoroughly dry. Any lumps must be broken up to assure a loose final mass.
4. Heat the water in the top part of a double boiler, add the salt, and bring to a boil.
5. Add the groats to the boiling water, and stir only once to prevent the mass from lumping. Cover, and cook for 20 minutes, fluffing once with a fork to separate. Turn out on a heated serving dish, and make a well in the center for the sauce.

6. Lift mushrooms out of the soaking water carefully so as not to stir up the sand that has settled to the bottom. Wash mushrooms to remove any traces of remaining sand.

7. Strain the soaking water through a fine sieve, add the mushrooms, bring to a boil, and simmer uncovered for 1 hour, or until mushrooms are tender.

8. Remove mushrooms from cooking water, and slice thin. Put water aside to use for sauce.

9. In a skillet, sauté onion in butter lightly, add mushrooms, stir well, and continue cooking for a few minutes. Add salt to taste, and blend well.

10. Stir the flour into the mushroom stock, and mix well until smooth.

11. Strain this thickening mixture over the mushroom-and-onion mixture in the skillet. Stir over medium heat until sauce thickens.

12. Garnish with chopped parsley and dill, and serve.

## Polenta with Porcini

**APPROXIMATE PREPARATION TIME:** 1½ **HOURS**
**MAKES** 4 **SERVINGS**

Polenta (yellow cornmeal) is a favorite dish of the Italians and is served thick, like a porridge, sliced, and covered with whatever suits their fancy. Here, the dish is covered with a rich extract of porcini, or *Boletus edulis.*

*1 ounce dried porcini*
*3 cups water*
*1 teaspoon salt*
*1 teaspoon sugar*
*1 tablespoon soy sauce*
*1 tablespoon chopped onions*
*2 cups water*
*Salt to taste*
*1 cup yellow cornmeal*
*1½ tablespoon arrowroot mixed with ⅓ cup water*

1. Combine the mushrooms, water, salt, sugar, soy sauce, and onions in a saucepan. Bring to a rapid boil, then let simmer for 20 minutes. This should cook down to 2 cups. Remove the mushrooms, and slice thin.

249

2.  Boil 2 cups of water, and add a little salt if desired. Gradually stir in the polenta (cornmeal), stirring constantly. Reduce the heat, and continue cooking. The polenta will thicken.

3.  When the polenta is thick enough, remove carefully from the pan, invert it onto a serving dish, and keep warm.

4.  Thicken the mushroom sauce with the arrowroot-and-water mixture and add back the mushrooms. Pour over the polenta, and serve. Or cut the polenta into serving slices, and surround it with some of the sauce.

## Hominy Grits with Mushrooms

**APPROXIMATE PREPARATION TIME: 1½ HOURS**
**MAKES 4 SERVINGS**

This makes an excellent side dish for duck or any game birds. Also, hominy can be made with dried mushrooms as well, as explained in the recipe for Partridge in Hominy with Morels and Caraway (page 181).

*⅓ cup chopped onions*
*3 tablespoons butter*
*1 pound chopped fresh mushrooms, wild or domestic*
*1 teaspoon salt*
*1 teaspoon sugar*
*1 tablespoon soy sauce*
*Water*
*¾ cup hominy grits*

1.  Sauté the onions in the butter until the onions are just transparent.

2.  Add the mushrooms to the onions and butter, and cook over a low flame for 20 minutes, covered. You want the mushrooms to draw as much water as possible without evaporating.

3.  Add the salt, sugar, and soy sauce to the mixture, and stir. Add enough water to bring the amount of liquid to 3 cups.

4.  Slowly stir in the hominy grits while the mixture simmers. To finish, cover, and cook for about 1 hour, stirring occasionally.

# Mushrooms with Vegetables

## Hunters' Potatoes

APPROXIMATE PREPARATION TIME: **2** HOURS

This is an old Polish dish, which was originated by hunters who needed a hearty meal out in the open during bear and wild boar season. They would take along sausage, raw vegetables, and potatoes, and when the time came, they made this dish, which would last for several days and even improve as it kept, because it takes several days for the flavors to blend into one experience. Made at home, Hunters' Potatoes are always best reheated. The hunters would add to the stew whatever they found in the wild, including mushrooms and game.

There are no specific amounts or measurements for this recipe, and no two versions of it are alike. The recipe given here lists just the basic ingredients. It can be made in a large or small quantity, but a larger quantity is suggested so that there are plenty of leftovers for succeeding days.

> *Bacon slices (enough to cover the bottom of the roasting pot)*
> *Sliced potatoes*
> *Sliced carrots*
> *Sliced mushrooms (preferably wild types of any sort)*
> *Sliced onions*
> *Sliced Polish sausage*
> *Several large white or red cabbage leaves (enough to cover the*
>     *entire top of the contents)*
> *Salt and pepper*

1. Cover the bottom of a large pot or dutch oven with the bacon.
2. Begin layering the ingredients. Covering the bottom with potatoes, then a layer of carrots, then mushrooms, then onions, then more potatoes, then sausage, and so on. Lightly salt and pepper each layer as you go along. When you get to the top, cover the whole with the cabbage, and fix a tight lid to the pot.
3. Start cooking over a low fire or in an oven set at 350°. In either case, it takes about 1 hour to cook. It's done when the potatoes are soft.

## Home-Fried Potatoes with Sautéed Mushrooms and Green Onions

APPROXIMATE PREPARATION TIME: 1 HOUR
MAKES 4 SERVINGS

This is a great accompaniment to a breakfast highlighting mushrooms!

*1 pound potatoes, peeled and sliced into ¼-inch rounds*
*Water*
*⅓ cup clarified butter (see page 51)*
*1 cup sliced scallions*
*2 cups sliced fresh mushrooms*
*Salt and pepper to taste*

1. Start boiling the potatoes in some lightly salted water. Cook until the potatoes are almost soft. Drain water, and let the potatoes cool.
2. In a large sauté pan, heat the butter, and add the scallions, sautéing until they are almost transparent. Add the mushrooms and potatoes, and sauté until the mushrooms are tender. Salt and pepper to taste.

## Souffléed Potatoes with Mushrooms

APPROXIMATE PREPARATION TIME: 2 HOURS
MAKES 4 SERVINGS

This is an ideal side dish for beef or furred game.

*2 pounds potatoes, peeled*
*Water*
*⅓ cup chopped onions*
*6 tablespoons butter*
*1 cup fresh mushrooms, chopped*
*1 cup heavy whipping cream*
*Dash cayenne pepper*
*Salt and pepper*
*1 egg*
*Paprika*

252

*Preheat oven to 425°.*

1. Start cooking the potatoes in the water. They are done when completely soft.
2. Sauté the onions in the butter until they are transparent. Add the mushrooms, and continue to cook for 2 minutes over medium heat.
3. Add the cream, cayenne pepper, and salt and pepper to taste. Remove from heat.
4. Begin to whip the potatoes, by hand or in a blender or food processor. Slowly add the mushroom mixture to it. You may have to vary the amount added, depending on the amount of liquid already in the potatoes from cooking.
5. When the potatoes are of a fluffy consistency, add the egg, and blend it in thoroughly. Place some of the potatoes in buttered ramekins, sprinkle with the paprika, and bake in the oven for 10 minutes, or until the potatoes begin to brown.

## Boiled Mushroomed Potatoes

Make a mushroom extract using an ounce of dried mushrooms, 4 cups of water, 1 teaspoon each of sugar and salt, and 1 tablespoon of soy sauce. Bring this to a boil, then let simmer for ½ hour. Remove the mushrooms, rinse, and chop them. Cut 2 potatoes into ½-inch-thick julienne slices. Bring the mushroom liquid back to a boil, add the potatoes, and boil them gently until they are cooked. Remove from the liquid, and cover with the chopped mushrooms and some parsley and fresh ground pepper.

## Baked Potato with Mushroom Butter and Scallions

Wrap some baked potatoes in aluminum foil. Place directly on an oven rack, and bake at 400° for 20 to 30 minutes or until the potatoes are soft. Remove the potatoes from the oven, remove the foil, and slit the potato crossways. Put some Mushroom Butter (see page 71) in the potato, sprinkle with some thin-sliced scallions, and serve.

253

# Mushrooms with Beans Flageolet Style

APPROXIMATE PREPARATION TIME: **3** HOURS
USEFUL ADVANCE PREPARATION: SOAK BEANS A DAY IN ADVANCE.
MAKES **4** SERVINGS

This recipe utilizes French flageolet beans and is the essential ingredient in a pheasant casserole with mushrooms. However, it may also be prepared with any dried beans such as red kidney beans or lentils.

*1 cup green flageolet beans*
*3 cups water*
*1 ounce dried mushrooms, preferably cepes*
*1 teaspoon salt*
*1 teaspoon sugar*
*1 tablespoon soy sauce*

1. Wash the beans thoroughly. Let drain, then cover with the water for 24 hours. The beans will absorb some of the water.

2. Cut the dried mushrooms into small pieces, then rinse. Add to the beans in the water.

3. Add the salt, sugar, and soy to the beans, and bring to a boil. Reduce the heat, and let simmer, covered. You will probably have to replace water, because some will evaporate during the cooking process. These beans will take several hours to cook. Stir them occasionally.

4. When the beans are soft, remove them from the heat, and serve. If you wish to reserve for later use, let stand for 1 hour, then place them in the refrigerator, and let them cool. The beans will hold for up to 5 days in the refrigerator.

# Mushrooms with Vegetables Polonaise Style

**APPROXIMATE PREPARATION TIME: 2 HOURS**
**MAKES 4 SERVINGS**

This is a classic Polish method for cooking vegetables. The simplicity of the polonaise sauce is startling and devastatingly effective. It is always a good idea to make more of this than needed, because of the length of time it takes to brown the bread crumbs. The remainder can be kept for 4 to 5 weeks in the refrigerator and simply combined with clarified butter (1 part clarified butter to 1 part polonaise crumbs) when ready to use.

*¼ pound butter*
*4 cups bread crumbs*
*½ cup freshly grated parmesan cheese*
*1 tablespoon poppy seeds*
*¼ cup water*
*1 pound fresh broccoli (or other green vegetable)*
*1 pound fresh mushrooms, sliced*
*¼ cup clarified butter (page 51)*
*Salt to taste*

1. Make the polonaise sauce by heating the butter in a large skillet. Let the butter brown. Add the bread crumbs, cheese, and poppy seeds while stirring.

2. Over medium to high heat, continue to stir the crumb mixture with the butter. Do *not* cease stirring unless you take the crumbs off the heat. They can burn instantly. The crumbs must be stirred until they turn a dark golden to brown color. This may take 30 minutes or more.

3. Remove the crumbs from the heat when they are done, and continue to stir for another 2 minutes. Transfer the crumbs to a mixing bowl.

4. In a pan with a little water at the bottom, add the broccoli, and place over high heat until the water begins to steam. Cover and let the broccoli steam for 5 minutes. Add the mushrooms, and let steam for 2 more minutes. Check the broccoli and mushrooms for doneness.

5. Cover about ¼ cup of the bread crumbs with ¼ cup clarified butter, and stir well. Remove the vegetables from the pan, and lightly salt them. Cover with the polonaise sauce.

# Sauerkraut with Dried Mushrooms and Peas

**APPROXIMATE PREPARATION TIME: 3 HOURS**
**USEFUL ADVANCE PREPARATION: SOAK DRIED PEAS OVERNIGHT.**
**MAKES 4 SERVINGS**

Humble sauerkraut is raised to lofty pinnacles with this interesting and deeply satisfying dish, which is great reheated, too. This is my mother's recipe.

*½ ounce dried cepes*
*1 cup water*
*Salt to taste*
*1 cup whole dried peas, soaked overnight*
*1 2½-pound can sauerkraut*
*1 small head fresh white cabbage*
*Water*
*1 teaspoon sugar*
*1 large onion, sliced thin*
*4 tablespoons butter*
*2 tablespoons flour*

1. Rinse the mushrooms thoroughly, then add to the water, and bring to a rapid boil. Let simmer, covered, for 30 minutes. Remove the mushrooms, and slice them thin, and return to liquid. Lightly salt the liquid.

2. Cook the peas in the soaking liquid with the mushrooms, until the peas are tender, about 1½ hours. Remove the peas.

3. Wash the sauerkraut well (depending on how sour you like it), and put it in a colander to drain.

4. Shred the cabbage, and place it in a 6-quart pot. Cover the cabbage with water, salt to taste, and bring it to a simmer over a medium heat.

5. Add the drained sauerkraut to cabbage, and simmer over a low heat.

6. Add the mushroom soaking liquid and sugar to the pot, and continue to simmer.

7. Sauté the onions in the butter until they are golden brown. When the butter is bubbling, add the flour, and brown it to a golden color.

8. Add the onion-butter mixture to the sauerkraut-cabbage. Add the peas. Continue to cook until it begins to thicken slightly. Adjust for salt, and serve.

CHAPTER THIRTEEN

# Some Recipes for Very Wild Mushrooms

Although the bulk of recipes in this book utilize mushrooms that can be bought in most specialty food stores, the following recipes are for people who hunt and pick their own in the wild. I emphasize that these mushrooms should be sought and used only by those who are expert at identifying mushrooms, people with many years of experience at picking.

For novices, information on mycological clubs and reference books are listed in the last chapter of this book.

### A Note About Exotic Wild Mushrooms

The principals of cooking with mushrooms are the same whether the mushrooms are available commercially or picked wild. There are, however, a few differences worth noting:

Fresh wild mushrooms take more care in washing. Coming directly from the earth, they are covered with soil and therefore bacteria, so careful and thorough washing is a must. For the varieties that get really soiled, like those in the genera *Lactarius*, *Russula*, and *Tricholoma*, soaking in warm water for a few minutes is a good idea, followed by thorough rinsing. But in that case, the mushrooms must be cooked or processed right away. (Do not soak the mushrooms for longer periods, like overnight, or you may discover fermented or rotted mushrooms in the morning.) An exception to the need for washing would be mushrooms that are to be dried for preserving. In that case just brush away the soil with a damp cloth; thorough cleaning and soaking are done when the dried mushrooms are reconstituted for use.

If you are going to preserve wild mushrooms for drying, consult the chart on pages 37 to 43 and choose only those recommended for that purpose. As a general rule, however, you will make life much easier for yourself if you limit yourself exclusively to those varieties that are firm and fairly clean when they are picked, genera like *Boletus* and *Suillus*.

Making extracts from blanching fresh mushrooms is generally a good way of starting an excellent wild mushroom soup. However, there are varieties of wild mushrooms like the *Armellariella mellea* or *Suillus luteus* that have viscous or slimy caps, and these produce an extract that is also slimy and even sometimes indigestible. Avoid using these liquids for cooking.

Apart from these notes, cooking wild mushrooms is the same as cooking domestic or dried mushrooms, as described earlier. In this brief chapter I am including some of our restaurant's recipes and those some mushroom-picker friends have shared with me over the years.

## Blewits with Pernod

APPROXIMATE PREPARATION TIME: **20** MINUTES
USEFUL ADVANCE PREPARATION: CLEAN AND SLICE BLEWITS.
MAKES **4** SERVINGS

This recipe was given to me by Alice Heitz, Joe's wife at Heitz Vineyard. It's a bold preparation for this well-loved mushroom.

> *½ pound fresh, cleaned blewits*
> *2 tablespoons melted butter*
> *2 tablespoons Pernod*
> *½ cup green onions, sliced thin*
> *½ cup cream*
> *Salt to taste*

1. Slice the blewits if large, or leave them whole if small.
2. Heat the butter in a saucepan. Add the Pernod, and continue heating for a minute. Add the mushrooms and green onions, and sauté for 2 minutes, or until they are tender.
3. Add the cream, and stir. Cook together until the cream is reduced slightly and thickened. Salt to taste, and serve.

258

## *Clitocybe nuda* Stuffed with Bryndza

**APPROXIMATE PREPARATION TIME: 1½ HOURS**
**MAKES 4 SERVINGS**

Bryndza is a cheese made from ewe's milk in the Tatra mountain region. Rymanów, Poland, produces some of the best Bryndza on the commercial market, but the very best is made in limited quantities in the secluded villages of the mountaineers. Bryndza is often available in Middle European stores under the name "Liptauer"; you may also substitute a good New York extra-sharp cheese or experiment with another cheese of your choice. We created this recipe after a visit to Poland, when the memory of that wonderful flavor was still fresh. We selected *Clitocybe nuda* for its flavor and its resistance to wilting in cooking.

*1 pound fresh or 1 cup canned caps of* Clitocybe nuda, *2 to 3*
   *inches wide*
*2 to 3 ounces stems and pieces of mushrooms*
*1 tablespoon butter*
*1 medium onion, chopped*
*1 rib celery*
*Several sprigs of parsley, cleaned and chopped coarse*
*2 ounces Bryndza cheese*
*1 egg*
*½ cup bread crumbs, seasoned with ½ teaspoon salt*
*Salt and pepper*

*Preheat oven to 350°.*

1. Clean mushrooms thoroughly, and cut off stems for use in stuffing. Chop mushrooms fine.
2. Melt butter, and sauté onions and mushroom pieces. Set aside for stuffing caps.
3. In a blender, mix onion, celery, parsley, and Bryndza with the egg.
4. By hand in a mixing bowl, blend the sautéed mushrooms with contents of blender and the bread crumbs into an even mass. Season.
5. If fresh mushrooms are being used, blanch them for about 3 minutes. Canned mushrooms need not be blanched.
6. Stuff the gilled side of the mushrooms with the stuffing mix.
7. Bake in the oven for about 45 minutes. Sprinkle with butter if you wish.

## Cream of Blewit Soup

APPROXIMATE PREPARATION TIME: 1 HOUR
MAKES 4 SERVINGS

This soup, from Helen Turley, the well-know Napa Valley wine-maker and cook, is best served with fresh sourdough bread, and a well-oaked Chardonnay.

*1 cup blewits, sliced thin*
*1 tablespoon fresh shallots, chopped*
*1 tablespoon butter, melted*
*1 cup half cream, half milk*
*1 cup rich chicken stock (pages 72–73)*
*1 teaspoon anisette*
*Salt and pepper to taste*
*4 egg yolks, beaten and mixed with ¼ cup cream*

1. Wash the mushrooms carefully, and sauté them with the shallots in the butter over a medium heat in a sauté pan. You want to draw the liquid out of the mushrooms, but you do not want to let it evaporate. Sauté for about 2 minutes.

2. Add the half-and-half, stock, anisette, and salt and pepper to taste.

3. Bring the mixture back up to heat, but do not let it boil excessively.

4. Slowly thicken the soup by adding the egg yolk-and-cream mixture, while stirring the soup gently. Stop adding when the soup is just shy of the proper consistency, and stir. Then take off the heat immediately, and let sit for 5 minutes before serving. You may have to stir the soup again before serving.

## Fresh Cepes Heitz-Style

APPROXIMATE PREPARATION TIME: 30 MINUTES
MAKES 4 SERVINGS

Another recipe from Alice Heitz, this one for making fresh *Boletus edulis*. They can serve as a unique first course for a dinner or as hors d'oeuvres for a cocktail party.

*1 pound fresh cepes that have been washed thoroughly and cut into*
*¼-inch slices*

*2 eggs, beaten*
*1½ cups cracker crumbs*
*¾ cup butter*

1. Dip the mushrooms into the eggs, and then cover with the crumbs.
2. Heat the butter, until it begins to bubble.
3. Start to sauté the mushrooms by adding as many as will fit onto the bottom of the pan. Sauté for 1½ minutes on each side, or until the crumbs are golden brown.
4. Salt to taste and serve.

## Honey Mushrooms with Sour Cream

APPROXIMATE PREPARATION TIME: **45** MINUTES
MAKES **4** SERVINGS

This is an excellent side dish for a dinner. Note the use of sour cream (or *crème fraîche*) for this dish. It is used to counteract the viscous character of this mushroom's cap.

*1½ pounds of mushroom caps, stems off*
*1 medium onion*
*4 tablespoons butter or margarine*
*Salt and white pepper*
*1 cup sour cream, or* crème fraîche
*1 pinch sugar*
*1 bunch chopped parsley (optional)*

1. Clean mushrooms, giving special attention to the presence of sand. Washing removes sand better than mere wiping.
2. Chop onion very fine.
3. Melt butter in a 10-inch skillet. Sauté onions until clear.
4. Remove stems, and reserve for other use. Add mushrooms, and cook, covered, over medium heat for at least 20 minutes. Remove cover, season lightly, and cook until most of moisture as evaporated but mushroom caps still retain their shape.
5. Reduce heat, add sour cream or *crème fraîche*, and a pinch of sugar, and stir while adjusting seasoning. When mixture is smooth and well blended, stir in chopped parsley, or serve plain.

## Oriental Mushrooms

APPROXIMATE PREPARATION TIME: 1 HOUR
USEFUL ADVANCE PREPARATION: SLICE AND CHOP INDICATED INGREDIENTS.
SUGGESTED WINE: SAUVIGNON BLANC
MAKES 4 SERVINGS

This recipe is from *Kitchen Magic with Mushrooms,* published by the Mycological Society of San Francisco. The method is a typical stir-fry treatment. It can be eaten as a main course or as part of a larger Oriental-style dinner. It goes well with steamed rice or any of the Chinese-style noodles.

*2 pounds cleaned matsutake, sliced thin*
*2 tablespoons peanut oil*
*1 small head bok choy, sliced as for cole slaw*
*1 8-ounce can bamboo shoots, cut into bite-sized pieces*
*1 8-ounce can water chestnuts, sliced thin*
*6 green onions, cut into 1-inch diagonal pieces*
*2 celery stalks, cut into 1-inch diagonal pieces*
*1 teaspoon fresh ginger, sliced fine*
*1 tablespoon rice wine vinegar*
*1 tablespoon soy sauce*
*½ cup rice wine (sake)*
*2 teaspoons sugar*
*2 teaspoons arrowroot*

1. In a wok or frying pan, sauté the mushrooms very rapidly in 2 tablespoons of the peanut oil, and set aside.

2. Sauté the vegetables in the rest of the peanut oil for 3 to 4 minutes, and add the mushrooms to the vegetables.

3. While keeping the vegetables warm, combine the ginger and liquid ingredients, and mix well.

4. Return the mushrooms and vegetables to the fire, and add the spices, liquid ingredients, and arrowroot. Cook, stirring constantly, until thoroughly blended and the sauce is well thickened. Serve with steamed rice or fried rice noodles.

## Scrambled Eggs with *Russulas*

APPROXIMATE PREPARATION TIME: **30** MINUTES
MAKES **4** SERVINGS

This recipe can be used for any of the genus of *Russula*, but also works very well for the genera *Lactarius* and *Tricholoma,* and for the edible *Amanita*s. It is a great breakfast dish. Onion or shallots can be sautéed with the mushrooms, but this addition is not necessary for excellent flavor.

> *2 tablespoons butter*
> *1 ounce ham or Polish sausage, chopped fine*
> *12 ounces* Russulas *of your choice, cleaned and chopped fine*
> *6 fresh eggs*
> *3 tablespoons cream*
> *Salt and pepper*

1. In a large frying pan, melt butter and sauté ham or sausage and mushrooms.
2. Mix the eggs with the cream, but do not beat. There should be some separation of the whites and yolks of the eggs.
3. Keeping the mushroom mixture on medium heat, pour eggs over, stirring slowly and continuously until the eggs begin to get slightly firm. Salt and pepper to taste. Remove pan from heat, stirring to achieve even consistency. Return briefly to heat if eggs are too soft—stirring, slowly stirring, until the eggs look firm enough and yet are not sticking to the pan. Season to taste, and serve.

## Baked Turkey and *Russula* Loaf

APPROXIMATE PREPARATION TIME: **3** HOURS
MAKES **4** SERVINGS

This delicious loaf rises above the modest status of meat loaf. Easily made, it challenges the pretensions of its beefy competition. It may be served both hot or cold, with a Chardonnay from Freemark Abbey.

263

*2 pounds boneless and skinless turkey meat*
*2 pounds* Russulas *of your choice*
*4 ounces butter*
*2 medium onions, chopped*
*½ fresh green pepper, chopped*
*2½ teaspoons salt*
*2 eggs*
*2 cups dried bread crumbs*
*¼ teaspoon freshly ground pepper*

*Preheat oven to 375°.*

1. Cube the turkey meat, and chop it coarse in a meat grinder.
2. Wash the mushrooms, and dice by hand into ¼-inch pieces.
3. Melt the butter in a 12-inch pan, and sauté onions and green peppers until they are lightly browned. Add the mushrooms, sprinkle with 1 teaspoon of the salt, and cook over a high flame until most but not all of the moisture cooks away. Too much remaining moisture will make the finished loaf soggy, while overcooking will make the mushrooms too dry. Stir while cooking, and when only a little moisture remains on the bottom of the pan, stop cooking and allow the mass to cool before mixing.
4. In a mixing bowl, mix the meat-and-mushroom mixture with the remaining ingredients, including the remaining 1½ teaspoons salt, until a sticky, cohesive mass is obtained, thoroughly mixed. Shape the mass into approximately the shape of a loaf.
5. Grease a loaf pan, and place the meat-and-mushroom loaf in the pan, pressing and patting until the mass is evenly distributed. Make diagonal scores on the loaf.
6. Bake the loaf in a 375° oven for about 1½ hours, or until a meat thermometer indicates an internal temperature of 170°.
7. Use a table knife to free the loaf from the sides of the pan. Invert the finished loaf onto a serving platter, and garnish with lots of fresh parsley.

## Stuffed *Russula xerampelina* as Prepared by David Bruce

APPROXIMATE PREPARATION TIME: 1 HOUR
MAKES 4 SERVINGS

This recipe was given to me by Dr. David Bruce of the David Bruce Wineries. *Russula xerampelina* (shrimp mushrooms) are among the best of the

*Russula*s, and are distinctive for their enormous, burgundy-color caps. They are very firm, which makes them excellent for stuffing. Extra-large domestic mushrooms provide good substitutes, as do the caps of extra-large shiitake. Serve with a Chardonnay.

> *16 medium* Russula xerampelina *or 12 large domestic mushroom*
>     *caps*
> *4 tablespoons olive oil*
> *2 tablespoons chopped parsley*
> *2 tablespoons chopped onion*
> *1 clove chopped garlic*
> *Salt and pepper*
> *Fine bread crumbs*

> *Preheat oven to 375°.*

1. Wash *Russula*s thoroughly or, using a soft-bristled brush, gently dry-clean domestic mushrooms. Separate caps and stems, reserving both. Do not peel caps of either mushroom. Chop stems fine, and set aside.

2. In a sauté pan, fry the caps, gills down, in 2 tablespoons of the olive oil for 2 minutes, or until they are brown. Turn over, lower the flame, and brown other side. Remove mushroom caps.

3. Add remaining olive oil to sauté pan. Add chopped stems, parsley, onion, and garlic, and cook 3 minutes. Add salt, pepper, and bread crumbs to taste (depending on how thick a stuffing you like). Stir carefully to be sure bread crumbs are evenly distributed throughout mixture.

4. Fill caps, and bake at 375° for 20 minutes.

## Marge Stafford's Mushrooms-in-the-Field

APPROXIMATE PREPARATION TIME: **15** MINUTES
SUGGESTED WINE: FREEMARK ABBEY CHARDONNAY
MAKES **4** SERVINGS

Only the best and firmest mushrooms should be used for this recipe. Of course, you don't *have* to eat these out of doors, but they taste the best in nature's restaurant, according to Marge Stafford of Napa, California, who shared her recipe with me. Firm caps of fresh *Russula*s are ideal. This is one of the simplest and most elegant mushroom preparations I know and represents a favorite method of longtime mushroom hunters for preparing wild mushrooms. It is really best eaten by itself with some toasted slices of French bread.

> *2 tablespoons cold-pressed extra virgin olive oil*
> *12 large caps fresh mushrooms, preferably wild, cleaned and sliced*
> *¼ inch thick*
> *Garlic powder, or fine-chopped fresh garlic*
> *Sea salt (Use kosher salt if sea salt is unavailable.)*

1. Heat the oil in a sauté pan to a light smoke.
2. Add the mushrooms, and cook on one side for 2 minutes.
3. Turn the mushrooms over, and lower the heat to a low flame. Sprinkle a little garlic powder and a little of the salt, which is coarse, over the mushrooms.
4. Cook the mushrooms 1 more minute, remove, and serve immediately. The salt does not have to be completely dissolved as this adds to the overall texture of the dish.


## Stir-Fried Chicken with Dried *Russulas*

APPROXIMATE PREPARATION TIME: **1** HOUR
USEFUL ADVANCE PREPARATION: RECONSTITUTE *RUSSULAS* OVERNIGHT IN
          CHARDONNAY.
MAKES **4** SERVINGS

"Dried *Russulas* that have been reconstituted have a salty character," Marge explained. "I don't use much salt in my diet, and using these mushrooms this way is perfect for getting a salt character without actually adding salt to the dish."

> *½ ounce dried* Russulas
> *2 cups good white wine, like a good Chardonnay*
> *2 tablespoons peanut oil*
> *1 cup broccoli flowers, cut into 1-inch pieces*
> *1½ pounds chicken cutlets, cut into 1-inch pieces*
> *2 cloves garlic, chopped*
> *1 cup fern tofu, cut into 1-inch cubes*

1. Reconstitute the *Russulas* in the chardonnay by soaking overnight. Remove the mushrooms from the wine. Rinse thoroughly.

266

2. Heat the oil in a wok until it begins to smoke.

3. Add the broccoli to the wok, and cook for 1 minute.

4. Add the mushrooms, chicken, and garlic, and cook for 1 minute.

5. Add the tofu, and continue to stir-fry for another 30 seconds. Serve immediately over rice or noodles.

## Raw *Lactarius* Salad

APPROXIMATE PREPARATION TIME: ½ HOUR
MAKES 4 SERVINGS

Some excellent species for this recipe are *Lactarius deliciosus, Lactarius subpurpureus,* and *Lactarius chelidonius.* Morels, cepes, and *Agaricus campestris* (meadow mushroom) are not suitable for this recipe.

> *½ pound fresh selected* Lactarius
> *⅔ cup olive oil*
> *Salt and freshly ground pepper*
> *⅓ cup vinegar*
> *1 small sweet onion, sliced*
> *A pinch of sugar (optional)*

1. Wash and slice mushrooms, handling carefully because they are very brittle. A sharp knife used with a long stroke will assure controlled cutting.

2. Place mushrooms in a salad bowl. Stir in the olive oil, adding salt and pepper to taste. Place vinegar in a 1-quart saucepan, bring to a boil, then remove from the heat.

3. Add onion and sugar to warm vinegar. Pour over the mushrooms. Chill for several hours.

4. Serve ice cold with rye bread, garnished with herbs of the season.

## Pickled *Lactarius*

APPROXIMATE PREPARATION TIME: THIS RECIPE INVOLVES FERMENTATION,
AND THE COMPLETE PROCESS TAKES SEVERAL WEEKS.
MAKES 4 SERVINGS

This recipe uses *Lactarius* preserved by the fermentation method. It is best to try out this recipe with a limited amount of mushrooms until you get the hang of it. Do not attempt it if you cannot store the mushrooms in a cool room during fermentation. A refrigerator can be used for storing, provided the temperature is not too low. For most, the result yields a new culinary experience not to be matched by eating any other wild mushrooms.

*2 pounds* Lactarius *wild mushrooms*
*2 tablespoons salt*
*2 bay leaves, crushed*
*1 teaspoon freshly ground pepper*
*½ teaspoon allspice, whole*
*2 ounces onion, sliced*

1.  After cutting off the stems, clean mushrooms carefully, and blanch for 3 minutes. Drain and cool.

2.  Select the smallest earthenware dish that will contain the mushrooms, and arrange the mushrooms in layers, distributing salt, spices, and onion evenly. Cover mushrooms with sterile gauze. Compress the mushrooms by laying a weighted plate on top. Store in a cool room, between 45 and 60°.

3.  In 3 days the released juices will cover the mushrooms. Should there be too little liquid to cover, make a salted* solution of boiled and cooled water, and cover. Check regularly, and remove any evidence of mold. The mushrooms will be ready for use after 2 weeks' fermentation time.

*Note: Use 1 ounce of kosher salt to 1 quart of water for this solution.

## *Coprinus* Egg and Cream Scramble

APPROXIMATE PREPARATION TIME: **30** MINUTES
MAKES **4** SERVINGS

Another good breakfast dish. The texture and flavor of this mushroom make it unique. Serve it with a warmed croissant.

*1 pound* Coprinus comatus
*2 tablespoons butter*
*½ cup chopped onion*
*Salt and pepper*
*½ cup cream*
*3 eggs*
*Chives, chopped, for garnish*

1. Wash, drain, and chop mushrooms. Slice into ¼-inch slices or, for a different effect, use small whole caps.

2. Melt butter in a 10-inch skillet, and sauté onion until just clear. Add *Coprinus* mushrooms and cover 10 minutes, or until the liquid is drawn.

3. Sauté mushrooms without cover until most of moisture has evaporated. Season.

4. Season cream lightly, and add to mushroom mixture. Stir to get an even and smooth mass. There shouldn't be any free moisture, but the mixture should also not be dry. Spread the loose mass evenly over the skillet.

5. Mix the eggs well without beating, and pour evenly over the mushroom-and-cream mixture.

6. Cover skillet, and cook over low to medium heat until the entire mixture is well set but not overdone, about 2 to 3 minutes. The lid should be lifted occasionally to check cooking progress. When finished, there will be a semisolid well-blended mass of mushrooms, cream, and eggs. Not having the firmness of an omelet, the dish will also not have its elegance. The taste will earn forgiveness. Garnish with fresh chopped chives.

## *Tricholoma* and Potato Soup

APPROXIMATE PREPARATION TIME: 1½ HOURS
USEFUL ADVANCE PREPARATION: PREPARE MEAT STOCK (PAGES 72–73) OR
      MAKE MEAT STOCK FROM PREPARED MIX OR BOULLION CUBES.
MAKES 4 SERVINGS

This soup can be made with *Russula*s or *Lactarius* as well as *Tricholoma*s. It is a big soup, using a meat stock for its considerable body. Use it as a luncheon dish along with a mushroom quiche (pages 104–107).

> *3 quarts meat stock*
> *1 pound fresh* Tricholoma *mushrooms*
> *¼ cup melted butter*
> *2 ounces onion, diced*
> *1 pound potatoes, peeled and diced (store in cold water until ready*
>     *to use)*
> *¾ cup flour*
> *Salt*
> *1 cup cream (1 additional cup if desired)*
> *Chopped parsley*

1.  Heat meat stock.

2.  Clean and cut mushrooms into thin slices, Sauté with the onions and butter, and put them into the meat stock to simmer for 1 hour. After 1 hour, add potatoes to pot, and cook until tender.

3.  Mix the flour in 1½ cups of the cooled stock, add to pot, and stir until smooth and slightly thickened, about 5 minutes.

4.  Adjust seasoning, and add cream. Stir. Garnish with chopped parsley, and serve.

## Pork Patties with *Clitopilus prunulus*

APPROXIMATE PREPARATION TIME: 1 HOUR
USEFUL ADVANCE PREPARATION: PREGRIND OR PURCHASE GROUND PORK.
SUGGESTED WINE: RAVENSWOOD ZINFANDEL
MAKES 4 SERVINGS

A great luncheon dish, this is best served with fresh, buttered corn on the cob.

*1 pound fresh* Clitopilus prunulus *mushrooms*
*1 medium onion, diced*
*7 tablespoons butter*
*1½ cups white bread soaked in milk and squeezed*
*2 tablespoons chopped parsley*
*Salt and pepper to taste*
*1 pound ground pork*
*1 whole egg*
*2 cups fresh bread crumbs*

1.  Sauté mushrooms and onions in 3 tablespoons butter until most of moisture has evaporated.

2.  Blend the mushrooms, onion, bread soaked in milk, parsley, salt, and pepper with the ground pork in a mixing bowl. Add egg, and mix thoroughly.

3.  Form mixture into 8 firm patties, and coat them with the bread crumbs.

4.  Add remaining 4 tablespoons butter to pan. After it melts and starts foaming, fry patties until they are brown and crisp.

## Pan-Fried *Lepiota procera*

APPROXIMATE PREPARATION TIME: **30** MINUTES
MAKES **4** SERVINGS

This wild mushroom, commonly known as the parasol mushroom, is one of the more flavorful, but its culinary treatment is simplicity itself. Pan-fried and served with fresh cole slaw, it makes a perfect lunch dish.

*1 large cap parasol mushroom*
*1 whole egg*
*4 tablespoons heavy cream*
*Salt and pepper to taste*
*4 ounces butter*
*1 cup fresh bread crumbs*

1. Do not wash the mushroom. Cut off the stem, and discard it. Brush off the hairlike surface of the cap.
2. Blend together egg and cream, and season.
3. In a skillet large enough to hold the mushroom, heat butter until it foams.
4. Dip mushroom in egg-and-cream mixture, cover mushroom with bread crumbs, and pat firmly.
5. Fry on both sides until nicely browned. Cook until the mushroom is browned; the time this takes will depend on the size of the mushroom.

## Naughty-Angel Popcorn

APPROXIMATE PREPARATION TIME: **1** HOUR
MAKES **4** SERVINGS

This is a fun snack dish or a finger-popping hors d'oeuvres. Put it out on the table just before sitting down to a large meal.

FOR THE DIPPING SAUCE:
*1 cup mayonnaise*
*1 teaspoon Tabasco sauce*
*2 teaspoons prepared relish*

271

FOR THE PUFFBALL:
*1 medium-to-large puffball*
*1 cup flour, sifted*
*3 eggs, beaten*
*1 cup fresh bread crumbs, lightly salted*
*4 cups cooking oil*

1. Cut the puffball into 1-inch cubes.
2. Prepare the dipping sauce by mixing together all ingredients thoroughly. Let stand for at least ½ hour before using.
3. For the puffball, place the flour, eggs, and bread crumbs each into its own pan or shallow bowl. Dredge the puffballs in the flour, then the egg, then the bread crumbs.
4. Bring the oil to a high heat, so that when you drop water into it, the water sizzles. The oil is then ready for frying.
5. Drop the coated puffballs into the oil 3 at a time; fry until browned. This will take only a few seconds. Place the finished puffball pieces on a paper towel to drain off the excess oil. Repeat until the puffball pieces are all used up.
6. Serve with the dipping sauce.

## Grilled Pigeon with Duriff and Ram's-Head

APPROXIMATE PREPARATION TIME: 1½ HOURS
MAKES 4 SERVINGS

The ram's head is a large, common fungus in a larger group known as the polypores, which grow in close association with or from decaying wood. The flesh is usually tough when raw, but softens on cooking. "Duriff" is another name for the grape Petite Sirah, and a wine by that name is made by Ken Burnap of Santa Cruz Mountain Winery in the Santa Cruz Mountains in California. The sauce of this dish is made from the wine and the mushrooms, and is cooked separately, then added to the dish later. Pigeon cooked in this way must be watched carefully during grilling so that the flesh does not burn. This dish should be washed down with generous amounts of Petite Sirah or a good Rhone wine.

*4 ready-to-cook young pigeons or squabs*
*Salt and pepper to taste*

*6 tablespoons melted butter*
*1 cup red wine, preferably Petite Sirah*
*4 teaspoons soy sauce*
*1 teaspoon red wine vinegar*
*2 tablespoons sugar*
*1 teaspoon fresh lemon juice*
*3 cups sliced ram's head mushrooms*
*2 cups chicken stock, lightly salted (see pages 72–73)*
*½ cup chopped onions*
*1½ tablespoons arrowroot mixed with water*

*Preheat broiler or prepare charcoal.*

1. Split the pigeons from the back, and pound them flat with a cleaver. Sprinkle with salt and pepper. Brush with 2 tablespoons melted butter.

2. Combine ingredients from the wine to the lemon juice, and set aside.

3. In a pot, cover the mushrooms with the chicken stock, and bring to a boil. The mushrooms are ready when they are tender, about ½ hour. This time will vary, depending on the age of the mushroom. Remove the mushrooms from the stock when finished. You will not use the stock, but it makes an excellent soup as a first course when this dish is served. Simply adjust for salt, and serve.

4. Sauté the onions in 2 tablespoons of the butter for 1 minute, add the mushrooms, and continue to sauté for 1 more minute. Add the wine-and-lemon juice liquid, and bring to a gentle simmer. Cover, and let simmer for 10 minutes. Replace lost liquid with water to maintain volume.

5. Grill or broil the pigeons for 15 minutes, skin side down on a broiler rack or skin side up on a grill. The idea here is to get most of the cooking done from the nonskin side of the birds.

6. Turn the birds and continue to broil or grill for about 10 minutes, until the skin is browned. The birds should be medium rare. When broiling, keep the birds about 8 inches from the source of heat, and coat repeatedly with remaining melted butter.

7. Thicken the sauce with the arrowroot-and-water mixture, and pour over the pigeons. Serve.

CHAPTER FOURTEEN

# *Mushroomless Desserts*

This is a mushroom cookbook. And we have a restaurant that specializes in cooking mushrooms. Customers there often ask me, with a wink or a guffaw, whether we serve desserts with mushrooms too. For the record, the answer is no, no, and once again, no. What we *do* have is one of the most creative dessert makers in the world—my wife, Heidi. I'm not being merely loyal when I say that. Of all the desserts I have eaten in my life in the great restaurants of this country, nothing even comes close to what Heidi conjures up in the recesses of her sugar-coated mind. I'm spoiled. I love it.

## Chocolate Mousse Cake

APPROXIMATE PREPARATION TIME: 1 HOUR
MAKES 12 SERVINGS

This is every chocolate lover's dream: rich and fudgy. You may want to serve this with some fresh raspberries and cream.

FOR THE CAKE:
*1½ pounds semisweet chocolate bits*
*1½ tablespoons water*

*9 ounces butter*
*1½ tablespoons sifted all-purpose flour*
*1½ tablespoons sugar*
*6 eggs separated*

**FOR THE GLAZE:**
*3 ounces chopped unsweetened chocolate*
*1 cup heavy cream*
*1 cup sugar*
*1 teaspoon corn syrup*
*1 whole egg*
*1 teaspoon vanilla extract*

*Preheat oven to 325°.*
*1 9-inch springform pan lined with wax paper*

1. In a double boiler, combine and melt together the semisweet chocolate bits, water, and butter. When mixture is smooth, remove from heat.

2. Mix together the flour and sugar, and add to the chocolate mixture. Slightly beat the egg yolks, and add them to the mixture. Let the chocolate mixture cool to room temperature.

3. Beat the egg whites until peaks form. Fold these whites gently into the chocolate mixture. Pour this batter into the prepared pan, and bake for 20 to 25 minutes. The center of the cake should still be soft and wobbly.

4. Take the cake out of the oven, and let cool. Refrigerate for 1 hour. Remove sides of pan. Cut away high rim at edges to make top of cake level. Invert onto cake platter. Remove bottom of pan and wax paper.

5. To prepare the glaze, combine the chocolate, cream, sugar, and corn syrup in a heavy saucepan. Stirring constantly, cook over low heat until smooth, about 15 minutes.

6. Turn flame or setting to medium heat, and let mixture cook 5 more minutes. Remove the mixture from heat, and let stand for 10 minutes. Beat the egg, and add to the glaze with the vanilla. Mix well.

7. Ice the cooled cake with the slightly warm glaze. The cake should be served at room temperature but will keep well in the refrigerator for several days.

8. Garnish with whipped cream.

275

## Orange-Poppyseed Cake

**APPROXIMATE PREPARATION TIME:** 1½ **HOURS**
**MAKES** 8 **TO** 10 **SERVINGS**

This is a wonderfully moist cake, great to take on picnics.

**FOR THE CAKE:**
*1 cup butter, softened*
*1 cup sugar*
*3 eggs, separated*
*1 teaspoon orange brandy, such as Grand Marnier*
*1 cup sour cream*
*Grated rind of 1 orange*
*½ cup poppy seeds*
*2 cups sifted all-purpose flour*
*1 teaspoon baking powder*
*1 teaspoon baking soda*

**FOR THE GLAZE**
*½ cup sugar*
*¼ cup orange juice*
*⅓ cup orange brandy, such as Grand Marnier*

*Preheat oven to 350°.*
*1 9-inch tube pan, buttered and floured*

1. To prepare the cake, cream together the butter, sugar, and egg yolks until fluffy. Add the orange brandy. Mix in the sour cream, orange rind, and poppy seeds.

2. Sift together the flour, baking powder, and baking soda. Add to butter mixture, and blend well.

3. Beat the egg whites until they form soft peaks, and fold them into the batter.

4. Pour combined mixture into the pan, and bake for about 50 minutes, or until it is done.

5. Make the glaze by stirring together the sugar, orange juice, and orange brandy. Do this until the sugar is dissolved. Cover the cake with this glaze while cake is still hot. Glaze will soak into cake. Serve this cake with fresh strawberries and some orange-flavored whipped cream.

# Almond Cream Cheesecake

APPROXIMATE PREPARATION TIME: 1¾ HOURS
MAKES 10 SERVINGS

This recipe was developed by my mother for the restaurant.

**FOR THE CRUST:**
*1 cup sifted all-purpose flour*
*½ teaspoon baking powder*
*3 tablespoons butter*
*1 whole egg*
*¼ cup sugar*
*1 teaspoon vanilla extract*

**FOR THE FILLING:**
*1½ pounds softened cream cheese*
*1 cup sugar*
*4 whole eggs*
*1½ tablespoons sifted all-purpose flour*
*¼ teaspoon salt*
*1 teaspoon vanilla extract*
*1 tablespoon fine-grated lemon rind*
*¾ cup ground toasted almonds*
*¼ cup heavy cream*
*¼ cup amaretto or similar almond liqueur*

*Preheat oven to 375°.*
*1 9-inch springform pan*

1. To make the crust, sift together the flour and baking powder. Cut in the butter, and set aside.

2. Beat together the egg, sugar, and vanilla until creamy.

3. Add the egg mixture to the flour mixture, and mix well. Wrap dough in wax paper, and chill in the refrigerator for 1 hour. Butter the springform pan.

4. Using as little flour as possible, roll out ½ of the dough for the bottom of the pan. Roll the rest out into strips for lining the sides of the pan. Press these strips into the inside of the pan until it is completely lined with the dough.

277

5. Prepare the filling by beating together the cream cheese and sugar until light and fluffy. Add remaining ingredients, mixing well after each addition.

6. Pour the filling into the dough-lined pan, and bake in the oven for 15 minutes. Turn the oven temperature down to 250°, and bake for 30 minutes more. Turn the oven off, and let the cake cool completely inside the oven.

7. Take cooled cake out of the oven, and gently remove the sides of the pan. Serve the cake slightly chilled.

## Monterey Lemon Torte

**APPROXIMATE PREPARATION TIME:** 1½ **HOURS**
**MAKES** 10 **TO** 12 **SERVINGS**

This dessert is named after our beloved Monterey, where Heidi and I were married. This torte would make a great finish for a special celebration dinner.

**FOR THE LEMON SPONGE CAKE:**
*6 eggs, separated*
*Pinch of salt*
*1 cup sugar*
*1 teaspoon fine-grated lemon rind*
*2 tablespoons fresh lemon juice*
*1 teaspoon vanilla*
*1 cup sifted all-purpose flour*

**FOR THE LEMON MOUSSE FILLING:**
*1 envelope plain gelatin, dissolved in ½ cup lemon juice*
*4 eggs, separated*
*1 cup sugar*
*1 tablespoon fine-grated lemon rind*
*¼ teaspoon salt*
*¾ cup heavy cream*

**FOR THE LEMON BUTTER-CREAM ICING:**
*¾ cup, room temperature unsalted butter*
*3 cups sifted confectioner's sugar*
*2 egg yolks*

*1 tablespoon fresh lemon juice*
*1 teaspoon fine-grated lemon rind*
*3 tablespoons heavy cream*

*Preheat oven to 350°.*
*9-inch cake pans, lined with lightly buttered wax paper, plus 1*
   *9-inch springform pan lined with* un*buttered waxpaper.*

1. To make the sponge cake, combine egg whites with salt, and beat until they form peaks. Add sugar gradually, and beat mixture until stiff.
2. Mix the egg yolks with the lemon rind, lemon juice, and vanilla until blended.
3. Pour yolk mixture into beaten egg whites, and combine gently.
4. Sprinkle flour on top, and fold carefully together. Do not overmix. Divide batter into the 3 prepared pans.
5. Bake approximately 20 to 30 minutes, or until the top springs back when pressed.
6. Invert pans onto wire racks, and let cool.
7. In a double boiler, prepare the lemon mousse filling. First mix together the gelatin-and-lemon juice mixture, egg yolks, and sugar.
8. Heat, and stir until the mixture coats a spoon, and the sugar and gelatin are completely dissolved.
9. Strain mixture through a sieve into a large bowl to remove any cooked egg lumps or particles. Add the grated lemon rind.
10. Add salt to egg whites and beat until peaks form. Fold into lemon-gelatin mixture. Let mixture cool to room temperature.
11. Whip the heavy cream, and fold gently into the lemon mixture.
12. To layer the cake with the filling, put one of the baked sponge cakes on the bottom of a springform pan. Cover top of the cake with half of the filling, then alternate with another layer of cake until the 3 layers of cake enclose 2 layers of the filling.
13. Refrigerate for several hours until the mousse filling has set. Invert the cake onto a platter, and remove the pan.
14. Prepare the butter-cream frosting by adding together the butter and sifted confectioner's sugar, and beating in an electric mixer until fluffy.
15. Add egg yolks, lemon juice, lemon rind, and heavy cream. Beat well after each addition until light and smooth.
16. Ice and decorate the cake. You may garnish with strawberry sauce made with puréed and sweetened strawberries. Keep refrigerated until ready to serve.

# Mocha Macadamia Nut Torte

**APPROXIMATE PREPARATION TIME:** $1\frac{1}{2}$ **HOURS**
**MAKES 10 TO 12 SERVINGS**

This cake consists of 3 layers of chocolate *génoise* (a very fine-textured French butter cake) with a rich filling of mocha, macadamia nuts, and mousse, topped with a lighter mocha cream icing. A *génoise* yields a firmer, moister texture than a conventional cake and is therefore more difficult to prepare. All ingredients *and* cooking implements must be at room temperature. Mixing bowls, beaters, and cooking pans should be warm (not hot) before the ingredients are added.

**FOR THE CHOCOLATE *GÉNOISE*:**
*6 large whole eggs*
*1 cup sugar*
*½ cup sifted all-purpose flour*
*½ cup dark, unsweetened cocoa*
*½ cup melted and clarified sweet butter (see page 51)*
*1 teaspoon vanilla extract*

**FOR THE MOCHA MACADAMIA MOUSSE:**
*1 cup semisweet chocolate bits*
*1 cup heated heavy cream*
*2 tablespoons instant coffee, undissolved*
*1 teaspoon vanilla extract*
*4 separated eggs*
*2 tablespoons confectioner's sugar*
*1 cup toasted macadamia nuts, chopped coarse*

**FOR THE MOCHA CREAM ICING:**
*2 cups heavy cream*
*½ cup confectioner's sugar*
*½ cup unsweetened cocoa*
*2 tablespoons instant coffee powder*
*Toasted whole macadamia nuts*

*Preheat oven to 350°.*
*3 9-inch cake pans, bottoms lined with lightly buttered wax paper*
*1 9-inch springform pan lined with unbuttered wax paper*

1. To prepare the *génoise,* first bring all ingredients to room temperature, and be sure that all cooking implements are warm.

2. Beat the eggs and sugar until light and fluffy in texture and thick and lemony in color.

3. Sift together the flour and cocoa, and carefully fold into the egg mixture.

4. Gently fold in the melted, still-warm* clarified butter and vanilla extract.

5. Divide this batter among the 3 pans, and bake each for 25 to 30 minutes, or until the cake springs back when pressed. After cakes are baked, loosen sides of cake pans, and immediately invert onto wire racks to cool.

6. To make the mousse, blend together the chocolate bits, heated cream, instant coffee, and vanilla in a food processor. After this mixture is very smooth, add the egg yolks. Blend well, and set aside.

7. In a mixing bowl, beat the egg whites until peaks form. Add confectioner's sugar, and beat until well blended. Fold the beaten egg whites into the chocolate mixture. Fold in the chopped macadamia nuts.

8. Line a 9-inch springform pan with wax paper. Put one of the chocolate cake layers on the bottom of the pan. Layer alternately with the mousse and cake. You should have 3 layers of cake and 2 layers of mousse. Refrigerate the cake, and let set overnight, or at least 5 hours.

9. When ready, invert onto a platter and remove the pan.

10. To make the mocha icing, whip together all the icing ingredients except the nuts, and beat until stiff.

11. Ice the cake with this mixture, and decorate with the whole nuts. Keep cake refrigerated until ready to serve.

*Note: If the butter is too warm, it will deflate the eggs. Slightly warm (70–75°) is the correct temperature.

## Meringue Tortelets with Amaretto Butter Cream

APPROXIMATE PREPARATION TIME: 1½ HOURS PLUS DRYING TIME
MAKES **8** SERVINGS

Make this dessert a day ahead of time. It improves from the contact of the butter cream with the meringues. Since this dessert is very rich and sweet, it would be best served after a somewhat lighter lunch or dinner.

281

**FOR THE MERINGUE ROUNDS:**
*4 egg whites*
*Pinch of salt*
*½ teaspoon cream of tartar*
*1⅓ cups sugar*
*½ cup fine-ground almonds*

**FOR THE AMARETTO BUTTER CREAM:**
*1½ cups unsalted butter, room temperature*
*3 cups sifted confectioner's sugar*
*4 large egg yolks*
*½ cup amaretto or similar almond liqueur*

**FOR THE PRALINE CRUMBS:**
*Pinch, cream of tartar*
*½ cup sugar*
*3 tablespoons water*
*¼ pound sliced almonds, toasted*

**FOR THE CHOCOLATE SAUCE:**
*4 ounces semisweet chocolate bits*
*¼ cup sugar*
*1 cup heavy cream*
*Pinch of salt*
*1 teaspoon vanilla*

*Preheat oven to 225° to 250°.*
*Line 2 cookie sheets with nonstick parchment or oven paper.*

1. To make the meringues, beat egg whites with salt and cream of tartar until stiff. Very slowly beat in the sugar. Gently fold in the ground almonds.

2. Using a pastry bag and a round no. 5 tip, form 24 meringue rounds on 2 parchment- or paper-lined cookie sheets. (If a pastry bag is not available, drop about 2 tablespoons of the meringue onto baking sheet, and spread to desired shape with a knife.) Each meringue should be about 3 inches in diameter and ½ inch high. Put the meringues into the oven, and bake for 30 minutes. Some meringues might need additional baking, depending on individual oven. Turn the oven off, and let the meringues dry completely in the oven, keeping the door closed. This drying process will take several hours but is best left overnight. The unused meringues may be kept in an airtight container for up to 2 weeks.

3. To make the amaretto butter-cream mixture, cream the butter in mixer, and add the sifted confectioner's sugar and the egg yolks. Mix well.

4. Add the amaretto, and continue to beat until the mixture is creamy and smooth.

5. Layer the baked and dried meringue rounds with the butter cream, using 3 meringues and 2 layers of butter cream for each tortelet. Set aside. If the butter cream is too soft, let chill in refrigerator until it reaches the right semistiff consistency. Also ice the sides of the tortelet, but not the top.

6. Prepare the praline crumbs by mixing together in a large frying pan the cream of tartar, sugar, and water. Bring to a boil. After sugar is dissolved, cook mixture without stirring until the syrup is 325° on a candy thermometer, or the syrup is light brown in color (this should take only a few minutes).

7. Add the toasted almonds. Mix well with the syrup, and pour onto a prepared cookie sheet that has been well-buttered. Separate almond lumps, and let cool.

8. Chop the sugar-coated nuts in a food processor into crumbs. Any crumbs unused may be stored for up to several weeks in a tightly sealed jar in the refrigerator.

9. Coat the sides of the tortelets with the crumbs by rolling the tortelets in them; the crumbs will stick to the butter cream. Store in refrigerator until ready to be garnished with with chocolate sauce.

10. To prepare the chocolate sauce, combine all the ingredients for it, except the vanilla, in the top of a double boiler. Cook about 20 to 25 minutes or until the temperature reaches 180°. To cool, place top of the double boiler in an ice bath, and beat with a wire whisk until the sauce is thick and creamy. Add the vanilla, and blend in. Pour over the tortelets just before serving.

## Apple Almond Tart

APPROXIMATE PREPARATION TIME: 1½ HOURS
MAKES 8 SERVINGS

This recipe works well for fresh apricots or peaches also.

FOR THE CRUST:
*⅓ cup lard or shortening*
*1 tablespoon butter*
*1 cup sifted all-purpose flour*
*½ teaspoon salt*
*⅓ cup ice-cold water*

283

**FOR THE FILLING:**
*3 large baking apples*
*¼ cup fresh lemon juice*
*1 egg*
*⅓ cup light corn syrup*
*⅓ cup sugar*
*1 tablespoon melted butter*
*½ teaspoon almond extract*
*¼ teaspoon salt*
*½ cup finely ground almonds*
*1 tablespoon all-purpose flour*

*Preheat oven to 400°.*
*1 9-inch tart pan with detachable bottom*

1. To make the crust, cut the lard and butter into the flour. Add salt, then ice-cold water. Mix until the dough forms a ball and all the flour has been absorbed. Do not overmix. Chill dough for 1 hour.

2. Roll dough into a large circle using as little flour as possible. Place in an unbuttered 9-inch tart pan. Chill the unbaked crust for 20 minutes.

3. Bake the crust in the oven for 10 minutes. To avoid excessive air bubbles and shrinkage during the baking time, weight the dough down with aluminum foil and some rice or beans. Remove foil with beans from crust, and bake crust an additional 5 minutes.

4. Reduce oven temperature to 350°, and remove pastry. Let stand until cool.

5. Prepare the filling by peeling and slicing the apples. Coat with the lemon juice. Arrange the apple slices in the tart shell.

6. Mix together the last 8 ingredients, and pour the mixture over the apples. Bake at 350° for ½ to ¾ hour or until the tart has a light brown color. Cool and serve.

## Kiwi-Raspberry Tart

**APPROXIMATE PREPARATION TIME: 1¾ HOURS**
**MAKES 10 SERVINGS**

This is a wonderfully refreshing dessert after a big dinner. You can substitute any of your favorite fresh fruits in this tart.

**FOR THE CRUST:**
*½ pound butter*
*3 cups sifted all-purpose flour*
*½ cup sugar*
*1 whole egg*
*1 egg yolk*
*1 teaspoon almond extract*

**FOR THE FRUIT AND PASTRY CREAM FILLING:**
*2 peeled kiwi, cut into slices*
*½ pint cleaned, fresh red raspberries*
*1 cup milk*
*¼ cup sifted all-purpose flour*
*½ cup sugar*
*3 egg yolks*
*1 teaspoon vanilla extract*
*½ teaspoon fine-grated orange rind*
*½ cup seedless raspberry jam*

*Preheat oven to 375°.*
*1 11-inch tart pan, with detachable bottom*

1. To prepare the pastry shell, in a mixing bowl cut the butter into the flour and sugar.

2. Beat together the egg, egg yolk, and almond extract. Combine the egg mixture with the flour mixture and blend well. Divide dough into 2 balls, and wrap with wax paper. Chill dough for ½ hour.

3. Take one of the balls, and roll it out with a little flour to fit into the pan. Save the other half of the dough for later use. Don't roll the dough too thin, or it will crack while it is baking. Line the pan with the dough, cover with aluminum foil, and weight it down with rice or beans. Bake for 10 minutes. Remove the lining and beans or rice, and let crust continue to bake for another 10 minutes or until light brown. Allow to cool.

4. In the meantime, prepare the filling. Clean and slice the fruit.

5. In a saucepan, mix together the milk, flour, and sugar, and cook, stirring constantly, over a low heat for 10 to 15 minutes, or until the floury taste is gone. Take off the heat.

6. Mix the egg yolks, vanilla extract, and orange rind with a small amount of the custard mixture, blend, and then add this back to the rest of

the custard. With a wire whisk stir, and bring the custard mixture back to a slow boil, but do not let it curdle. Take off the heat, and let the custard cool. To avoid formation of a skin on top, cover it with some plastic wrap.

7. Fill the crust with the pastry cream. Arrange the fruit in a decorative pattern on top of the cream filling.

8. In a small saucepan, heat the raspberry jam, and glaze the fruit by pouring some of liquified jam gently over it. Serve tart slightly chilled.

### Raspberry Pear Stefan

APPROXIMATE PREPARATION TIME: 1½ HOURS
MAKES 6 SERVINGS

These delicious poached pears are nested on sweetened whipped cream and *génoise* rounds, then glazed with a raspberry sauce. The dish is named for my son Stefan. For an extra touch here, fill the center of the pears with a chocolate nougat, or use white chocolate mousse instead of the whipped cream. All parts can be made several days ahead of time and then can be assembled just before serving.

FOR THE PEARS:
*6 pears with stems (preferably Bartlett)*
*Water*
*¼ cup fresh lemon juice*
*1 cup sugar*
*¼ cup brandy*
*1 inch stick of vanilla bean*

FOR THE *GÉNOISE*:
*6 whole eggs*
*1 cup sugar*
*1 cup sifted all-purpose flour*
*½ teaspoon vanilla extract*
*1 teaspoon fine-grated lemon rind*
*½ cup clarified butter, room temperature (see page 51)*

FOR THE RASPBERRY SAUCE AND FINISH:
*1 pint of cleaned, fresh raspberries, or 1 10-ounce package frozen*
*    unsweetened raspberries*

*½ cup confectioner's sugar*
*½ pint whipping cream*
*2 tablespoons sugar*


*Preheat oven to 325°.*
*1 11-by-16-by-1-inch cookie sheet*

1. Peel and core the pears, leaving stems on.
2. Place the pears in a medium-size stainless steel pot, and cover them with water. Add lemon juice and sugar. Bring to a boil, and simmer the pears until they are tender but not too soft, about 15 minutes (time depends on ripeness of pears).
3. Cool the pears in the juice. Then gently stir in the brandy, and add the vanilla bean. Set aside.
4. To prepare the *génoise,* first bring all ingredients to room temperature, and be sure that all cooking implements are warm.
5. Beat the eggs and sugar until the mixture is fluffy and light and thick in texture and lemony in color. Fold in sifted flour. Add the vanilla extract and the lemon rind. Fold in the slightly warmed clarified butter. The mixture should be well-blended without being overmixed.
6. Pour the batter into the pan, which has been lined with buttered oven or parchment paper, and bake in the oven for 20 to 30 minutes, or until the *génoise* is golden brown. Remove the *génoise* from oven, and immediately invert onto a wire rack, and let cool. Pull off parchment paper, and cut 6 3-inch *génoise* rounds out of the sheet of *génoise.* Cut 6 additional rounds and freeze for later use.
7. To make raspberry sauce and finish, puree the raspberries, and sweeten with the confectioner's sugar. Strain through a sieve to remove the seeds. Beat whipping cream with 2 tablespoons of sugar until stiff.
8. To serve, place each piece of the *génoise* on a serving dish. Put about 2 tablespoons of the sweetened whipped cream on top of each piece of *génoise.* Also fill the core of the pears with whipped cream. Place the pears on the whipped cream and *génoise* rounds. Cover pears with the raspberry sauce. Serve immediately.

## White Chocolate Mousse with Strawberry Sauce

**APPROXIMATE PREPARATION TIME:** ¾ HOUR
**MAKES 8 TO 10 SERVINGS**

This creamy, light, but rich mousse would be a grand finale of any dinner party.

*½ cup sugar*
*¼ cup water*
*1 pound high-grade white chocolate, chopped*
*2 cups whipping cream*
*½ cup egg whites, room temperature*
*1 pint cleaned, fresh strawberries, or 1 10-ounce package frozen*
     *unsweetened strawberries*
*½ cup confectioner's sugar*

1. Combine sugar and water in a saucepan, and bring to a slow boil. Stir to dissolve sugar. Cook syrup 3 to 5 minutes.
2. In double boiler, combine white chocolate with ½ cup of the whipping cream. Begin to heat, and stir until melted and smooth.
3. Beat egg whites until they form soft peaks. Gradually add hot sugar syrup while continuing to beat egg whites.
4. Fold the melted white chocolate into the beaten egg whites. Let mixture cool to room temperature.
5. Whip cream until stiff. Chill for a few minutes in refrigerator. It is important that the white chocolate mixture be completely cooled before it is blended with the whipped cream. Fold whipped cream into white chocolate mixture. Do *not* overmix. Refrigerate for 1 hour before serving.
6. Puree the strawberries with the confectioner's sugar. Serve mousse in chilled champagne saucers, and surround it with the sauce.

## Blueberry-Peach Trifle

**APPROXIMATE PREPARATION TIME:** 1 HOUR
**MAKES 6 SERVINGS**

This is not a traditional trifle, but is one of our most popular desserts. It is refreshing yet substantial.

*1 pint washed, fresh blueberries*
*½ cup confectioner's sugar*
*1½ cups sweetened whipped cream*
*6 génoise rounds (see pages 286–287)*
*½ cup cream sherry*
*6 scoops vanilla ice cream*
*6 peach halves, cooked or canned*

1. Make the blueberry sauce by pureeing the blueberries with the sugar.
2. Assemble the trifles. Cover the bottoms of the dessert dishes with 2 tablespoons each of the whipped cream. Place the *génoise* rounds on top. Moisten each of the *génoise* with some of the cream sherry. Add 1 large scoop of vanilla ice cream on top of each *génoise*. Place the peach halves on top of the ice cream, and cover with the sauce. Serve immediately.

## Heidi's Favorite Double Chocolate Soufflé

**APPROXIMATE PREPARATION TIME:** 1½ **HOURS**
**MAKES** 6 **SERVINGS**

A light yet dramatic dessert.

*2 tablespoons granulated sugar*
*3 tablespoons melted butter*
*3 tablespoons all-purpose flour*
*2 tablespoons unsweetened cocoa*
*1 cup hot milk*
*½ cup granulated sugar*
*Dash of salt*
*2 ounces bitter baking chocolate, chopped finely*
*5 egg yolks*
*7 egg whites*
*½ teaspoon cream of tartar*
*Confectioner's sugar*

*Preheat oven to 350°.*

1. Butter a 1-quart soufflé dish. Attach a buttered collar to the rim of the

soufflé dish,* and sprinkle the inside of the dish and collar with 2 tablespoons of granulated sugar.

2. In a double boiler combine butter, flour, and unsweetened cocoa. Cook for a few minutes. Add hot milk, and cook, stirring constantly, until mixture is thick and creamy.

3. Add the sugar, salt, and baking chocolate. Continue stirring until the mixture is smooth.

4. Remove from the heat, and using a wire whisk, beat the mixture for 1 minute. Beat the egg yolks lightly, and add to the mixture; continue beating until smooth. Let the mixture cool.

5. Beat the egg whites with the cream of tartar until stiff. Fold egg whites into chocolate mixture, and blend thoroughly.

6. Place batter in the prepared soufflé dish, and bake for 25 minutes, or until the soufflé begins to brown around the edges. Remove from oven. Dust with confectioner's sugar, and serve immediately. Serve with some lightly sweetened whipped cream on the side, or some chocolate sauce as described on pages 282–283.

*Note: To prepare the collar, fold and butter a 24-inch piece of parchment paper or wax paper. Wrap it around the outside of the soufflé dish and attach with string. The collar should stand up about 3 inches higher than the edge of the soufflé dish.

## Pineapple-Lime Sorbet

APPROXIMATE PREPARATION TIME: **45** MINUTES
MAKES **8** TO **10** SERVINGS

A refreshing summertime dessert; for an extra touch, serve with almond macaroons (see page 293).

> *4 cups pineapple puree (from 1 large ripe pineapple)*
> *1¾ cup sugar*
> *1¾ cup water*
> *¼ cup fresh lime juice*
> *1 tablespoon fine-grated lime rind*
> *2 tablespoons rum*
> *¼ cup egg whites*

1. Pass the pineapple puree through a food mill to eliminate some of the fiber.

2. Make a sugar syrup by combining sugar and water in a small saucepan, and heating to a gentle boil over medium heat. The syrup is ready when the sugar has dissolved, about 3 to 5 minutes. It should read 235° on a candy thermometer.

3. Add lime juice and rind to the pineapple puree. Then add syrup to sweeten to taste. Add rum, and blend well.

4. Beat the egg whites to soft peaks, and combine with pineapple-syrup mixture, although egg whites will not be completely absorbed.

5. Pour mixture into ice-cream maker (either the electric or manual kind), and let freeze for 25 minutes. Serve in tall stem glasses garnished with fresh fruit and a mint sprig.

## Persimmon Pudding with Pecans

APPROXIMATE PREPARATION TIME: 1 HOUR
MAKES 8 TO 10 SERVINGS

This is a very moist and almost cakelike pudding. It does not refrigerate well and is therefore best eaten the same day. Use only very ripe persimmons, that is, persimmons which are dark brown and very soft to the touch. It will take about seven to ten days after purchase for firm persimmons to ripen.

*2 cups mashed, sieved, very ripe persimmon pulp*
*3 eggs, beaten*
*1¾ cups milk*
*2 cups sifted flour*
*½ teaspoon baking soda*
*1 teaspoon salt*
*½ cup sugar*
*1 teaspoon ground coriander*
*3 tablespoons melted butter*
*½ cup pecans*
*¼ pint whipped cream*
*A pinch of nutmeg*

*Preheat oven to 325°.*
*1 9-inch tube pan coated with butter and flour*

1. In a large mixing bowl, mix together persimmon pulp, eggs, and milk.

2. Sift together the next 5 ingredients.

3. Add these dry ingredients to the persimmon mixture. Mix well. Blend in butter.

4. Pour batter into prepared pan. Sprinkle the pecans on top of the batter. Bake for about 40 minutes, or until a toothpick comes out clean. (Note that the finished cake will shrink, somewhat like a soufflé.) Invert cake onto platter when still warm. Garnish with whipped cream and a pinch of nutmeg.


## Chocolate Mint Cookies

APPROXIMATE PREPARATION TIME: **45** MINUTES PLUS CHILLING TIME
MAKES **24** COOKIES

These are a delightful ending to any dinner. They have become a favorite and anticipated finish to dinner at Joe's.

*1 cup sugar*
*¼ cup melted butter*
*2 ounces unsweetened melted chocolate*
*2 whole eggs*
*1 teaspoon vanilla extract*
*½ teaspoon mint extract*
*1 cup sifted all-purpose flour*
*1 teaspoon baking powder*
*½ teaspoon salt*
*1 cup confectioner's sugar*

*Preheat oven to 325°.*

1. In mixing bowl, combine first 6 ingredients. Blend well.
2. Sift together flour, baking powder, and salt.
3. Add the 2 mixtures together, and blend well. Cover and chill dough overnight in refrigerator.
4. Place confectioner's sugar in a small bowl. Drop ½ teaspoon dough into the sugar, and roll into a small ball. Press ball onto a greased cookie sheet lined with wax paper. Proceed to do this with the rest of the dough.
5. Bake for 5 minutes, taking care not to overbake. Cookies should still be soft to touch when finished baking. Let cool before removing from cookie sheet.

# Almond Macaroons

APPROXIMATE PREPARATION TIME: 1 HOUR
MAKES 24 MACAROONS

Wonderful and chewy.

*1 cup almond paste*
*1 cup confectioner's sugar*
*3 egg whites*
*A dash of salt*
*½ teaspoon vanilla extract*
*½ cup sugar*

*Preheat oven to 300°.*

1. Line 2 cookie sheets with wax paper.
2. In a food processor, blend together the almond paste and confectioner's sugar. Add the egg whites, and blend until dough has a smooth consistency. Add salt and vanilla extract, and blend.
3. Using a pastry bag and a tip with a round no. 5 tip, squeeze a small amount of dough about 1 inch in diameter onto the cookie sheet. (If a pastry bag is not available, use a ½ teaspoon of dough, and drop it onto cookie sheet.) Proceed until all the dough has been used. The pieces of dough should be about ½-inch apart from one another. Sprinkle with sugar, and bake for 20 minutes or until light brown.
4. Spread out some damp cloths on a flat surface. To remove macaroons, place the cookie sheets on top of these cloths. The moisture from the cloths will loosen the cookies from the sheets of paper. Using a spatula, remove, and serve. These cookies can be stored in an airtight container to maintain moisture for several weeks.

## Meringue Mushrooms

APPROXIMATE PREPARATION TIME: 7½ HOURS
MAKES **24** COOKIES

These are mushroom-shaped cookies, made with baked meringues. Use these also to garnish cakes.

*3 egg whites*
*⅛ teaspoon cream of tartar*
*¾ teaspoon vanilla extract*
*¾ cup sugar*
*1 ounce semisweet melted chocolate*
*1 teaspoon unsweetened cocoa powder*

*Preheat oven to 225°.*

1. Line 2 cookie sheets with wax paper.
2. In a mixing bowl, beat together the egg whites, cream of tartar, and vanilla extract until peaks form. Add sugar in a very slow stream, while the egg whites are still being beaten. Continue beating egg whites until they are stiff and glossy and the sugar is dissolved.
3. On the first cookie sheet, make the mushroom caps. Do this by taking half the meringue, and putting it in a pastry bag fitted with a no. 5 tip. Start squeezing out 1-inch-diameter rounds of meringue onto the sheet, ½ inch apart. If a pastry bag is not available, fold a piece of parchment paper into a cone. Cut off the tip to leave a ½-inch opening.
4. On the second cookie sheet, make the stems for the mushrooms. You do this with the same tip and bag you used for the caps, only this time squeeze the meringue out so that each one sticks up as much as possible, looking like a finger about 1¼ to 1½ inches high.
5. Bake the meringues in the oven for 1 hour. Turn the oven off, and let the meringues dry inside completely. This should take about 6 hours.
6. When the caps and stems are completely cool and dry, make a small hole in the bottom of each cap and fill with some of the melted chocolate. Attach the stems to the caps where the chocolate has been put. Let the chocolate harden, then dust the meringues with the cocoa powder before serving. Put these meringues in an airtight container for storing. They will keep up to a week.

## Banana Date Nut Bread

APPROXIMATE PREPARATION TIME: $1\frac{1}{2}$ HOURS
MAKES 8 TO 10 SERVINGS

This makes a moist breakfast bread. Or serve it for dessert, accompanied by some vanilla or maple walnut ice cream.

> *3 large, ripe bananas*
> *1 cup sugar*
> *¼ cup softened butter*
> *1 whole egg*
> *1 teaspoon baking soda*
> *1½ cups sifted all-purpose flour*
> *1 teaspoon salt*
> *1 teaspoon vanilla extract*
> *½ cup chopped walnuts*
> *1 cup dates, chopped fine*
>
> *Preheat oven to 325°.*
> *2 5-by-9-inch buttered loaf pans*

1. Puree bananas. In mixing bowl, mix together sugar, butter, and egg, and add pureed bananas.

2. Sift together baking soda, flour, and salt, and combine with the banana mixture. Add vanilla, walnuts, and chopped dates. Blend well.

3. Pour into prepared pan, and bake for 50 minutes or until a toothpick comes out clean after piercing. Invert bread onto a wire rack, and let cool. Serve. The other loaf can be stored in the freezer.

My favorite variation of this recipe is to substitute 6 ounces of fresh cranberries for the dates.

**CHAPTER FIFTEEN**

# Situations and Menus

## Situations

This section is designed to help you use some of the ideas in this book in some of those awkward situations a real cook confronts on a regular basis. For example, let's say you come home with an ounce of dried morels. How do you justify spending seven or eight dollars for what looks like little more than a garnish? You make a meal out of it! This chapter will show you how. Or suppose, on a hike, you happen to encounter some mushrooms that you recognize—because you are an experienced picker—as deliciously edible. There's a menu here for making a four-course supper from a pound of fresh wild mushrooms. And so on.

Having come so far in your introduction to the variety of mushroom cookery, I would hate to see you stopped by momentary difficulties. This chapter may make things a little easier.

### Situation One

*Your neighbor has come over to share some fresh wild mushrooms she just bought for you. She hands you exactly five medium-sized caps.*

Your neighbor's sudden generosity notwithstanding, five caps is not much to work with. And by allowing them to sit around for a few days while you wait for inspiration to strike, you will cause them to go bad. What *do* you do?

First (and this is true for *all* fresh mushrooms you have), inspect the mushrooms. Chances are that they will not be in perfect shape, since mushrooms start deteriorating from the moment they are picked. Decide then and there that you are going to use them immediately.

Reject the temptation to put them in the refrigerator for a few more days, or hours. Refrigeration is the worst thing you can do, because it is only for mushrooms that are very fresh and can take a few days there. Even domestic mushrooms off a retail shelf should be used as soon as possible; they will have been out of the ground for several days already and, worse, will have been displayed outside a refrigerated area, which hastens their deterioration.

Another temptation to avoid is to throw them away just because they are drying on the edges or are developing some dark spots. These are signs of age, but not necessarily of total decay, and most mushrooms can still be used at this point.

Start by washing the mushrooms to remove the dirt. Any dry spots will revive during this process.

Then put the mushrooms in a saucepan and just barely cover with some water. Bring this to a boil, then turn down the heat and simmer for 10 minutes. This should produce 1 cup of mushroom blanching liquid. The mushrooms are now sterilized and will cease to deteriorate for the time being.

Separate them from the liquid by straining it through a sieve. After this process, you will wonder what happened to the mushrooms. They will probably look a little bedraggled. What do you do with *that?* Well, they are excellent for slicing and adding to any dish for that night's supper.

Then look again at your liquid. This is your real source of flavor.

The easiest and best way to handle it is to use it as a clear mushroom soup, the way you would a consommé. Follow the procedure for flavoring as explained on pages 57–58. Slice about 1 teaspoon of fresh scallions, add them to the liquid, then add a pinch of fresh herbs. Bring back to a simmer, and serve when ready, adding back the mushrooms, sliced, if you prefer. This is the best way to maximize the flavor from those few mushrooms. Nothing fancy here, just elegant flavor. (This method is reliable except for certain types of mushrooms.)

Another approach would be to slice the mushrooms and prepare them as an appetizer for one. Sauté 2 tablespoons of chopped onion in 1 tablespoon of melted butter. When the onions are transparent, add the mushrooms, and sauté according to one of the sauté methods described on pages 119–121. Serve on toast.

### Situation Two

*You're cleaning out your refrigerator, and you find, to your horror, some mushrooms (domestic) that you have left over from the salad you made for a dinner party almost two weeks ago!*

This is a situation that happens everywhere, every day. In most cases the mushrooms will have browned somewhat. If they have a distinctly rotten odor that offends you, then just dump them. But if their earthy, "mushroomy" smell still lingers, you can do something with them. First, wash the mushrooms thoroughly. Smell them again. If the odor signaling decay is still strong, throw them away. However, if it has abated and they smell all right, then prepare them for cooking.

What you are going to do is make duxelles with them because duxelles require cooking and flavoring, just what you need to rescue the mushrooms. The process is simple and provides one of the most powerful ways to trap and save mushroom flavor. Refer to the methods described on pages 60–67 for preparing duxelles. Remember, you don't have to use the duxelles right away. You can freeze them until you decide how you wish to use them. If you are pressed for time and wish to expedite the preparation of the duxelles, blend the mushrooms in a food processor or blender, instead of chopping them fine as most of the recipes require. Then proceed as directed.

But remember, these mushrooms *must* be cooked, whether chopped or pureed.

### Situation Three

*You overbought domestic mushrooms. There are more there than you can possibly use, but you don't want to waste what's left. The mushrooms are in good condition.*

The mushrooms may be in good shape now, but we know they will not stay that way for long. Fresh domestic mushrooms will retain their firm, snowy-white appearance for three days, maximum, before they begin to turn brown. It is important, therefore, that you cook these mushrooms if you want to keep them for longer than a few days in the refrigerator. Cooking sterilizes them and halts the enzymatic action that causes mushrooms to break down. The following are ideas for small amounts of mushrooms:

- Braise the mushrooms in onions, butter, and spice (see pages 124–125). Thicken them with a little arrowroot or cornstarch as described elsewhere.
- Make a simple Domestic Cream of Mushroom Soup (see page 102). For smaller amounts than that described in the recipe, intensify their flavor by covering them with a little water. Bring to a boil and cook down the liquid until it is barely noticeable. Add cream and milk, and season with salt, sugar, and soy sauce in the same proportions as indicated for the Cream of Mushroom Soup.
- Make duxelles (see pages 60–67).

These methods insure that you will have at least usable mushrooms for ten days. The braised mushrooms and duxelles can be frozen for longer storage.

### Situation Four

*You've gone and done it! You've either picked them or gone hog-wild in a gourmet shop, but you're now in possession of twenty-five to fifty caps of fresh wild mushrooms. This is about two to three pounds. You want to make a dinner using these mushrooms as a focal point or by themselves.*

Now you have the makings for a mushroom feast! You can feed four people four courses each, each course being a different way of using the same wild mushrooms. Here's your menu:

**FRESH WILD MUSHROOM SOUP** *(see page 101)*
**MUSHROOM FRITTERS** *(see pages 114–115)*
**JOE'S PICKLED MARTINI MUSHROOMS** *(see page 138)*
**MUSHROOMS IN BÉCHAMEL SAUCE I** *(see pages 126–127)*

Wash and clean all the mushrooms. Separate ¼ pound of the smallest and firmest caps for the pickled mushrooms. Begin to make the pickled mushrooms as described. When they are covered with the marinade, place in the refrigerator to cool. These should be cold when served, so give yourself at least 2 hours' chilling time. This is meant to be a palate cleanser between courses.

Prepare the batter for the fritters. Select the least appealing in appearance for this dish; you'll need ½ pound sliced mushrooms to make the fritters.

Separate the rest of the mushrooms in the following manner: Set aside 1 pound for the soup, and use the rest of the mushrooms for the main course.

Prepare in turn the soup and fritters. Serve the pickled mushrooms as a palate cleanser, two or three per person, depending on the size of the caps, along with a fresh green such as arugula or romaine. Finish with the Mushrooms in Béchamel Sauce. Serve with a rich, woody Chardonnay from California, perhaps from the Chalone vineyard.


## Situation Five

*You've hit the jackpot! A day in the woods, and your bushel baskets are brimming with morels—more than you can possibly eat.*

Okay. You've just brought in basket after basket of fresh morels. You've never seen so many, but you just couldn't let them sit out there. What now?

Well, bushels of fresh mushrooms must be processed immediately, or they won't be worth having by the next morning. Since you probably don't have the facilities to store large quantities by refrigeration, what you must do is stop the enzymatic action right away.

The tendency in this situation is to process all the mushrooms the same way, by canning, salting, or drying. But I think you ought to consider storing the morels several ways.

First of all, avoid canning unless you are very good at it. The mushrooms must be blanched for this operation and then specific measures and precautions must be taken to ensure complete sterilization, and the end result is still only tasteless canned mushrooms.

Start by dividing the mushrooms in half. One half should consist of the less attractive or broken caps. Use these for drying. See Chapter 16 for specific methods of drying. Dried morels are very useful for sauces and extracts. But don't waste the best-looking caps on drying, a technique that simply will not allow them to reconstitute attractively.

Use the other half of the mushrooms for sautéing and freezing. Yes— I said freezing. Although I prefer other preservation methods, there are times when freezing is best. Remember, in this case you have a large amount of fresh mushrooms that *must* be preserved.

Prepare them in the way described for Morels Rosenthal (see pages 122–123), that is, sautéing them in butter, onions, and sweet green peppers. The mushrooms will draw a large amount of their own liquid and shrink down to a manageable size. Go ahead and salt the mushrooms as described in the recipe. When you are done, you will have a mass of morels cooked in their own juices, salted and ready to eat. Simply store the mushrooms in quart or half-gallon plastic containers in your freezer. You will be surprised at how an enormous-looking bunch of mushrooms can cook down.

The chances are that you will not have a pot large enough to hold nearly all the mushrooms you have picked. In that case, fill your largest pot with mushrooms, and cover the bottom of the pot with water. Then cover the pot, and raise the heat to high. The water on the bottom will boil and begin to steam, and will cook the mushrooms, which will soon be almost covered by their own liquid. After they are covered like this, let them boil for another 5 minutes to ensure maximum liquid extraction from the mushrooms. Then repeat until all the mushrooms are cooked. In a separate sauté pan, cook the onions and green peppers in the butter, the amount depending on the amount of mushrooms you have. Add this mixture to the cooked mushrooms, apportioning to several pots if one is not large enough to contain the entire mixture. Blend thoroughly, and then freeze. A bushel basket will yield no more than 5 quarts of sautéed mushrooms. And the nice thing is that, on defrosting, all you have to do is heat them and thicken the sauce as you desire.

If it's not morels you've picked but chanterelles (or any other wild mushrooms) the above-mentioned method of sautéing or freezing will also work. I'd suggest that you skip the green peppers during the sauté step, however, since their flavor best complements that of morels. The only other mushrooms that should be held for drying are boletes, black trumpet mushrooms, or mushrooms from which you would like to try to make a mushroom extract. Finally, if you want to preserve the natural texture of mushrooms for an extended period, try brining (or salting) them, as described in Chapter 16.

By the way, make sure that you keep some of the mushrooms you've just picked for consuming fresh. Often, in the rush of preserving, you forget to leave out some freshly picked mushrooms to enjoy immediately with family and friends. Scoop out several generous handfuls of mushrooms and put them in the refrigerator until you are ready to make them. This is still the most exhilarating way to enjoy mushrooms—fresh and still redolent of the forest or field from which they were plucked. Use a simple preparation such as sautéing them with butter and onion, perhaps blending into the mixture a dollop or two of *crème fraîche* just before serving.

### Situation Six

*Either you've just received as a gift, or you've treated yourself to, one fresh truffle. One.*

People who are curious about food buy truffles at least once in their life. In my case I received a truffle as a gift one Christmas. It sat and sat and—finally ended up in the garbage can. Why? Because I was intimidated by it. It was like having royalty in the living room. I enjoyed knowing it was there, but didn't know what to do with it. Now I try to remember one thing—truffles are food and are meant to be eaten. Furthermore, they must be used immediately, because they lose their wicked intensity quickly. Even if you do nothing more than grate the truffle onto a salad, it's still better than leaving it in your refrigerator. The white truffle from Piedmont, Italy, is the one you are most likely to see in a store. The directions can also be used for a black truffle.

But now back to the situation at hand. To make a dinner from one truffle, you do the following:

Brush the truffle with a coarse, dry cloth to remove any dirt. Cut the truffle in half. Wrap one half carefully and place it back in the refrigerator. Cut the truffle you have into very thin slices. Place these slices in a small jar with a tight-fitting lid. Cover the truffle slices with some Wild Turkey Bourbon, or any other brand of bourbon or brandy. Cover the jar with the lid tightly, and let sit for twenty-four hours, at least.

You now have the makings for a dinner consisting of the following:

TRUFFLED RICE *(see pages 245–246)*
TRUFFLE AND BOURBON SAUCE *(see page 86)*

You will have just enough left of your refrigerated half truffle to make rice for four. The slices steeping in the bourbon are to be used in the sauce for a meat dish, such as beef or veal, which can be cooked however you like.

## Situation Seven

*You have finally decided to venture over to that apothecary jar in your favorite gourmet food store. You buy an ounce of dried cepes.*

It doesn't look like much, but you've just purchased enough flavor for a full lunch.

CEPE LIQUOR *(see pages 93–94)*
CEPE SOUFFLÉ *(see pages 116–117)*

Reconstitute the mushrooms by adding the ounce of cepes to 2 cups of water. Bring to a boil, then let simmer for 20 minutes. The liquid should be very dark, and you should add back enough water to retain 2 cups. Separate the mushrooms from the liquid. Strain the liquid, and save for the soup. Thoroughly rinse the mushrooms and make Purée of Cepes (page 69) from them for the soufflé. Serve with a chilled Grenache rosé.

### Situation Eight

*You tried the menu for Situation Seven and were pleased with the results. You went back to the gourmet shop and bought an ounce of dried morels.*

The procedure for 1 ounce of morels is basically the same as for an ounce of cepes. But let's do something for dinner this time.

**CHRISTOPHER SOUP** *(see pages 94–95)*
**FILET OF SOLE IN PARCHMENT WITH MOREL DUXELLES** *(see page 66)*

Reconstitute the morels the same way you did the cepes in the procedure for Situation Seven. Use the liquid for the soup as described in the recipe for Christopher Soup. Make the duxelles from the mushrooms; the mushrooms from the reconstitution will be sufficient. Cut 4 pieces of sole weighing 5 to 7 ounces each. Cover each piece of fish with some of the duxelles, then wrap the fish in the parchment paper (see page 145) and bake at 350° for 15 minutes. Serve immediately, accompanied by one of the less woody Chardonnays like a Heitz, Iron Horse, or Acacia.

## Menus for All Seasons

Any occasion can call for the use of mushrooms, whether a dinner party or a simple evening snack. The following menu ideas range from the quick and simple to the sumptuous and lengthy.

### Breakfast

A continental breakfast with mushrooms as the theme would be the following:

RED OR BLACK CURRANT JUICE
CROISSANTS WITH MUSHROOM BUTTER *(see pages 71 and 113)*
BAGELS WITH SMOKED SALMON DUXELLES *(see page 63)* AND CREAM CHEESE
BLENDED FRENCH ROAST AND COLOMBIAN COFFEE
OR KEEMUN BLACK TEA

A more elaborate approach would be this:

FRESH WINEBERRIES AND BLACKBERRIES WITH APRICOT
LIQUEUR
SCRAMBLED EGGS WITH MORELS *(see pages 108–109)*
HOME-FRIED POTATOES WITH SAUTÉED MUSHROOMS AND GREEN ONIONS *(see page 252)*
WHOLE WHEAT TOAST WITH SWEET DUXELLES *(see page 62)*
KONA COFFEE
OR GUNPOWDER TEA

## Brunch and Lunch

The following represent some ideas for midday meals.

PICKLED MUSHROOMS WITH ROCKET (ARUGULA) *(see page 139)*
POACHED OYSTERS CALLOWHILL *(see page 163)*
IRON HORSE CHARDONNAY
BLUEBERRY-PEACH TRIFLE *(see pages 288–289)*

HELEN TURLEY'S SAUTÉED ENOKI AND APPLES WITH CALVADOS *(see page 122)*
POLENTA WITH PORCINI *(see pages 249–250)*
STAG'S LEAP GAMAY BEAUJOLAIS
CHOCOLATE MINT COOKIES *(see page 292)*

## Cookout

A midday cookout on a grille using some mushrooms might comprise the following:

GRILLED OYSTER MUSHROOMS *(see page 131)*
TENDERLOIN EN BROCHETTE *(see page 194)*
MIRASSOU HARVEST ZINFANDEL
KIWI-RASPBERRY TART *(see pages 284–286)*

# Special Dinners

## An All-Mushroom Dinner

FRESH WILD MUSHROOM SOUP *(see page 101)*
SAUTÉED MUSHROOMS—I, LOW-HEAT METHOD *(see page 119)*
RAYMOND CHARDONNAY
CEPE SOUFFLÉ *(see pages 116–117)*
Z-D PINOT NOIR
MUSHROOMS KRACÓW STYLE *(see pages 127–128)*
MATANZAS CREEK CHARDONNAY, ESTATE BOTTLED
MERINGUE MUSHROOMS *(see page 294)*

## A Mushroom and Game Dinner

CEPE LIQUOR *(see pages 93–94)*
QUAIL WITH CHANTERELLES, TRUFFLES, AND PINE NUTS *(see page 178)*
FREEMARK ABBEY CHARDONNAY
WILD BOAR ZRAZY WITH MORELS *(see pages 229–230)*
DAVID BRUCE PINOT NOIR
BEAR SOBIESKI WITH CROISSANTS *(see pages 234–235)*
MONTEREY PENINSULA WINERY CABERNET SAUVIGNON
ORANGE-POPPYSEED CAKE *(see pages 275–276)*
FELTON-EMPIRE LATE HARVEST GEWÜRZTRAMINER

CHAPTER SIXTEEN

# *Caveats and New Friends*

## Caveats

Up to this point I have described various ways that mushrooms can be used for cooking. As you are now aware, each species of mushroom has its own personality, which makes it more suitable for some dishes than others, and you need not be confined to using supermarket mushrooms, because wild types are available. The latter are rarely in fresh form, but this fact need not preclude your use of them, because the dried and canned forms are excellent flavor enhancers. I have also made available, but not emphasized, recipes using fresh wild mushrooms. In this chapter I will talk briefly about gathering fresh wild mushrooms and how to go about doing it.

First, the caveats.

### Picking Wild Mushrooms

It should come as no surprise to anyone that I warn people not to try picking their own wild mushrooms without prior experience. This is not a sport for beginners. The danger is quite real, even though (contrary to popular belief) the vast majority of wild mushrooms are quite safe, and your statistical chances of being poisoned are small.

The problem is that the toxic varieties (e.g., *Amanita phalloides,* death cap) grow in large quantities. The mushrooms in the *Amanita* genus are the most deadly; they are also the most sophisticated genetically and often the most brightly colored because they do not have to camouflage themselves for survival purposes. In other words, they are able to be bright and colorful precisely because they do not have to "hide" themselves from animals and insects that normally feed on mushrooms. (On the other hand, most of the best wild mushrooms grow the closest to the ground and are well hidden from view until you are up close to them. They have developed these features to blend in with the environment so that they are less likely to be eaten by hungry denizens of the forest.)

Further, a number of poisonous mushrooms actually resemble some very good and edible types and are often mistaken for them. For instance, there is an excellent mushroom called the *Lepiota naucina,* which grows in grass in the early fall in Pennsylvania. It looks almost identical to the *Amanitas verna* and *virosa* (fool's mushroom and destroying angel), which are two of the five deadliest mushrooms known. All three are pure white. I have seen the *Lepiota procera* (parasol mushroom) in the grass adjoining woods, and upon looking into the woods have spotted the *Amanitas virosa* and *verna* not more than thirty feet away! There are definite identifying characteristics for each of these species, but for a beginner the differences may go unnoticed and lead to a deadly mistake.

Poisonings have happened several times in my native Reading. The most dramatic case occurred in 1960 when a woman accidentally gave her family the deadly poisonous *Amanita phalloides.* Two of the five family members who ate the mushrooms died. The astonishing thing was that this mushroom was not supposed to exist anywhere in the United States outside of California. My father's positive identification of the mushroom is the first recorded outside California. Now the mushroom is rampant around Reading and, in fact, all over the East. Another incident occurred only four years ago with the same mushroom. A woman who had been picking mushrooms for years picked some of the *Amanita phalloides,* pickled them, and gave them to her neighbor, who died after eating them. The woman who pickled the mushrooms was not harmed, because she had not gotten around to trying them. I remember the person from the hospital bringing that jar of pickled mushrooms to the restaurant. We opened them and dumped them into a stainless steel bowl. My father started weeping when he realized what they were. It was as if someone from another planet had wanted to offer an earthling baby a present to play with and brought rattlesnakes as the gift. So it was with the woman who innocently gave her neighbor the fatal mushrooms.

If from the above stories you think I am trying to scare you, you're right. Poisoning is a real possibility, the chances being greater than one would be led to believe from the relatively few poisonous varieties that exist.

Now the good news: The above warnings apply mainly to the arrogant and the ignorant. For the rest of us, mushroom hunting is, in many ways, like shopping in the supermarket. You know enough not to drink floor cleaner, but this knowledge had to be acquired at some point. It is exactly the same with wild mushrooms. Once you have become familiar with identification techniques, you will know what to avoid and what to pick for your own table. And once you have learned to pick your own mushrooms, you'll realize how much fun it is and how rewarding a hobby it can be.

But before I get to ways of developing mushroom hunting as a hobby, I would like to discuss methods of picking and preserving mushrooms.

### Handling Your Harvest

Finding your own cache of wild mushrooms can be a thrilling and exhausting experience. There are those glorious Sunday afternoons when the forests are literally carpeted with wild mushrooms. Yet, if you plan to pick a large amount of mushrooms, a few things are helpful to know. Filling bushel baskets is satisfying to the ego and great for snapshots, but consider the mushrooms at the bottom of the basket. While you are huffing and puffing and crawling from one spot to another, the unfortunate mushrooms that went into the basket first are getting squashed under the weight of succeeding layers. You'll find an unwanted purée by the time you get them home, because mushrooms are the most brittle when fresh from the ground. The best way to avoid this is to fill only half your basket.

If you don't have sufficient baskets for all you want to pick (and even if you do), separate the stem from the cap. This way the mushroom caps will lie roughly in parallel rows. A higher percentage of what you recover will be whole caps. Also, while you're at it, cut away the dirty base of the stem. It will save you work later on. Keep your basket as free as possible from leaves, pine needles, and grass.

## Preserving Your Own Mushrooms

Clean your harvest of mushrooms as soon as possible after returning home. Your method of cleaning is determined by the process you choose for preserving them. These are indicated for each method. There are three good ways to preserve mushrooms—drying, brining, and canning—and they all have their advantages and drawbacks. Before you decide which technique to use, decide what condition you want the mushrooms to be in when you resurrect them from their embalmed state: For creating mushroom extracts for cooking, drying is the best method; for preserving mushrooms in their most natural shape and texture, brining is best; canning is good but risky and the least preferred among the methods.

## Drying Mushrooms

**ADVANTAGES:** Easy, quick, and safe. Lasts a long time. Reconstitutes to yield excellent extracts for cooking.

**DISADVANTAGES:** Reconstituted mushrooms look limp and lifeless. Method can be used for very few types of mushrooms.

**BEST FOR:** Morels, all types of boletes (of which the cepe is a species), and black chanterelles (also called black trumpet mushroom, trumpet-of-death, and false truffle).

**DISCUSSION AND METHOD:** Drying is the most common method for preserving mushrooms worldwide. The Chinese use it extensively, as do the Japanese. Up until few years ago the black forest mushroom or shiitake was only available dried. The culinary advantages to drying have been discussed elsewhere in this book as have the criteria for deciding whether a mushroom should be dried or not. To recapitulate briefly, any mushroom can be dried, but if the resulting product is limp and cannot yield a distinctive extract, then it is not worth the effort. This is in fact the case with most mushrooms. Chanterelles, for instance, are not good for drying, because their extract is difficult to use and the mushrooms themselves lose their flavor and reconstitute to a rubbery texture. Most mushrooms simply shrivel up, and upon reconstitution their shapes are rather pathetic-looking. However, dried mushrooms do last a long time when properly stored, and if the right types are used, they yield extracts that can be the source of wonderful flavor.

If you decide to dry your mushrooms, the first thing you must realize is that the drying method is the most extreme in terms of altering form and shape. Water constitutes over 90 percent of the mushroom's mass, and once the water is evaporated out, the mushroom will never again look anything like its original form. Drying is like removing furniture from a room. An empty room is a mere shell, because its character came from the way the furniture

309

was arranged inside it. Reconstituting mushrooms in water is like returning the furniture to the room by dumping all of it in a pile in the middle—same room, same furniture, but different end result.

To proceed with drying, remove all the visible dirt, using a dry rag, a paring knife, or a soft brush. *Do not rinse the mushrooms in water.* After all, you're going to dry them to get the water out, so why make it more difficult by adding more to the mushrooms? When all the mushrooms are cleaned, begin drying. There are several methods for doing this, but the principles are the same: (1) The mushrooms should not touch each other during drying, because where they touch may not dry; (2) air circulation is the most important factor, so place the mushrooms on a grill rack, where the airflow can circulate; and (3) allow the area of drying to be properly ventilated so that fresh air can come in while moisturized air can flow out.

When finished, the mushrooms do not have to be crisp to the touch, but should still be slightly flexible. Longer, slower drying on low heat is safer than faster drying on high heat, because the latter method may toast the mushrooms. But if the fresh mushrooms are very wet, the heat must not be too low, or they may rot before they dry. In this situation start drying on a higher setting for an hour, watching the mushrooms closely, then lower the heat to normal. Whole mushrooms take longer to dry than sliced ones and require more close watching. If the mushrooms picked are quite large (4 inches or more across the top) slice them into smaller pieces. Mushrooms sliced fairly thin dry the quickest and easiest, and reconstitute the fastest. Do not cut whole mushrooms into chunks for drying purposes because this results in a product that looks awful when reconstituted.

To dry mushrooms in a gas or electric oven, place them on a rack, separated from one another, and leave the oven door open a crack, about 2 inches. Set the electric oven on its lowest setting, and the gas oven on its lowest setting or just on pilot. The first two hours in drying are the most important, because you will determine during that time the rate at which the mushrooms are drying. If the edges have not yet begun to dry at 2 hours, you will need to increase the setting another 20°. If the mushrooms are about half dried already at this time, you must be careful that the outside does not toast before the whole mushroom is dried. Either lower the setting or keep close watch on their progress. You can make electric drying racks with canvas covers and venting space at the top, and these work very well, but observe safety precautions with them. The total drying time for the mushrooms will be 15 to 24 hours. Commercial dehydrators are also available. Follow the directions that accompany these appliances.

When the mushrooms are dried, wrap them in plastic bags and seal them. The idea is to keep them dry once you have processed them. The mushrooms kept like this will last six months to a year but not much longer. The reason is that during the mushroom's growth, tiny bugs find their way into the mushrooms. These bugs are killed during drying, but their eggs survive and will eventually hatch, and hatched larvae will begin feeding on the mushrooms; one day you may discover that the bag of mushrooms you so deliberately dried has become a pile of dust crawling with little creatures. Don't be alarmed too fast, however; it may take a year or more before this becomes a problem. Nevertheless, check the bags every month or so for evidence of these bugs. Also, it is possible to retard this hatching process by simply *freezing* the dried mushrooms. If you do this, they will last indefinitely.

## Canning Mushrooms

ADVANTAGES: Basic shape of mushroom is maintained. Can be used for any type of mushrooms.

DISADVANTAGES: A lengthy process, demanding extraordinary care and sanitation. Danger of botulism. Some textural character of mushrooms lost.

BEST FOR: All mushrooms.

DISCUSSION AND METHOD: Home canning has long been a tried and true method of preserving foods. It works well for mushrooms also *if you are proficient at canning low-acid foods*. If you are not, *don't*. Canning is an anaerobic means of preservation. An anaerobic (without oxygen) atmosphere is a breeding ground for a bacterium known as *Clostridium botulinum*. Acid kills botulinum, so you are relatively safe in canning, say, tomatoes. But with low-acid foods such as mushrooms, great care and caution must be taken to kill all spores of this bacterium so that they don't have a chance to multiply. This means boiling *everything* that comes into contact with the mushrooms during processing, including spoons, pots, and, of course, the jars.

I am not going to recommend a method for canning mushrooms. Instead I refer you to the United States Department of Agriculture for their literature on home canning. Several good books on the subect can be found in your bookstore. However, I do recommend that when you plan to use a jar of home-canned mushrooms, you first pour the contents of the jar into a pan, cover them with fresh water, and boil them for 30 minutes before using. If the toxin from the bacterium is present, boiling will destroy it.

If you decide to can mushrooms, start by soaking the mushrooms in a bath of hot water. This will help loosen the dirt on the mushrooms. Then rinse the dirt off with a spray or under running water without breaking up the mushroom. When the mushrooms are cleaned, blanch them in a pot of water. Do this by bringing the water to a boil and adding the mushrooms to it. Remove the mushrooms as soon as the pot returns to a full boil. Rinse the mushrooms thoroughly again, and bring to a boil a second time. Then proceed with the canning method.

Canned mushrooms retain a fair amount of their original flavor, even though they do become limp in the process. The method of canning is not as drastic as drying, because the mushrooms do not lose all of their moisture, although some of it is lost, then recovered during boiling. To return to an earlier analogy, canning is like removing some of the furniture from the room but not all of it, thus retaining most of its original character. Its usefulness comes from its universal application to all kinds of mushrooms.

## Brining Mushrooms

**ADVANTAGES:** Maintains original shape and texture of mushrooms. Can be used for all mushrooms.

**DISADVANTAGES:** Lengthy period required for desalting.

**BEST FOR:** All mushrooms.

**DISCUSSION AND METHOD:** If you really want to maintain wild mushrooms in the form closest to fresh, then this is your method. Salting mushrooms for preservation is a very useful alternative to canning or drying. Preservation by salting is easily carried out at home. After cleaning and blanching, fresh mushrooms can be preserved in a salt solution. The quantity of brine to be prepared should equal about ½ the capacity of the container that will hold the mushrooms. The container should be earthenware or glass. To prepare the brining solution, place the required amount of water—determined by the number of jars you intend to fill—in a pot and add 7 ounces of kosher salt for each quart of water. Bring to a boil, and stir until the salt is dissolved. Cool the brine before using.

While the brine is cooling, clean the mushrooms as described in the steps for the canning method. Prepare a 5-percent salt solution (1½ ounces salt for each quart of water), and blanch the mushrooms in it for 5 minutes after the water has come to a boil. Drain and cool the mushrooms. Scald the earthenware or glass container to be used for the brining. Arrange the mushrooms layer by layer, gills or pores down, until the container is nearly filled, *covering each layer with the cooled brine.* Place a weighted cover over the mushrooms. Cover everything with clean cheesecloth. Thereafter mushrooms can be added or withdrawn for use as desired. *Be sure mushrooms are always covered with brine and all signs of molding are removed. When necessary, add brine solution to cover.* For use, first desalt in fresh cold water for 48 hours; this time can be cut by frequent water changes, or by placing the mushrooms in a vessel that allows some drainage at the bottom; run water continuously from a spigot over the mushrooms, constantly replacing the water that flows out the bottom. Using this method, the mushrooms should be desalted in about 2 hours. Taste the mushrooms occasionally for salt. Once desalted, mushrooms can be used as you would fresh ones.

In my opinion this is the best preservation method of all, unless you are drying them to obtain an extract. The immersion in salt draws water out of the mushrooms without disturbing the cellular structure, so that when the mushrooms are desalted, their shape and texture remain virtually the same as when they are fresh. Again, the analogy: The furniture is removed but then returned to the same relative positions as before, although on a smaller scale. However, not all the water is regained, so the mushrooms are somewhat smaller than fresh.

### Freezing

Some readers may wonder why freezing is not mentioned. The reason is that freezing from the raw state does little to preserve the original character of the mushrooms. The cellular structure of the mushroom is ruptured completely in the process. The exception to this is when the mushrooms are going to be frozen for only a day or so. Then the method works fine, and the mushrooms return to their original shape. And, as we have seen (page 311), dried mushrooms can be frozen successfully.

Freezing does have an important place, however, in maintaining prepared mushroom dishes like braised mushrooms. Let's say, for instance, that you would like to use your find in a vegetable dish in some future meal and would like to sauté the mushrooms in butter and onion. Clean and cook them according to your chosen method (remembering to retain a good deal of the liquid) and then store them in containers for freezing. When the time comes to use them, pull the prepared mushrooms from the freezer, defrost, and proceed. Soups are also excellent saved this way.

So if you pick a large batch of fresh mushrooms and are sure you know how you will want them prepared, cook them in a large batch right away and preserve the dish in the freezer.

# Learning About Wild Mushrooms

Learning about wild mushrooms involves a two-step process. First, become familiar with mushrooms and the means of identification by reading some books that deal with the subject, some of which are listed in the Bibliography. Second, join a club or organization that regularly meets and goes on forays for wild mushrooms. What you learn in the books will do you no good until you see for yourself what mushrooms look like in the wild. And there is no thrill like the one you get from correctly identifying your first wild mushroom. It becomes addictive. Find the club that is nearest you and join if you can. All the current known mycological clubs in the country are listed below. Of these the largest and best-equipped is the North American Mycological Association, which has many local affiliates. Not only does the association conduct forays, but it is a rich source of literature and educational material.

The following is a list of mycological clubs, small and large, which are now active in the United States.

### Addresses

North American Mycological Society (NAMA)
4245 Redinger Road
Portsmouth, Ohio
45662

### Alaska

Glacier Bay Mycological Society
P.O. Box 65
Gustavus, Alaska 99826

### Arkansas

Arkansas Mycological Society
Box 365
S.R. 1
Mount Ida, Arkansas 71957

## California

Mycological Society of San Francisco
Box 11321
San Francisco, California 94101

Humboldt County Mycological Society
Box 4419
Arcata, California 95521

Los Angeles Mycological Society
900 Exposition Boulevard
Los Angeles, California 90007

Mendocino County Mycological Society
Box 87
Philo, California 95466

## Colorado

Colorado Mycological Society
3024 S. Winona Court
Denver, Colorado 80236

Pikes Peak Mycological Society
2507 Alteza Place
Colorado Springs, Colorado 80917

## Connecticut

Nutmeg Mycological Society
Box 530
Groton, Connecticut 06340–0530

Connecticut Valley Mycological Association
Job Pond Road
Portland, Connecticut 06480

## Iowa

Prairie States Mushroom Club
310 Central Drive
Pella, Iowa 50219

## Idaho

North Idaho Mycological Association
W. Highway 1980 95
Coeur d'Alene, Idaho 13814

Southern Idaho Mycological Association
Box 843
Boise, Idaho 83701

## Illinois

Illinois Mycological Association
4020 Amelia Avenue
Lyons, Illinois 60534

## Massachusetts

Berkshire Mycological Society
Pleasant Valley Sanctuary
Lenox, Massachusetts 02140

Boston Mycological Club
4 Beverly Road
Bedford, Massachusetts 01730

## Maryland and Washington, D.C.

Mycological Association of Washington
25725 Long Corner Road
Gaithersburg, Maryland 20879

### Michigan

Michigan Mushroom Hunters' Club
7626 Auburn Street
Utica, Michigan 48087

West Michigan Mycological Society
923 E. Ludington Avenue
Ludington, Michigan 49431

### Minnesota

Minnesota Mushroom Society
4128 7th Street NE
Minneapolis, Minnesota 55421

### Mississippi

New Orleans Mycological Society
Route 4
Box 111–A
Ocean Springs, Mississippi 39564

### New Hampshire

Montshire Mycological Club
Jones Hill Road
Enfield, New Hampshire 03748

New Hampshire Mycological Society
3 Wellesley Drive
Milford, New Hampshire 03055

### New Jersey

New Jersey Mycological Association
802 N. Vosseller Avenue
Martinsville, New Jersey 08836

## New York

Central New York Mycological Society
E&F Biology
State University of New York
Syracuse, New York 13207

Connecticut-Westchester Mycological Society
Box 137–B
Route 3
Pound Ridge, New York 10576

Eastern Long Island Mycological Club
840 Clearview Avenue
Southold, Long Island, New York 11971

Mid-Hudson Mycological Association
Box 136
Verbank Road
Millbrook, New York 12545

New York Mycological Society
562 West End Avenue
New York, New York 10024

Long Island Mycological Society
1620 160th Street
Whitestone, New York 11357

## North Carolina

Asheville Mushroom Club
Nature Center
Gashes Creek Road
Asheville, North Carolina 28805

Triangle Area Mushroom Club
700 Morreene Road
G–11
Durham, North Carolina 27705

## Oregon

Florence Mushroom Club
Sillcoos Station
Westlake, Oregon 97493

Lincoln County Mycological Society
6504 S.W. Inlet
Lincoln City, Oregon 97367

Mt. Mazama Mycological Society
417 Garfield Street
Medford, Oregon 97501

North American Truffling Society
2340 W. Nob Hill, SE
Salem, Oregon 97302

Oregon Coast Mycological Society
Box 1590
Florence, Oregon 97438

Oregon Mycological Society
6548 SE 30th
Portland, Oregon 97202

Willamette Valley Mushroom Society
2340 W. Nob Hill SE
Salem, Oregon 97302

## Ohio

Ohio Mycological Society
RD 3
Sunset Drive
c/o Johnson
Export, Pennsylvania 15632

## Texas

Texas Mycological Society
2110 Wilcrest
151
Houston, Texas 77042

## Washington

Central Washington Mycological Society
Box 2214
Yakima, Washington 98907

Jefferson County Mycological Society
Rt. 1
Box 451–S
Port Ludlow, Washington 98365

Kitsap Peninsula Mycological Society
Box 265
Bremerton, Washington 98310

Olympic Mountain Mycological Society
P.O. Box 251
Forks, Washington 98331

Pacific Northwest Key Council
124 Panorama Drive
Chehalis, Washington 98532

Snohomish County Mycological Society
Box 2822
Claremont Street
Everett, Washington 98203

South Sound Mycological Society
111 Archwook Drive
448
Olympia, Washington 98502

Spokane Mushroom Club
No. 2601 Barker Road, No. 5
Otis Orchards, Washington 99027

Tacoma Mushroom Club
8306 Mount Tacoma Drive, SW
Tacoma, Washington 98498

Tri-Cities Mycological Society
Rt. 1
Box 5250
Richland, Washington 99352

Wenatchee Valley Mushroom Society
Rt. 1
Box 314
Everett, Washington 98203

Puget Sound Mycological Society
2559 NE 96th Street
Seattle, Washington 98115

### Wisconsin

N.W. Wisconsin Mycological Society
311 Ash Street
Frederic, Wisconsin 54837

Parkside Mycological Club
5219 85th Street
Kenosha, Wisconsin 53142

Wisconsin Mycological Society
Room 614
MPM
800 W. Wells
Milwaukee, Wisconsin 53233

## Canada

Assoc. de Myco. de Montreal
5955 rue Labreche (292)
Ville Laval, Province of Quebec
Canada HOA 1GO

Cercle de Mycologues de Quebec, Agriculture
Laval University
Quebec City, Province of Quebec
Canada G1K 7P4

Cercle de Mycologues de Rimouski
University of Quebec
Rimouski, Province of Quebec
Canada

Cercle de Mycologues de Sherbrooke
University of Sherbrooke
Sherbrooke, Province of Quebec
Canada

Club des Mycologues des Laurentides
1020, Chemin de la Pisciculture
Case Postale 26
St-Faustin, Province of Quebec
Canada JOT 2 GO

# Bibliography

*(Asterisks denote books most useful for beginners.)*

*Ainsworth, G. D. *Dictionary of the Fungi*. Kew, Surrey: Commonwealth Mycological Institute, 1971.

Alexopoulos, C. J. *Introductory Mycology*. Minneapolis: Burgess Publishing Co., 1962.

————. *Laboratory Manual for Introductory Mycology*. Minneapolis: Burgess Publishing Co., 1962.

Atkinson, G. F. *Mushrooms: Edible and Poisonous*. New York: Hafner Publishing Co., 1961.

*Aurora, David. *Mushrooms Demystified*. San Francisco: Ten Speed Press, 1986.

Berger, Dr. Karl. *Mykologisches Wörterbuch in Acht Sprachen*. Jena: Verlag Gustav Fischer, 1980.

Bessey, E. A. *Morphology and Taxonomy of Fungi*. New York: Hafner Publishing Co., 1961.

Bigelow, H. E., and H. D. Thiers. *Studies on Higher Fungi*. Vaduz: J. Cramer, 1975.

Cash, Edith H. *A Mycological English-Latin Glossary*. New York: Hafner Publishing Co., 1965.

Cernhorski and Machura. *Pilzbibel: Markt und Giftpilze*. Vienna: Verlag Karl Kuhne, 1947.

Clemençon, Heinz. *Les Quatre Saisons des Champignons,* 2 vols. Lausanne: Piantanida, 1980.

Clements, Frederic E., and Cornelius L. Shear. *The Genera of Fungi.* New York: Hafner Publishing Co., 1931.

Coker, W. C. *The Club and Coral Mushrooms of the United States.* Chapel Hill: University of North Carolina Press, 1923; New York: Dover reprint, 1974.

Coker, W. C., and A. H. Beers. *The Boleti of North Carolina.* Chapel Hill: University of North Carolina Press, 1943.

————. *The Stipitate Hydnums of the United States.* Chapel Hill: University of North Carolina Press, 1951.

Coker, W. C., and J. N. Couch. *The Gastromycetes of the United States.* Chapel Hill: University of North Carolina Press, 1928; New York: Dover reprint, 1974.

Corner, E. J. H. *A Monograph of Thelephora.* Berlin: J. Cramer, 1968.

Costantin, M. J., and M. L. DuFour. *Nouvelle Flore des Champignons.* Paris: Libraire Générale de l'Enseignement, 1947.

Dahnke, R. M., and S. M. Dahnke. *700 Pilze in Farben.* Stuttgart: AT Verlag Aarau, 1980.

Dickinson, Colin, and John Lucas. *The Encyclopedia of Mushrooms.* New York: G. P. Putnam and Son, 1979.

Erhart, Josef, and Marie Erhartova. *Houby ve Fotografii.* Prague: Statni Zemedelske Nakladatelstvi, 1977.

Farlow, William G. *Icones Farlowianae.* Cambridge, Mass.: The Farlow Herbarium and Library, 1929.

Findlay, W. P. K. *Wayside and Woodland Fungi.* London: F. Warne and Co., 1967.

Gerhardt, Ewald. *Pilzfuhrer.* Munich: B1V Verlagsgesellschaft, 1981.

*Groves, J. Walton. *Edible and Poisonous Mushrooms of Canada.* Ottawa: Canada Department of Agriculture, 1962.

Guillot, Jean. *Les Champignons.* Paris: Fernand Nathan, 1983.

Guirard, Irena. *Grzyby i Potrawy z Grzybów.* Warsaw: Państwowe Wydawnictwo Gospodarcze, 1956.

Guminska, Barbara, and Wladyslaw Wojewód. *Grzyby Owocnikowe i ich Oznaczania.* Warsaw: Państwowe Wydawnictwo Rolnicze i Leśne, 1968.

Gussow, H. T., and W. S. Odell. *Mushrooms and Toadstools.* Ottawa: F. A. Acland, 1927.

Guzman, Gaston. *The Genus Psilocybe.* Vaduz: J. Cramer, 1983.

Haas, H., and G. Gossner. *Pilze Mitteleuropas*. Stuttgart: Frankische Verlags-handlung, 1966.

Halling, Roy E. *The Genus Collybia*. Braunschweig: J. Cramer, 1983.

*Hard, M. E. *Mushrooms, Edible and Otherwise*. New York: Hafner Publishing Co., 1961.

*Hawksworth, D. L., B. C. Sutton, and G. C. Ainsworth. *Ainsworth and Bisby's Dictionary of the Fungi*. Kew, Surrey: Commonwealth Mycological Institute, 1983.

Hawlik, W. J. *Waldpilzzucht für jedermann*. Munich: Verlag Dr. Richter, 1983.

Hesler, L. R. *Entoloma in Southeastern America*. Berlin: J. Cramer, 1967.

*————. *Mushrooms of the Great Smokies*. Knoxville: University of Tennessee Press, 1960.

Hesler, L. R., and A. H. Smith. *North American Species of Hygrophorus*. Knoxville: University of Tennessee Press, 1963.

————. *North American Species of Lactarius*. Ann Arbor: University of Michigan Press, 1979.

Jahn, H. *Mitteleuropäische Porlinge*. Berlin: J. Cramer, 1970.

Jenkins, D. T. *A Taxonomic and Nomenclatural Study of the Genus Amanita, Section Amanita for North America*. Vaduz: J. Cramer, 1977.

Kaufman, C. H. *The Agaricaceae of Michigan*, 2 vols. New York: Johnson Reprint, 1981.

Kavaler, Lucy. *Mushrooms, Molds, and Miracles*. New York: John Day, 1965.

Kleijn, Von H. *Grosses Fotobuch der Pilze*. Garden City, N.Y. Doubleday, 1962.

*————. *Mushrooms and Other Fungi—Their Form and Color*. New York: Doubleday, 1962.

Kornerup, A., and J. H. Wanscher. *Methuen Handbook of Color*. London: Methuen and Co., 1963.

Kreisel, H. *Grundzeuge Eines Natürlichen Systems der Pilze*. Berlin: J. Cramer, 1969.

Krieger, Louis C. *The Mushroom Handbook*. New York: Dover, 1967.

Kühner, R., and H. Romagnesi. *Flore Analytique des Champignons Supérieurs*. Paris: Masson et Cie., 1953.

Langa, J. E., and M. Lange. *600 Pilze in Farben*. Munich: B1V Verlagsgesellschaft, 1961.

*Largent, D. L. *How to Identify Mushrooms to Genus II: Macroscopic Features*. Eureka, Calif.: Mad River Press, n.d.

## BIBLIOGRAPHY

*Largent, D. L., and H. P. Thiers. *How to Identify Mushrooms to Genus II: Field Identification of Genera.* Eureka, Calif.: Mad River Press, n.d.

*Largent, David, David Johnson, and Roy Watling. *How to Identify Mushrooms to Genus III: Microscopic Features.* Eureka: Calif.: Mad River Press, n.d.

*Lincoff, Gary. *The Audubon Society Field Guide to North American Mushrooms.* New York: Knopf, 1981.

Marshall, Nina L. *The Mushroom Book.* New York: Doubleday, 1902.

*McIlvaine, Charles. *One Thousand American Fungi.* Indianapolis: Bowen-Merrill, 1900.

Meixner, A. *Chemische Farbreaktionen von Pilzen.* Vaduz: J. Cramer, 1975.

Michael, Edmund, Bruno Hennig, and Hanns Kreisel. *Handbuch für Pilzfreunde,* 4 vols. Jena: Verlag Gustav Fischer, 1977.

*Miller, Orson K. *Mushrooms of North America.* New York: E. P. Dutton, 1978.

Moser, Meinhard. *Agarics and Boleti.* London: Phillips, 1983.

*Needham, G. H. *The Microscope.* Springfield, Ill.: Charles Thomas, 1968.

Nespiak, Andrzej. *Grzyby (Mycota) Tom VII: Basidiomycetes, Agaricales, Cortinariaceae, Cortinarius.* Warsaw: Państwowe Wydawnictwo Naukowe, 1975.

Oetker, Dr. A. *Pilz Kochbuch.* Bielefeld: Verlag Rudolf A. Oetker, 1963.

*Pacioni, Giovanni. *Guide to Mushrooms.* New York: Simon & Schuster, 1981.

Peck, Charles H. *Memoir of the New York State Museum.* Albany: State University of New York, 1900.

*Phillips, Roger. *Mushrooms and Other Fungi of Great Britain and Europe.* London: Ward Lock, 1981.

Pilat, Albert. *Mushrooms.* London: Spring Books, n.d.

———. *Mushrooms and Other Fungi.* London: Peter Neville, 1961.

Pilat, Albert, and O. Usak. *Maty Atlas Grzybów.* Warsaw: Państwowe Wydawnictwo Rolnicae i Leśne, 1978.

Pomerleau, René. *Les Amanites du Quebec.* Quebec: Naturaliste, 1966.

Rayner, R. W. *A Mycological Color Chart.* Kew, Surrey: Commonwealth Mycological Institute, 1970.

Richter, J. *Austernpilz Kochbuch.* Munich: Verlag Dr. Richter, 1984.

Richter, Dr. *Wilpilz Kochbuch.* Munich: Verlag Dr. Richter, 1981.

Richter, Nora. *Champignon Kochbuch.* Munich: Verlag Dr. Richter, 1981.

———. *Die Schönsten Gerichte.* Munich: Verlag Dr. Richter, 1981.

Rinaldi, A., and V. Tyndalo. *The Complete Book of Mushrooms.* New York: Crown Publishers, 1972.

Rolf, R. T., and F. W. Rolf. *The Romance of the Fungus World*. New York: Dover, 1924.

Sass, John, E. *Botanical Microtechnique,* Ames: Iowa State University Press, 3d ed., 1958.

*Seymour, Jacqueline. *Mushrooms and Toadstools*. New York: Crescent Books, 1978.

*Shaffer, Robert L. *Keys to Genera of Higher Fungi*. Ann Arbor: University of Michigan Biological Station, 1968.

Singer, Rolf. *Agaricales in Modern Taxonomy*. Tucumán, Argentina: Universidad Nacional de Tucumán, 1949.

*Smith, A. H. *The Mushroom Hunter's Field Guide*. Ann Arbor: University of Michigan Press, 1974.

*———. *Mushrooms in Their Natural Habitat,* 2 vols. Portland, Oregon: Sawyer's, 1949.

———. *North American Species of Mycena*. Ann Arbor: University of Michigan Press, 1947.

———. *North American Species of Psathyrella*. New York: Memoirs of the New York Botanical Garden, 1972.

Smith, A. H., and L. R. Hesler. *The North American Species of Pholiota*. New York: Hafner Publishing Co., 1968.

*Smith, A. H., H. V. Smith, and Nancy S. Weber. *How to Know the Gilled Mushrooms*. Dubuque, Iowa: William C. Brown, 1979.

*Smith, A. H., and H. Thiers. *The Boletes of Michigan,* Ann Arbor: University of Michigan Press, 1971.

Smith, Helen V., and A. H. Smith. *The Non-Gilled Fleshy Fungi*. Dubuque: William C. Brown, 1973.

Snell, W. H., and E. A. Dick. *The Boleti of Northeast North America*. Lehre: J. Cramer, 1970.

*———. *A Glossary of Mycology*. Cambridge, Mass.: Harvard University Press, 1971.

Stevens, R. B. *Mycology Guidebook*. Seattle: University of Washington Press, 1974.

Stuntz, Daniel E. *How to Identify Mushrooms to Genus IV: Keys to Families and Genera*. Eureka, Calif.: Mad River Press, n.d.

Tosco, Uberto. *La Cueillette des Champignons*. Paris: Grange Battellière, 1969.

United States Department of Commerce, *The ISCC-N.B.S. Method of Designating Colors and a Dictionary of Color Names*. Washington, D.C.: National Bureau of Standards, 1955.

## BIBLIOGRAPHY

Von Frieden, Lucius. *Mushrooms of the World*. New York: Bobbs-Merrill, 1969.

Wasson, R. Gordon. *The Wondrous Mushroom*. New York: McGraw-Hill, 1980.

———. *Soma: The Divine Mushroom*. New York: Harcourt, Brace and World, 1968.

*Watling, Roy. *How to Identify Mushrooms to Genus IV: Cultural and Developmental Features*. Eureka, Calif.: Mad River Press, n.d.

Wells, V. L., and P. E. Kempton. *A Preliminary Study of Clavariadelphus in North America*. Ann Arbor: Michigan Botanist, 1968.

Wilczek, Lech. *Grzbów Jest w Bród*. Warsaw: Nasza Ksiegarnia, 1967.

Zeitlmayer, Limus. *Knaurs Pilzbuch*. Berlin: Droemersche Verlag, 1955.

# INDEX

*Jack Czarnecki is the third-generation chief proprietor of* Joe's, *which opened in Reading, Pennsylvania, in 1916 as a workingman's bar, specializing in serving wild mushroom soup made from mushrooms Joe himself had gathered in the pine forests outside of town. It has since gone on to become one of the nation's most distinguished and innovative dining establishments, receiving the Travel-Holiday Award for Fine Dining and a Four-Star rating from the Mobil Guide. Joe's has also been the subject of feature articles in the* New York Times, Travel & Leisure, Gourmet, Town & Country, Esquire, *and elsewhere.*

*Educated at Phillips Academy in Andover, Massachusetts, and the University of California at Davis, Mr. Czarnecki also attended the Cornell University School of Hotel Administration. He lives with his wife and three children in Wyomissing, Pennsylvania, where the family enjoys hunting for wild mushrooms, using them the way his father and grandfather had for so many years.*